sappi
tree spotting

KWAZULU-NATAL

COAST AND MIDLANDS

IDENTIFICATION MADE EASY

Rina Grant and Val Thomas
Illustrations by Joan van Gogh

Jacana

Acknowledgements

Sappi Tree Spotting KwaZulu-Natal has taken two years of intensive research and testing to reach publication. Jacana is grateful to all the people from many different fields who contributed their time and commitment to produce this superb publication. We would like specifically to thank the following individuals and organisations for their dedication, time and expertise during the project.

We sincerely thank Professor Kader Asmal, Minister of Water Affairs and Forestry, for his support and for writing the foreword.

The research and development of **Sappi Tree Spotting KwaZulu-Natal** was carried out by the Jacana Team, primarily Dr Rina Grant and Val Thomas. This would not have been possible without the assistance of the following scientists: Holger Eckardt (Botanist KNP); Wayne Lotter (Exotic plant specialist); Anne Rennie; Guin Zambatis. We would also like to acknowledge the following researchers: Duan Biggs; Oonsie Biggs; Penelope Troloppe; Jutta von Breytenbach, Jan Korf and Riette Smit (Dendrological Society); Neels van Tonder (Bonsai Friend).

Many people gave generously of their time and we thank them for their invaluable assistance: Dr Toni Milewski, Geoff Nichols, John Rushworth, Lynn Troloppe and Joanne Lankester for their contributions to the editing of the book; Keryn Adcock, David Johnson (NPB Botanist) and the rangers at Hluhluwe Park for their involvement.

Our special thanks to Joan van Gogh for the beautiful artwork which will assist tree spotters to discover and identify trees of KwaZulu-Natal. We would also like to acknowledge and thank Sally MacLarty for her contributions to the line-artwork.

We sincerely thank the following organisations and individuals for their photographs: Anka Agency International; Pitta Joffe; Piet van Wyk; Anthony Bannister (CSIR); The Jacana Team (Dr Rina Grant, Peter Thomas, Val Thomas and Gary van der Merwe).

We would like to thank the various companies and individuals for their expert help in the production of the maps: Gordon Lumby (Cartographics) for layout and DTP; The National Botanical Institute for the use of data from the Herbarium, Pretoria (PRE) Computerised Information Systems (PRECIS), in particular Hannelie Snyman and Trevor Arnold; and Jutta von Breytenbach (The Dendrological Society) for the Tree Distribution Maps.

The polished surfaces of the wood samples were photographed by André Pretorius and Gary van der Merwe, by courtesy of Stephanie Dyer, Division of Water Environment and Forestry Technology (Environmentek) CSIR, Timber Utilisation Programme, Forestek. The wood ornaments were donated to Pretoria University by the late WEC van Wyk and photographed by courtesy of Magda Nel and Professor AE van Wyk (Department of Botany).

The book was designed by Jacana and Nix Hampel, and the cover by David Selfe Designs. The Desktop Publishing was carried out by Jacana, Concept Training, Resolution, Steven Clutty and Shelley Nortier. We thank them all for their creative input.

We are proud to acknowledge the work of the entire Jacana Team who have contributed in their specialised fields to produce **Sappi Tree Spotting KwaZulu-Natal**: Maren Bodenstein, Carol Broomhall, Ryan Francois, Liz Godfrey, Dr Rina Grant, Nix Hampel, Zann Hoad, Nafeesa Karrim, Mirela Kerns, Maisie Mbali, Andrea Meeson, Obed Molobe, Debbie Munro, Fortune Ncube, Mpume Ncube, Davidson Ndebele, Jannett Ndebele, David Ngwenya, Conor O'Neal, Jenny Prangley, Angela Price, Joan Sibiya, Natasha Stretton, Mariette Strydom, Peter Thomas, Val Thomas, Pamela Thompson, Gary van der Merwe, Jenny van der Walt and Debbie White.

Finally we would like to thank Sappi Limited for their vision and commitment in helping to fund the research and development of a book that we believe will significantly add towards helping South Africans and our visitors to be aware of, care for, protect and enjoy our magnificent KwaZulu-Natal trees.

Foreword

For many people, KwaZulu-Natal evokes a lush-green picture. From the warm ocean to the east, to the towering Drakensberg in the west, Nature has bestowed an above-average rainfall upon much of the region. Over the millennia, the plants have responded to this bounty with a bounty of their own. KwaZulu-Natal is a fascinating mix of ecological opportunities, what with its Coastal Forests, Bushveld-Savannah, Mangrove Forests, Wetlands, Grasslands, Afromontane Forests and more.

Because of increased ecological awareness worldwide, more and more people are becoming interested in the role trees play in the environment. This emphasises the need for books which make it easy, and enjoyable, to identify trees in their natural environments.

It is therefore with great pleasure that we can welcome the extension of the truly excellent **Sappi Tree Spotting** series, with the publication of this volume on KwaZulu-Natal.

As our environment and wilderness areas come under greater and greater pressure, there is a growing need for concern and awareness.

Raised public awareness highlights the need for knowledge and understanding. Ecological relationships and processes, and the role of plants in general, and trees in particular, are complex. Scientific terminology and jargon sometimes further complicates explanations.

The **Sappi Tree Spotting** series, and the KwaZulu-Natal edition in particular, come as a very welcome tool for those people and organisations attempting to address these problems. It also helps to remind us of our responsibility to conserve the ecological integrity of our natural systems, and to take special care in clearing invading alien plants, which are seen as the single greatest threat to our biological diversity and ecological health.

The knowledge, enthusiasm and commitment that Jacana has lavished on producing these books bodes well for the botanical, ecological and spiritual benefits of the user. I have no hesitation in recommending the individual books, and the series as a whole, and in commending Sappi for their foresight and support.

Professor Kader Asmal, M.P.
Minister of Water Affairs and Forestry

sappi

KwaZulu-Natal, known for its rolling green hills and lush vegetation, is home to more than 750 species of indigenous trees that have evolved under the sub-tropical climate along the coastlines and the drier, colder climate of the Midlands and Drakensberg. In comparison to the whole of Europe, which has fewer than 100 species, KwaZulu-Natal is noted for its abundance of floral diversity.

Approximately 25% of unplanted land on Sappi tree farms is unplanted and managed for environmental purposes, which is closely monitored on an ongoing basis, under the guidance of the company's environmental management team. In line with this approach, Sappi Forests is presently finalising its environmental management system and is seeking certification according to the international ISO 14 000 standard. In KwaZulu-Natal, Sappi is guardian of four Natural Heritage Sites and 48 Sites of Conservation Significance.

As a significant landowner in this region, Sappi takes care in the way we manage our landholdings. Sappi supports the work of various nature conservation agencies and remains committed to a number of environmental sponsorships in an effort to crreate understanding and appreciation for the richness and diversity of our environment.

Sappi is therefore proud to bring to you the third edition in the Tree Spotting series, **KwaZulu-Natal (Coast and Midlands).** We wish you many enjoyable moments spotting trees in this beautiful province.

Valley Bushveld at the Windy Hill Tree Farm in KwaZulu-Natal.

The National Botanical Institute (NBI)

The mission of the National Botanical Institute is to promote the sustainable use, conservation, appreciation and enjoyment of the exceptionally rich plant life of South Africa, for the benefit of all its people.

The NBI is an autonomous, state-supported, statutory organisation, which has its head office in the Kirstenbosch National Botanical Garden. It has physical resources such as the eight National Botanical Gardens, three Herbaria and two Research Units. In addition, it boasts the human resources of many highly qualified scientists, horticulturists, academics and support staff.

National Botanical Gardens

The eight National Botanical Gardens propagate and display the unique wealth and diversity of South African flora.
The Natal National Botanical Garden is situated in Mayor's Walk, Pietermaritzburg.

Herbaria

The combined collections of dried plant material of the three NBI herbaria, in Durban, Cape Town and Pretoria, contain over 1,5 million specimens of mainly Southern African plant material. They are an invaluable resource to researchers throughout the African continent, as well as internationally.

Education

Environmental Education, both within the National Botanical Gardens and working with communities on greening projects country-wide, is a major priority of the National Botanical Institute.

Research

The Conservation Biology Research Programme focuses on conservation of plant diversity and plant resources in Southern Africa.

Many plants could prove invaluable to humans in terms of new food crops or medicinally as cures for diseases for which, at present, there are no cures. However, many are being eradicated before their potential has been investigated.
The Stress Ecology Research Programme focuses on responses of vegetation to environmental stress and global change. These are crucial questions facing mankind to which answers must be found before it is too late.

Botanical Society membership

Members of the public who are interested in the work of the NBI can join their nearest branch of the Botanical Society, or can visit their local National Botanical Garden.

NBI and Sappi Tree Spotting

As a sheer coincidence of positive energy the early phase of planning the Tree Spotting series overlapped with the NBI publication of the *Low and Rebelo Vegetation Map of South Africa* (see page 8).
Defining the boundaries of each Tree Spotting book, and the zones within each boundary, was automatically facilitated by this essential piece of scientific work. As part of the information about each tree, there are mini maps of their South African distribution. The information for each of these maps was supplied by the NBI from data collected throughout the country.
It is services and relationships such as these that make the NBI an unique and invaluable asset to South Africa.

Botanical Society of South Africa

The Botanical Society aims to support the National Botanical Institute and to promote the conservation, cultivation, study and wise use of the indigenous plants of Southern Africa for the benefit of all.

The Botanical Society is a non-governmental organisation with 12 branches throughout the country. Most of these support the National Botanical Gardens.

Botanical Society Branches' Membership

Information and application forms are obtainable from the various National Botanical Gardens, Botanical Society head office or branches.

Head office: Kirstenbosch

Tel: (021) 797-2090 Fax: (021) 797-2376
Private Bag X10, Newlands, 7725
New members are welcome.
Members enjoy the following benefits:

- The privilege of visiting any of South Africa's National Botanical Gardens free of charge.
- The opportunity to create an indigenous garden from your annual allocation of free seed.
- First hand experience can be gained of our magnificent indigenous plants on organised hikes and outings.
- The opportunity to increase your knowledge by attending demonstrations and lectures.
- The pleasure of receiving Veld & Flora, our quarterly magazine full of interesting articles, free of charge.
- A discount of 10% on plants and books purchased at Kirstenbosch Gardens, Cape Town and at the Witwatersrand National Botanical Garden, Roodepoort.
- The opportunity to support and participate in plant conservation and environmental education projects and to assist with development projects for the National Botanical Institute.

Botanical Society Branches and Botanical Gardens

Botanical Society Branches

Bankenveld Branch	(011) 958-1750
Bredasdorp / Napier Branch	(02841) 42587
Durban Branch	082 444 2083
Free State Branch	(051) 436-3612
Garden Route Branch	(044) 874-1558
Johannesburg Branch	(011) 788-7571
Kirstenbosch Branch	(021) 762-1166
Kogelberg Branch	(028) 272-9311
Lowveld Branch	(013) 752-5531
Pietermaritzburg Branch	(0331) 44-3585
Pretoria Branch	(012) 804-3149
Villiersdorp Branch	(0225) 32244

Botanical Gardens

Free State National Botanical Garden	(051) 436-3612
Harold Porter National Botanical Garden	(028) 272-9311
Karoo National Botanical Garden	(0231) 70785
Kirstenbosch National Botanical Garden	(021) 762-1166
Lowveld National Botanical Garden	(013) 752-5531
Natal National Botanical Garden	(0331) 44-3585
Pretoria National Botanical Garden	(012) 804-3149
Witwatersrand National Botanical Garden	(011) 958-1750

Dendrological Society

Arborum silvarumque conservatio salus mundi est. – The conservation of trees and forests is the salvation of the world (literally translated).

The Dendrological Foundation

When the Dendrological Foundation was formed in 1979 by Dr F. von Breitenbach, the terms "Dendrology" and "Dendrologist" were fairly unknown in South Africa. The Foundation was created as an independent, non-profit, non-racial association aimed at the promotion of the knowledge of trees. This was with particular emphasis on the protection, planting and preservation of indigenous tree-dominated ecosystems.

Early projects were carried out:
- to standardise the common English and Afrikaans tree names, and species' numbers
- to standardise the ethnic names
- to create a "Big Tree Register" of the biggest trees of any species in South Africa
- to publish the *"Dendron"* newsletter

"Dendron" has been published ever since 1979 on a more or less regular basis. In 1981 the first issue of the Journal of Dendrology appeared containing more scientific essays on all aspects of dendrology.

Dendrological Society

In 1980 the Dendrological Society was formed. The aims of the Society were similar to those of the earlier Foundation, focusing on conservation and education.

Tree conservation cannot succeed without the active participation of both city dwellers and country people. In order to preserve trees, people have to love and respect them and to do this, they at least have to know their names or their families.
Many of the Society's activities support this basic philosophy.

- The Society runs Tree Knowledge Courses which aim to spread the joy of trees through information.
- The Society provides a Tree Identification Service for members who submit specimens for identification.
- Tree Number Plates are available from the Society. They are made in a high-quality ABS-material with the National tree number, and the botanical and common names in Afrikaans and English. They are also available with an ethnic common name in place of Afrikaans. Contact Jutta von Breitenbach for further information.

Publications of the Dendrological Society

- "National List of Indigenous Trees" (1995) in its third, revised edition
- "National List of Introduced Trees" (1984) in its second, revised edition
- The first volume of the "Tree Atlas of Southern Africa" (1992) which is to be followed by another 22 volumes

Branches

Branches around the country are named after a tree species or a significant geographical feature.
- "Magalies" – Pretoria
  (012) 567-4009 Jutta von Breitenbach
- "Umdoni" – Durban
- "Celtis" – Pietermaritzburg
- "Kameeldoring" – Potgietersrus
- "Erythrina"– Pietersburg
- "Atalaya" – Port Elizabeth
- "Wolkberg" – Tzaneen
- "Tafelberg" – Cape Town
- "Witwatersrand" – Johannesburg
- "Boekenhout" – Witbank
- "Langeberg" – Swellendam
- "Olienhout" – Groot Marico
- "Soutpansberg" – Louis Trichardt
- "Outeniqua" – Knysna
- "Vaal" – Meyerton
- "Kwambonambi" – Zululand

The Society is growing annually and looks forward to new members.

Tree Society

*The Tree Society of Southern Africa has been actively involved
in promoting the awareness and preservation of our natural heritage since 1946.*

Our members are tree enthusiasts from all
walks of life, including professional botanists,
who will gladly extend your knowledge. Some
members provide background information on
the geology, history and fauna of the areas.

Tree Society outings
Enjoy the opportunity of walking on the wild
side of nature in undisturbed places!
• Day outings are organised to local areas of
  particular botanical interest. Please contact
  the Wildlife / Botanical Society.
• Weekend and long weekend outings further
  afield, Waterberg, Mpumalanga, and
  occasionally KwaZulu-Natal, give the
  opportunity to meet our country members.
• Invitation to landowners! The Society
  compiles checklists while on outings. It
  identifies any rare indigenous or invasive
  exotic plants. Specimens collected are
  deposited in recognised herbaria, to help build
  the archive of scientific knowledge on plants.

Education
• The Tree Society has been instrumental in
  establishing three prizes for excellence in
  the field of Plant Systematics at the
  University of the Witwatersrand.
• The Society has and will consider offering
  assistance to deserving students to
  further their studies in the field of botany.
• In co-operation with the C.E. Moss
  Herbarium, Department of Botany,
  University of the Witwatersrand, the Society
  offers courses on tree identification. These
  courses consist of illustrated lectures and the
  use of microscopes. These take place under
  the guidance of botanists, which should help
  you to identify trees in the field.
• On request, courses can be organised which
  concentrate on trees in a specific area.

Tree Society publications
The Society actively promotes the production
and sale of books on indigenous trees and,
when available, has books for sale.
Membership entitles you to the following:
• *"Trees in South Africa"* – The Society
  Journal is published twice a year with
  research and items of botanical interest
  written by amateur and professional
  botanists.
• *"Peltophorum"* – The Society Newsletter is
  published twice yearly and gives reports on
  outings and a "Diary of Events" of
  forthcoming outings and courses.
• *"Combretaceae"* by Denzil Carr –
  a comprehensive and definitive account of
  the Bushwillow family.

Society membership
Please contact the Society for further details:
Tel / Fax: (011) 465-6045   Walter Barker
Tel: (011) 316-1426   Cheryl Dehning
Fax: (011) 316-1095
For information about courses contact:
Renee or Kevin Balkwill
Tel: (011) 716-4006
or e-mail: kevinb@gecko.biol.wts.ac.za

Contents

TREES GREET YOU

The colours of the tabs on the side of each page cross-correlate with the Contents and have nothing to do with the Ecozones.

YOU FIND TREES BY ECOZONE AND HABITAT

Lebombo Wattle
Newtonia hildebrandtii SA Tree no 191
This special tree is found almost exclusively in the Sand Forests of the Coast. It is a huge, single-stemmed tree (10 - 25 m), with a moderate rounded canopy. The trunk is often buttressed, and the older branches and twigs contort like old arthritic fingers, while young stems and branches are smooth and have pinkish bands.
The fine, twice compound leaves grow on thick twigs towards the outer edge of the canopy. Creamy-white flower-spikes appear from October to December. They develop into long, slender, wine-red pods that turn dark brown before splitting down one side (April to September), to show the papery, reddish-brown seeds on the flat pod surface.

1

How to use this book

English name/Scientific species name/Scientific family name
English family name/Other South African names

These identify the specific tree. The majority of the names in different South African languages are listed according to the National List of Indigenous Trees, compiled by Dr F von Breitenbach. The Dendrological Society has collected the official names of South African trees in 9 of our 11 languages. There is further information about tree names on page 389.

Where you'll find this tree easily

As with the cross-section diagram below, the **red tree icon** shows the easiest place to find the tree. The **green tree icons** show the other Habitats where the tree is likely to be found.

Ecozone blocks

The blocks that are coloured show the Ecozones in which you can find this tree easily.

The colours and their letters are the same ones you will find on the Maps – pages 406 - 409.

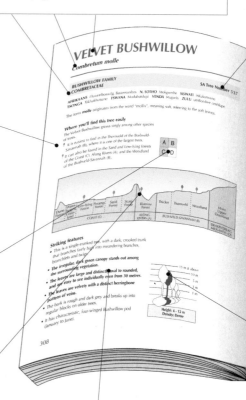

Cross-section diagram of KwaZulu-Natal

The **red tree icon** show the Habitat where it is easiest to find the tree. The **green tree icons** show the Habitat to look in as second choice. Note that the icons of trees are proportionately too large for the scale of the landscape.

Striking Features of mature trees

These are features of mature trees which will help you find an example of the tree with the greatest ease.

The bold items are those Striking Features which are the most important in helping you with positive identification.

South African tree number

The numbers are according to the National List of Indigenous Trees, compiled by Dr F von Breitenbach.

Line drawing

This drawing will indicate the most important Striking Feature that will help you to differentiate the tree from any others.

Artwork of the tree

Trees vary greatly and no single photograph or illustration can represent every tree you will find. However this artwork gives an overall impression of the size and the common form of mature trees, which are easiest to find. It emphasises the Striking Features listed on the opposite page.

Identification tab

For easy reference the colour-coded tabs indicate **Sappi Tree Spotting** groups, as well as the specific tree. These same groups are colour-coded in the Contents (page x). The green colour-codes are purely to separate sections of the book – they have no correlation to Ecozones.

Dendrological Society record tree

This information is from the society's register indicating the largest tree of this species currently registered. The location of the tree is also given. See further information on the Grids (Record breaking trees) page 400.

309

BUSHVELD-SAVANNA – THORNVELD
Big Tree – Velvet Bushwillow

Density and height icon

This will help you form a more accurate Search Image.
The tree which is coloured gives an idea of the average height of mature trees you will find easiest to identify in KwaZulu-Natal, in comparison with other common trees. The height is given in metres.
The density of the colour indicates the average, summer density of the leaves and branches, as well as the resultant density of the shade.

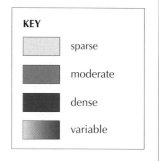

KEY

	sparse
	moderate
	dense
	variable

How to use this book
(continued)

Wood samples and ornaments

Many South African trees have beautiful wood that is workable for carving, turning or furniture. Where possible a picture of the polished wood, as well as a finished product, are included to show the texture and the colour. Not all the workable timbers are included in the book.

These pictures should help with the appreciation of the value, beauty and diversity of South Africa's indigenous woods, and should encourage sustainable usage. Wasteful chopping and burning of our rarer trees is leading to a number of them becoming "endangered" in the wild, although none of these trees are covered here. The photographs of these wood samples were taken courtesy of the CSIR, Pretoria. Sets of wood samples and technical details of different woods can be obtained from CSIR (Environmentek) - (012) 841-3683. The photographs of the ornaments were taken courtesy of Prof A E van Wyk, University of Pretoria.

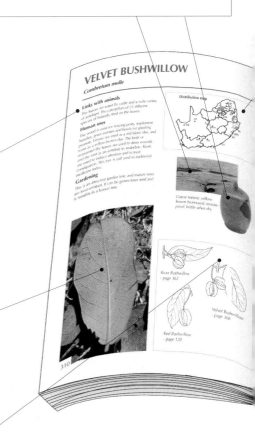

General information and usages

Details of interest about the tree, in relation to people and to animals, as well as gardening, are given here.

Photograph/Look-alike diagram

These are **photographs** of the tree, or its features, chosen to increase either your information or your pleasure!

In some trees there is a **diagram** in this position which covers look-alike trees. Wherever relevant, confusing look-alike trees are also covered in the text on this page.

Map of South Africa

This is an adaptation from maps supplied by the National Botanical Institute in Pretoria, and the Dendrological Society.

Abbreviations:

		GR:	Graaff Reinet	PE:	Port Elizabeth
BLM:	Bloemfontein	JHB:	Johannesburg	PS:	Port Shepstone
BW:	Beaufort West	K:	Kimberley	RB:	Richard's Bay
CT:	Cape Town	MB:	Mossel Bay	SC:	Sun City
DBN:	Durban	N:	Nelspruit	SPR:	Springbok
EL:	East London	P:	Pietersburg	UP:	Upington

Growth details

These details will help you to check your identification. They build up a wider Search Image so you can find the same tree elsewhere. For each specific tree the size of the leaves, flowers, fruit and/or pods are shown in relation to one another. However this size relationship does not carry through proportionately from one species to another.

Seasonal changes

This grid is to help you find trees at different times of the year. However, KwaZulu-Natal Habitats offer varying protection, therefore it is an average guide only.

- The information will vary from year to year depending on temperature and rainfall.
- The information also varies from Ecozone to Ecozone and within Habitats.
- The colours represent the months during which the leaves, flowers, fruit / pods are most likely to be seen.
- The colours themselves are a very rough guide only. You should refer to the artwork for more accurate colours.
- Pale yellow is used for inconspicuous flowers or pods.
- Whether a pod has seeds or not, it is shown on the grid, while it is still visible on the tree.

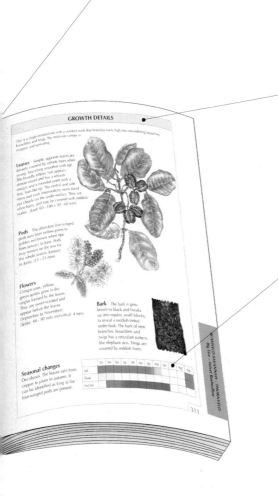

How Sappi Tree Spotting works

Umfolozi Nature Reserve, with its superb accommodation, network of roads and unsurpassed Bushveld Habitat offers the ideal African holiday.

How Sappi Tree Spotting works

The main aim of this book is to introduce outdoor enthusiasts to the exciting hobby of tree spotting. It is also written to offer experts a new interpretation of trees accroding to where they grow naturally.

KwaZulu-Natal is known as the Green Province, with a very wide variety of trees growing from the wind-blown coastline to the cold exposed slopes of the Drakensberg Mountains.

Due to this extraordinarily wide variety of tree species, it is difficult for newcomers to get to know the trees here. It can be very frustrating using traditional keys in tree books, unless you have information about the tree in different seasons, in different areas, and have some botanical background. However, once you know the trees in this book, you will recognise most of the common trees in the KwaZulu-Natal coast and higher Midlands.

DEFINITION OF KWAZULU-NATAL COAST AND MIDLANDS

The primary objective of **Sappi Tree Spotting** is to simplify the understanding of tree distribution by vegetation zones, and through this, to promote recreational tree spotting in South Africa. Therefore, with the exception of the southern border, the standard political boundaries of KwaZulu-Natal have only served as a starting point.

A detailed vegetation map, published by the National Botanical Institute in 1996, was adapted by Jacana to define most of the boundaries, and to create the four Ecozones covered in this book.*

This map is available from the NBI. Details of the NBI, its activities in South Africa and its contribution to this book are on page vi.

The area of the province that is covered in this book, stretches from the coastline in the east, to the Drakensberg Midlands in the west. The northern border is formed by the drier Sour and Sweet Bushveld of Mpumalanga. The coastal vegetation of the Eastern Cape has many trees that are not common along the KwaZulu-Natal coast, therefore the southern border is the same as the provincial boundary.

Low, AB and Rebelo, GG: Vegetation of South Africa, Lesotho and Swaziland, Department of Environmental Affairs and Tourism, Pretoria, 1996

A- Along Rivers

B- Bushveld-Savannah

C- Coast

D- Drakensberg Midlands

Northern Province

Mpumalanga

North-West

Gauteng

SWAZI-LAND

Free State

KwaZulu-Natal

D B

A

C

Northern Cape

LESOTHO

D

SOUTH AFRICA

ATLANTIC OCEAN

Eastern Cape

INDIAN OCEAN

Western Cape

Patterns of tree distribution

The patterns that influence which trees grow where, and how they grow, have been simplified in this book. The fundamentals that govern any area, and its pattern of trees, are the same all over the world. These are primarily the altitude, the climate and how close the area is to the coast or to other water. Information provided on this page is purely for those readers who wish to confirm data presented throughout the book.

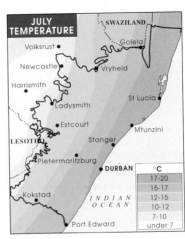

Altitude
Altitude varies from sea level along the coast, to 1 400 m in the Moist Upper Grassland of the Drakensberg Midlands.

Rainfall
It is a summer rainfall area. Mean annual rainfall ranges from a 400 mm high in the Drakensberg Midlands, to over 1 500 mm along the Coast. The humidity is also high along the Coast during most of the year.

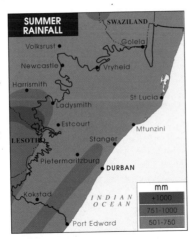

Temperature
The summers are hot over most of the area, with mean annual temperatures between 22 - 28°C. In the Drakensberg Midlands it is cooler, with temperatures dropping in winter and frost occuring regularly.

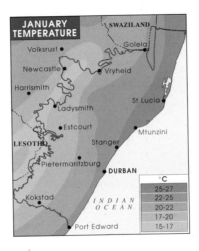

WHY THIS BOOK IS DIFFERENT

Sappi Tree Spotting is a creative new way to make the most of the outdoors. It is designed to do for trees what Roberts and Newman have done for birds. Two years of intensive, scientific, field and market research have gone into fine-tuning a simple and innovative method of getting to know trees in their natural environments. Until recently trees have remained inaccessible to all but the most devoted, botanically minded, tree-key followers.

With **Sappi Tree Spotting** this changes in a number of ways.

• **Simple language**
The average recreational tree spotter will never use 'pubescent' when hairy will do! Learning to know and love trees need not only be for the botanically trained.

• **Summarised information**
The book helps the readers by means of accessible, easy-to-use information like: height and shade density icons; grids indicating seasonal changes; maps and information blocks which direct you to the most convenient park, lodge or game reserve. It also gives information on modern and traditional uses for trees and their gardening possibilities.

• **Creation of Search Images using Striking Features**

• **Finding trees by Ecozone and Habitat**
The above two points are the most important innovations which make **Sappi Tree Spotting** successful. They are discussed in detail below and on the following page.

CREATE A SEARCH IMAGE USING STRIKING FEATURES

Finding a tree that you do not know is like looking for a stranger in a crowded room. You need to have a clear Search Image of certain Striking Features that you can visualise. For example, you might be looking for a grey-haired, old man, smoking a pipe.

Most tree species covered in this book have a specific shape and pattern that will help you find them. This pattern is so strongly encoded that it is repeated to a greater or lesser degree in each individual tree. As you get to know these patterns of growth, you will learn to recognise many trees at a glance. For example, your Search Image could be for a large, single-trunked tree, with rough-bark, and small, simple, toothed leaves.

To create a Search Image you should have a clear idea about a number of important things.

After reading the description of the tree, visualise at least some of the following:
• the tree's likely size
• the trunk form
• how this trunk splits up into branches, branchlets and twigs
• the form and density of the canopy
• the shape, size and colour of the leaves, flowers, fruit or pods

Once you have a Search Image of a tree, it is easy to find in one of the two ways described on the following pages:
• Trees Greet You
• You find Trees by Ecozone or Habitat

TREES GREET YOU - pages 44 - 143

The first method of identifying a tree is if its flowers, pods, leaves or bark are very striking. The most outstanding Distinctive Striking Features of each tree are shown in colour visuals, on pages 44 - 59.

Some trees can be identified easily because of their Unique form, like the huge, hand-shaped leaves of the Common Cabbage Tree, perched on the top of the extraordinarily corky trunk, page 90.

The unique trees are on pages 72 - 97.
Other trees greet you with Seasonal Features that cannot be missed – like the flowers or fruit of the White Gardenia, page 136, which distinguish this tree throughout the year. Seasonally Striking trees are on pages 100 - 143.

None of these trees need a complex system of 'keying', because they are instantly recognisable, in many instances even from a distance.

YOU FIND TREES BY ECOZONE AND HABITAT - pages 146 - 373

Most trees are easy to find, as long as you look for the right trees in the right places. For example, the Paperbark Acacia, page 348, flourishes in the open spaces of a Habitat called Moist Upper Grassland, which is in Ecozone (D), Drakensberg Midlands.

The Powder-puff Trees, page 168, crowd together, with their feet in the water, in the Swamp Forest Habitat of Ecozone (C), Coast.

With its wide variety of different Habitats and incredible diversity of tree types within these Habitats, KwaZulu-Natal offers an exciting challenge to tree-spotters.

Sappi Tree Spotting KwaZulu-Natal divides the region into four Ecozones with 14 Habitats, all of which are easy to recognise.

- Maps, on pages 406 - 409, will lead you to finding the Ecozone you are in.
- Pages 12 - 29 give detailed information about the Ecozones and Habitats, and of the types of trees that can be found in them.
- You will find a step-by-step guide on how to find trees by Ecozone and Habitat on pages 30 - 31.

You find trees by Ecozone

In this book the KwaZulu-Natal area is divided into four Ecozones: A, B, C and D. These Ecozones each have their own distinctive Habitats. All these Ecozones and Habitats are discussed from pages 12 - 31. The Ecozone profile below is featured on all species' pages.

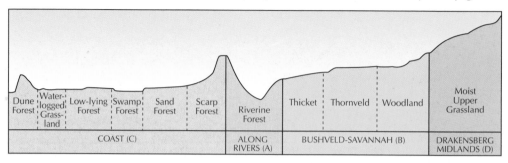

Dune Forest	Water-logged Grass-land	Low-lying Forest	Swamp Forest	Sand Forest	Scarp Forest	Riverine Forest	Thicket	Thornveld	Woodland	Moist Upper Grassland
COAST (C)						ALONG RIVERS (A)	BUSHVELD-SAVANNAH (B)			DRAKENSBERG MIDLANDS (D)

To make the Ecozones easier to remember, **Sappi Tree Spotting** has named them Along Rivers (A), Bushveld-Savannah (B), Coast (C) and Drakensberg Midlands (D). This order does not follow the natural sequence of coast, river, savannah and midland.

These Ecozones A, B, C and D, have been adapted from the vegetation zones of the NBI Map, referred to below. For details about the NBI, see page vi.

Each Ecozone has a specific colour and consists of the NBI zones listed below. For detailed maps of KwaZulu-Natal Ecozones, see pages 406 - 409.

A   Along Rivers
NBI Zone: 5

B   Bushveld-Savannah
NBI Zones: 24 and 26, and 25 to 900 m above sea level

C   Coast
NBI Zone: 23

D   Drakensberg Midlands
NBI Zone: 42, as well as the higher lying areas of Zone 25, above 900 m above sea level.

On the following pages each Ecozone, and the Habitats of B and C, are described in detail. Next to many of these are descriptions of trees with which they are specifically associated. Most of these trees do not occur **throughout** KwaZulu-Natal, and have **not** been included in the main body of the book. These trees are marked with this asterisk.*

Ecozone A – Along Rivers

This Ecozone stretches from the Coastal Forest to about 900 metres above sea level along the permanent rivers. At 900 metres the winter temperatures are too low to allow tree growth in unprotected areas. Along the Coast there are other factors such as soil type and sea winds, that alter the characteristic vegetation Along Rivers. The rainfall in this Ecozone varies from 400 to 800 mm, and temperatures are mild. Some parts of the valleys are fairly arid due to the drying effect of the Berg winds that blow through them.

Trees in Ecozone A form dense forests with canopies touching and with very little grass growing underneath. Some of the largest and most spectacular trees such as the Sycamore Cluster Fig, page 366, and the Fever Tree Acacia, page 74, are found in this Ecozone.

This area is mostly used for small stock farming. A number of reserves have been proclaimed (see page 380), but it is difficult to assess the percentage that is specifically conserved.

* **White Stinkwood** *Celtis africana*
SA Tree no 39
This is often a huge tree with a straight trunk and smooth, pale grey bark. The bright green leaves have three veins from the base, and the top two thirds of the margin are toothed. This tree can be confused with Pigeonwood, page 194. It is included in the Forest Trail, page 69, and in **Sappi Tree Spotting Highveld***.*

The vegetation surrounding the rivers is very variable. Rivers are not easy areas in which to start tree spotting – unless you look for the four trees listed on page 364, which are easily found.

Ecozone B – Bushveld-Savannah

This Ecozone lies between 400 and 900 metres above sea level. It is a summer rainfall area with a mean annual rainfall between 700 and 1 000 mm. The summer temperature averages from 26 - 28°C, and frost seldom occurs in winter. Ecozone B is more undulating than the Coast (C). Thorn trees dominate the vegetation because they thrive on the fertile, clay soils.

There are large, grassy plains in between. Most of the game farms and parks of KwaZulu-Natal fall in this Ecozone. It is fairly well conserved with 6,5% under conservation.

Most of the unconserved areas are used for cattle farming where the larger natural vegetation is fairly well protected.

This diagram illustrates the Habitats of the Bushveld-Savannah (B). Five different Habitats are found here, each with its own variety of trees. The Thickets tend to be near rivers, and the Rocky Outcrops and Termite Mounds occur in the Thornveld, Woodlands and Thickets. These are discussed in more detail on pages 19 - 22.

Diagram illustrating the Habitats of the Bushveld-Savannah (B), pages 19 - 22.

River   Thicket   Rocky Outcrop   Thornveld   Termite Mound   Woodland

The Bushveld-Savannah is the most common Ecozone in all the Game Reserves of KwaZulu-Natal. The Umbrella Thorn Acacias are the most striking.

Ecozone C – Coast

Due to the effect of the warm Mozambique Current, this Ecozone is tropical. The rainfall, of 1 000 - 1 500 mm per year, is high, as is the humidity, and there are only two months with low rainfall. Mean temperatures for the summer and winter are between 22 and 25°C, and frost hardly ever occurs here. This whole Ecozone is below 400 metres above sea level. It is fairly flat or slightly undulating, and rises quite steeply further from the coast. The climate varies over short distances towards the mountains. Therefore the vegetation also differs in the higher and lower lying habitats, and in areas inside and outside the river valleys.

Most of this Ecozone is covered in forests. These are densely wooded areas with intertwined canopies and very little undergrowth and grass cover. Distinct Habitats have been created by landform, together with sea winds, rain and mist. The distribution of these Habitats is illustrated in the diagram below.

The area is intensely utilised for sugar-cane and timber. Exotic species are common and now grow in large parts of the unconserved areas. However, due to the size of the Lake St Lucia area, 14,03% of the Ecozone is conserved.

The diagram below illustrates the Habitats of the Coast (C), pages 23 - 29.

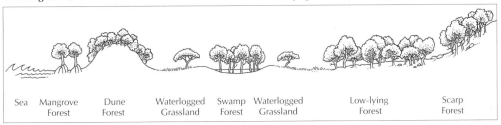

| Sea | Mangrove Forest | Dune Forest | Waterlogged Grassland | Swamp Forest | Waterlogged Grassland | Low-lying Forest | Scarp Forest |

The KwaZulu-Natal Coast is a mixture of vast cultivated, or urbanised areas and well preserved natural Habitats, which are wonderful for tree spotting.

Ecozone D – Drakensberg Midlands

This Ecozone lies at the foot of the Drakensberg mountains from 900 to about 1400 metres above sea level. Frost occurs regularly in winter, and summer temperatures average between 22° and 26°C. The mean annual rainfall is 660 - 1 000 mm, and falls mainly in summer in the form of thunderstorms. This Ecozone is very undulating and is traversed by many streams, running off the mountains. The soils are shallow and rocky. Due to the shallow soils and the inhibiting effects of fire and frost on trees, grassland is plentiful. Throughout the grassland there are only a few species of trees, either scattered or in groups. Within this predominantly grassy Ecozone there are wooded kloofs. However, these are not covered in this book, because many of the trees here differ from those in the rest of KwaZulu-Natal. They are covered in a separate book, **Sappi Tree Spotting Highveld**, which deals with the trees of higher altitudes.

The commercial farms are mostly cattle farms, but crop-farming and forestry are also important. Natural vegetation can still be found on most of the cattle farms, but only 2,52% of this Ecozone is specifically conserved.

* **Outeniqua and Real Yellowwoods**
Podocarpus falcatus & Podocarpus latifolius
SA Tree nos 16 & 18
*Yellowwoods are found in the Kloofs of this Ecozone – but this Habitat is not covered in this book. Both species can grow to be exceptionally tall, exceeding 30 metres. The leaves are long and thin, and may have a bluish tinge. The bark and leaves are characteristic, and are illustrated in the Forest Trail, page 66. These trees are covered in detail in **Sappi Tree Spotting Highveld**.*

Rivers cut through the moist upper farmlands of the Drakensberg Midlands, and are wooded. Here you will find magnificent Yellowwoods, shown above.

You find trees by Habitat

Each of the four Ecozones is divided into various Habitats.

Habitats are smaller, more uniform areas of vegetation, within each Ecozone, that are individually recognisable. Each Habitat has a different combination and density of tree species.

A number of different Habitats make up each Ecozone (see page 18).

Habitats in KwaZulu-Natal are the result of a number of different influences:

- distance from the sea
- coastal winds
- proximity to rivers
- underground water level
- altitude
- soil type
- rainfall

The following diagrams explain terminology used in Sappi Tree Spotting – see page 15.

Grassland
Wide open expanses of grassland have only a few scattered groups, or individual trees.

Thornveld
The trees stand apart individually, and there are many thorn trees. Grass grows between the trees.

Thickets
Smaller trees grow very close together, often in stands of one species. There is little grass growing in the under-storey.

Woodland
The canopies of trees touch and there is very little grass growth in the under-storey.

Forest
The canopies of trees overlap and there is no grass growth in the under-storey.

Ngoye Forest, near Mtunzini, is a wonderful pristine forest.

SUMMARY OF HABITATS IN EACH ECOZONE

Ecozone A – Along Rivers

These are the forests along the major rivers, running from about 400 - 900 metres above sea level. There is only one Habitat, Riverine Forest (see page 13).

Habitat	Description
Riverine Forest	Densely wooded river valley (see page 13).

Ecozone B – Bushveld-Savannah

This is open Savannah from 400 - 900 metres above sea level (see page 14).

Habitats	Description
Thickets	Densely wooded groups of similar-sized, small trees of mainly one species (see page 19).
Thornveld	Scattered thorn trees on grassland (see page 20).
Woodland	Densely wooded areas of tall trees of many different species (see page 21).
Rocky Outcrops and Hillsides	Scattered trees of various sizes where rocks provide good drainage and protection (see page 22).
Termite Mounds	Small, densely wooded islands growing on old, unused termite mounds (see page 22).

Ecozone C – Coast

This is a strip along the coastline of about 400 metres above sea level and is mainly dense forests (see page 15).

Habitats	Description
Mangrove Forest	Specialised forests, along sheltered shores with muddy flats, at river mouths (see page 23).
Dune Forest	High, forested dunes along the sandy shore (see page 24).
Sand Forest	Forests on well-drained, deep, sandy soils north of the St Lucia lakes (see page 25).
Swamp Forest	Forests in low-lying areas, where the soil surface is below the water table (see page 26).
Waterlogged Grassland	Low-lying grassland, often along swamps, where the surface soil is just above the water table (see page 27).
Low-lying Forest	Dense forests between the Dune Forest, and the higher-lying Scarp Forests, or Bushveld-Savannah (see page 28).
Scarp Forest	Dense coastal forests on seaward-facing gorges, or on high coastal ridges (see page 29).

Ecozone D – Drakensberg Midlands

This is found at the foot of the Drakensberg from 900 to 1 400 metres above sea level (see page 16).

Habitat	Description
Moist Upper Grassland	Scattered thorn trees on grassland (see page 16).
Kloofs	Densely wooded, high-lying forests are not in this book. They are covered in **Sappi Tree Spotting Highveld.**

Thickets – Ecozone Bushveld-Savannah (B)

Thickets are patches of a single type of tree, growing densely to the exclusion of other species. In this book, to be classified as Thickets the mature height of these trees is usually less than three metres. They are found in low-lying areas, especially along drainage lines where the rainfall and soil conditions are unsuitable for tall trees to grow. The most striking of these Thickets are formed by the Magic Guarri, page 256.

Thorny Thickets often grow in places where the soil has been disturbed. The trees spring up at the same time and persist until thinned by fire. The Sickle Bush commonly forms this type of Thicket, page 264.

The Red Thorn Acacia, page 260, grows in dense uniform Thickets but can also be found growing as an umbrella tree in the Thornveld. It is easiest to identify by its leaves which form a sleeve around the thick branchlets.

* River Climbing Thorn Acacia
Acacia schweinfurthii
SA Tree no 184.1
This is a robust climber with dark green leaves that can form impenetrable Thickets. It can easily be confused with the Flame Thorn Acacia, page 108. The strong, hooked thorns of the River Climbing Thorn are arranged in rows on dark lines on pale branchlets. The scented flower-balls are creamy-white (October to March) and the pods are pale brown (March to June).

Thornveld – Ecozone Bushveld-Savannah (B)

A very large area of the Bushveld-Savannah (B) is covered by scattered thorn trees that grow far apart, their canopies seldom touching.
Tall, deciduous, broad-leaved trees such as the Velvet Bushwillow, page 308, and the Marula, page 304, stand out above the thorn trees. The umbrella-like canopies of many of these thorn trees, are very characteristic of the Thornveld. One of the most magnificent is the Black Monkey Thorn Acacia, page 312.

Umbrella canopies

Thick- or deep-umbrella canopy	Moderate-umbrella canopy	Thin-umbrella canopy

Black Monkey Thorn Acacia, page 312	Scented Thorn Acacia, page 316	Umbrella Thorn Acacia, page 320
Large tree with striking, dark green leaves; dense, thick-umbrella canopy.	*Smallest of the umbrella trees and less dense; bottle-green, stiff leaves; moderate-umbrella canopy.*	*Dense, grey-green, thin-umbrella canopy.*

The umbrella thorn trees are very striking in the Thornveld and are easy to identify. Here the thick-umbrella canopy of the Black Monkey Thorn Acacia is easy to recognise.

Woodland – Ecozone Bushveld-Savannah (B)

The Woodland is densely covered by tall trees with canopies touching, but not intertwining. The canopies allow enough light for sun-loving plants such as grasses to grow beneath them. *Acacias* are generally scarce in Woodland, so that most types of trees have relatively broad leaves.

Woodland is usually found on well-drained, hilly slopes, where enough moisture is available for tree growth. On the more protected hills, Woodland consists mostly of broad-leaved trees such as the Red Ivory, page 282. In the lower lying areas Cape Ash, page 274, and Natal Mahogany, page 278 are common.

Many different species of trees grow close together in the Woodland with their canopies touching. This is a difficult place for tree spotters to start.

* **Resin Tree species** *Ozoroa* species
SA Tree nos 371 - 377
The Resin Tree can be identified easily by its long, narrow leaves and distinct herringbone veins, shown on page 53. It has milky, resinous sap, and kidney shaped fruit growing in loose clusters. It can be confused with the Red Beech, page 234.

Rocky Outcrops and Termite Mounds – Ecozone Bushveld-Savannah (B)

The slopes of Rocky Outcrops have well-drained, shallow soils, and trees such as the Crow-berry Karree, page 326, can be found here.

Termite Mounds are rich in nutrients, and contain more moisture than the surrounding areas. Dense clumps of trees compete for the relatively small, but rewarding space. The most common large trees on the Termite Mounds are the White Milkwood, page 342, and the Weeping Boer-bean, page 338.

Weeping Boer-bean is very common, and easiest to find on Termite Mounds.

* **Dwarf Coral Tree** *Erythrina humeana*
SA Tree no 243.1
This is a small, deciduous tree often found on rocky slopes. The leaves are long (300 mm), dark olive-green above, and pale green below. The flowers are deep red and usually sparse (see page 338).

Mangrove Forest – Ecozone Coast (C)

This forest only develops in warm climates, on the sheltered shores of the Indian and Pacific oceans. Before the arrival of agricultural settlers, mangroves grew all along the east coast of Southern Africa, where streams or rivers enter the sea. Mangroves grow between the high-watermark of spring tide and the mean sea level, and are common in marine bays and tidal estuaries.

They are specially adapted to cope with very salty water. Due to evaporation, the areas settled by trees become more and more salty, and a source of fresh water is needed. The rivers provide muddy soil for the trees to grow in, and decrease the salt content of the soil by flushing the area with fresh water at low tide.

The Mangrove Forest has a unique group of animals and fish associated with it, making use of the protection of the trees and roots.

Management measures are being implemented to save some of the most threatened remaining Mangrove Forest such as those at Richard's Bay and Durban.

* Red Mangrove *Rhizophora mucronata*
SA Tree no 526
This tree is only found in mature Mangrove Forests and is more widespread worldwide than either the Black or White Mangroves, discussed on pages 160 - 167. It is smaller than either of these trees, with dark bark, sharp pointed leaves, four-petalled flower-stars, and very long cigar-shaped fruit (300 - 450 mm). Its roots stand high above the soil and water surface, forming a branched stilt or prop.

The best Mangrove Forests are found in the Parks of the St Lucia Estuary.

Dune Forest – Ecozone Coast (C)

The Dune Forest is best developed north of Cape St Lucia along the eastern coast. It has been formed by the wind over millions of years, creating some of the tallest vegetated dunes in the world – some as high as 200 metres above sea level.

These dunes act as a wind barrier. They therefore catch the sand blown from the beaches, as well as the rain and moisture provided by the sea mists. The soils are very low in nutrients, and trees must be able to withstand the onslaught of the salt-laden winds from the sea. These factors limit the species that can grow here. Because of the direction and strength of the winds, the evergreen trees growing on the dunes often have a clipped hedge appearance.

The canopies are tightly interlaced, and very few plants are found in the under-storey. However, trees may grow up to 20 metres and many species of orchids, ferns and lichen are found growing on the trees themselves.

The Coastal Red Milkwood, page 154, and the Coast Silver Oak, page 150, are dominant species in most of the Dune Forests. In areas that have been cleared, the White Pear, page 198, and a coastal form of the Sweet Thorn Acacia, page 352, can be found. This area has been used for sugar-cane farming, forestry and has also been mined.

* **White Milkwood**
Sideroxylon inerme
SA Tree no 579
This tree is a common tree in the Dune Forest and can be identified by its distinctive, regular blocked bark, as well as dark, leathery leaves with a yellow central vein. It is described in detail on page 342, because it is easier to identify first on Termite Mounds in the Bushveld Savannah.

Very few trees are able to grow in the harsh conditions of the Dune Forest and these species are very easy to get to know.

Sand Forest – Ecozone Coast (C)

The Sand Forest lies north of the St Lucia Lake system towards Kosi Bay and the Pongola River.

The depth of the sand varies from a thickness of 4 - 20 metres, and there is very little surface run-off when it rains. These sandy soils are low in nutrients and this limits the species of trees that can grow here. However, trees that prefer well-drained soils grow very tall, and some unique trees such as the Lebombo Wattle, page 1, can be found here. Other prominent trees are the Date Palm, page 72, Fever Tree Acacia, page 74, Black Monkey Orange, page 146, Lala Palm, page 78, Sneezewood, page 238, and Silver Cluster-leaf shown here.

Because of the lack of surface water, this area is very sparsely populated, and cattle farming is the main form of land use, especially along the Pongola River, and Mozi and Mkuzi swamp areas.

The Lala Palm is one of the common trees of the Sand Forest. Many trees grow here that can only be found in this Habitat, but it is an easy place for tree spotting.

✳ Silver Cluster-leaf *Terminalia sericea*
SA Tree no 551
This tree is very common in the Sand Forest of the Coast (C), where it is often one of the tallest trees. The branches leave the trunk horizontally at different levels to form distinct, flat layers. The simple leaves are clustered towards the tips of the branchlets, and young leaves have silver hairs, giving the tree a characteristic silvery shine. This tree is covered in detail in **Sappi Tree Spotting Lowveld.**

Swamp Forest – Ecozone Coast (C)

The land behind the coastal dunes is undulating. Rain water and mist, caught by the dunes, filters out behind the dunes, to form vleis, pans and swamps in the depressions.

Swamps are covered by fresh water throughout the year and this robs the soil of oxygen. These conditions only suit specialised trees. As a result, Swamp Forests, unlike other forests in KwaZulu-Natal, contain very few types of trees.

The trees of the Swamp Forests form a dense canopy and are more or less of an even height. One of the most striking trees of these forests is the unique Kosi Palm, shown here. The Wild Cotton Tree, page 88, and the Powder-puff Tree, page 168, form dense groves along the edge of the water.

The Kosi Palm has the longest leaves of any tree worldwide, and only flowers once in its lifetime.

These Swamp Forest patches were never extensive, but many have been cleared for agricultural development.

* **Kosi Palm (Rafia Palm)** *Raphia australis*
SA Tree no 26
These are very large palms with a single trunk and huge leaves that grow from the tip of the trunk to form a V-shaped canopy. These compound, blue-green leaves are the longest of any plant worldwide and can be over 9 metres long. The tree dies after producing large, oval fruit that takes two years to mature, and is covered by red-brown, shiny scales. Palm Nut Vultures eat the fruit.

Waterlogged Grassland – Ecozone Coast (C)

These are low-lying areas with a fairly dry surface, but waterlogged soils below. They are covered by grassland and a few scattered trees. The grassy patches are maintained by fire and grazing, especially by Hippopotamus.

Some of the more striking trees that can grow here are the Water Berry, page 172, Broom Cluster Fig, page 182, Wild Poplar and False Cabbage Tree. The Wild Medlar, page 176, is found in the drier areas.

The conservation status of this specialised Habitat is not easy to assess.

Waterberries are very characteristic of these Waterlogged Grasslands because they are well adapted to permanently wet soils. This is a very easy Habitat to spot trees in, as the number of species is limited.

* **Wild Poplar** *Macaranga capensis*
SA Tree no 335
The smooth, whitish or yellow bark is striking in the Swamp Forests. The leaves are poplar-like with smooth or slightly toothed margins and are very large (120 x 100 mm). There are 3 - 5 veins from the base, and the yellow-tinged veins are prominent on the under-surface. In autumn the yellow leaves are striking.

Low-lying Forest – Ecozone Coast (C)

To the west of the wetlands and lakes, the Coast becomes much drier. The clay content of the soils is higher and soils are nutritious. Due to the increased nutrients that are available to trees, and the relatively high rainfall, an exceptionally wide variety of trees can be found here. Many of the main roads along the Coast traverse this forest, and most visitors to KwaZulu-Natal are therefore familiar with it.

Most of these trees are evergreen and the canopy height ranges from 10 - 30 metres. Especially in disturbed areas there are many woody creepers and climbers, such as the Thorny Rope, page 226, and Climbing Flat-bean, page 100. The forest canopy is formed by densely intertwining, tall trees such as the White Ironwood, page 242, and Red Beech, page 234.

Trees found below the canopy have less light and warmth and are much smaller, with thinner trunks and often sparser leaves. Trees such as the

A wide variety of trees grow in the Low-lying Forests therefore this is not an easy area to first learn about the trees of the Coast (C).

Large-leaved Dragon Tree, page 80, and various Gardenias, page 138, are found here. Along the forest margins are trees that need sun but do not grow very tall. These are the Tassel Berry, page 124, Tinderwood, page 128, Sickle Bush, page 264, and Cross-berry Raisin, page 104.

These forests have been extensively cleared to make way for forestry and sugar-cane farming, and only about 10% of their original extent remains.

✳ **Forest Mahogany**
Trichelia dregeana
SA Tree no 300
This tree is very similar to the Natal Mahogany, page 278, except that the tips of the leaflets are more pointed. The Forest Mahogany is more common south of Stanger, while the Natal Mahogany is found in the north.

Scarp Forest – Ecozone Coast (C)

Scarp Forests are found on south- and east-facing slopes, or in gorges of high coastal ridges, where Rocky Outcrops or krantzes form protected areas for trees. Many of the trees of the Low-lying Forest can also be found in the higher-lying Scarp Forest.

The canopy of the trees varies in height, and climbers are abundant. Some very striking trees grow in this forest. Both the Forest Elder, page 112, and False Cabbage Tree, shown here, speckle the forests with white when they flower.

Due to the ruggedness of the terrain, this forest has not been utilised much for agriculture, and substantial parts still survive, with large areas conserved.

✳ **False Cabbage Tree** *Schefflera umbellifera*
SA Tree no 566
The False Cabbage Tree has a dense, round canopy with compound, hand-shaped leaves. The 3 - 5 leaflets have very wavy margins. Small, pale yellow flowers form a large, round spike (umbel), and make the tree particularly conspicuous in the Scarp Forest from January to May. Other cabbage trees are compared on page 92.

Ngoye Forest near Mtunzini is one of the best pristine Coastal Scarp Forests in KwaZulu-Natal. It is also the only place where Green Barbets are found.

Find trees by Ecozone and Habitat - A Seven Step Guide

Every time you want to find a tree, follow the steps below.
It will soon become second nature.

① Decide where you are. In which Ecozone is this?

To identify specific trees you must first work out where you are. Turn to the Maps on pages 406 - 409, and note in which Ecozone you are.
Example: Ecozone B – Bushveld-Savannah

② In which Habitat are you?

The descriptions on pages 11 - 29 give details of the Ecozones and their Habitats. Decide which of these applies to you.
Example: Thornveld

③ Which trees can you find in your Ecozone and Habitat?

On pages 32 - 35, you will find the Tree List for your Ecozone. Read this and make a note of the three or four trees you are most likely to find, and mark their pages.
Example: Black Monkey Thorn Acacia to Velvet Bushwillow

ECOZONE B — BUSHVELD-S

	Thornveld		Rocky Outcr
Page	**Tree**	**Page**	**Tree**
252	Black Monkey		Common Cabbage
256	Thorn Acacia	312	Tree
260	Buffalo-thorn	292	Crow-berry Karree
264	Marula	304	Hook Thorn Acacia
340	Umbrella Thorn		Red-stem Corkwoo
328	Acacia	352	Spike-thorn
220	Velvet Bushwillow	308	Brack Thorn Acacia

④ Create Search Images for these trees

Look at the pictures and read the Striking Features of each of these trees. In the same way as you would create a mental picture of a blonde child, with a green shirt eating an ice-cream, imagine the Striking Features of the trees you are hoping to find.

Black Monkey Thorn Acacia
Striking features

• **This is the tallest of the umbrella trees in the Thornveld, being single-trunked, often high-branching, with a dense, dark green, semi-circular to deep-umbrella canopy.**

• The twice compound leaves are short and stiff, stand upright and hardly move in the wind.

• The bark is dark, rough, and forms deep, lengthways fissures exposing yellowish under-bark.

⑤ Match your Search Images to nearby trees

Look at the larger, mature trees nearby and see if you can find one that has similar Striking Features to any of your Search Images.

⑥ Check the details

When you find a tree, check the details more carefully. Check all the Striking Features, then read the details about the leaf, flower, pod and bark. If you have any problems with any of the terms in the text, read 'How to meet a tree' pages 36 - 41.

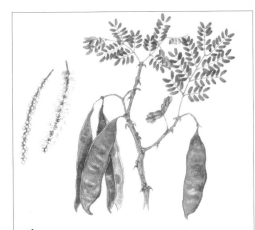

Flowers   White flower-spikes in small groups appear long after the leaves in late spring or summer (October to January). (50 - 100 x 10 - 20 mm)

⑦ How successful were you?

Successful?

That's great! Remember the key to enjoyable, long-term tree spotting is to focus on all the Striking Features – not only on one conspicuous pod or flower that is seasonal. One of the excitements and satisfactions of learning about trees is that they are not like birds. Once you know a bird it is the same wherever you go. Trees even vary from Habitat to Habitat, or Ecozone to Ecozone, and vary greatly in different parts of the country.

Not sure?

Look around. Are there any other similar trees you could check? If not, move on and find another tree to help you confirm your identification.

Unsuccessful?

Don't lose heart. Think of how often you saw one of the Big Five disappear into the bush as you rounded the corner. The joy of tree spotting is that trees in the wild are everywhere you look, all year round and they don't fly or run away when you approach. Simply try another spot and another tree.

Ecozone Tree List

This is the list of trees you are most likely to find in each Habitat. The trees you should look for first are shown at the top of the list in the darker colour.

* This list includes Look-alike trees, trees from the Forest Trail (pages 60 - 69), trees in the Distinctive Striking Features section (pages 44 - 59), and trees identified in the introductory pages.

ECOZONE A – ALONG RIVERS

Riverine Forest

Tree	Page	Tree	Page
Brack Thorn Acacia	358	*Red-stem Corkwood	94
Date Palm	72	*River Climbing	
Fever Tree Acacia	74	Thorn Acacia	19
River Bushwillow	362	Scented Thorn	
Sycamore Cluster		Acacia	316
Fig	366	Small Knobwood	218
Tamboti	370	Sneezewood	238
Black Monkey		Spike-thorn	334
Thorn Acacia	312	*Spiny Gardenia	138
*Broad-leaved		Sweet Thorn Acacia	352
Coral Tree	212	Tassel Berry	124
Broom Cluster Fig	182	Thorny Elm	222
*Brown Ivory	284	Thorny Rope	226
Buffalo-thorn	292	Tinderwood	128
Bush Guarri	270	*Toad Tree	62
Cape Ash	274	Umbrella Thorn	
Cape Beech	206	Acacia	320
Climbing Flat-bean	100	Umzimbeet	132
Coast Silver Oak	150	Velvet Bushwillow	308
Common Cabbage		Water Berry	172
Tree	90	Weeping Boer-bean	338
Common Poison		White Ironwood	242
Bush	186	White Milkwood	342
Coral Tree	210	White Pear	198
Cross-berry Raisin	104	*White Stinkwood	13
Crow-berry Karree	326	Wild Medlar	176
*False Horsewood	220	Wild Mulberry	202
Flame Thorn Acacia	108	Wild Olive	286
Forest Elder	112	Wild Pear	140
Forest Karree	230	Wild Plum	246
*Forest Mahogany	28	*Wild Poplar	
*Green Monkey			
Orange	148		
Knob Thorn Acacia	296		
Kooboo-berry	116		
Lala Palm	78		
Large-leaved Albizia	300		
Large-leaved Dragon			
Tree	80		
Marula	304		
Mitzeeri	214		
Natal Banana	82		
*Natal Fig	184, 368		
*Natal Forest			
Cabbage Tree	92		
Natal Mahogany	278		
Paperbark Acacia	348		
Pigeonwood	194		
Red Beech	234		
Red Ivory	282		
Red-leaved Rock Fig	368		

Rocky Outcrops

Tree	Page
Common Cabbage	
Tree	90
Crow-berry Karree	326
Hook Thorn Acacia	330
Red-stem Corkwood	94
Spike-thorn	334
Brack Thorn Acacia	358
*Broad-leaved	
Coral Tree	212
*Cape Gardenia	138
Common Poison	
Bush	186
*Common	
Wild Fig	184, 368
*Dwarf Coral Tree	22
*False Horsewood	220
*Horsewood	220
*Mountain Cabbage	
Tree	92
*Red-leaved Rock Fig	368
*Resin Tree	21
*Rock Cabbage Tree	92
Rubber Euphorbia	84
Small Knobwood	218
*Small-leaved	
Guarri	258, 272
Tree Euphorbia	86
White Gardenia	136

ECOZONE B

Termite Mounds

Tree	Page
Weeping Boer-bean	338
White Milkwood	342
Bush Guarri	270
Magic Guarri	256
*Dwarf Coral Tree	44

BUSHVELD-SAVANNAH

Thicket		Thornveld		Woodland			
Tree	**Page**	**Tree**	**Page**	**Tree**	**Page**	**Tree**	**Page**
Camphor Bush	252	Black Monkey		Bush Guarri	270	Red Ivory	282
Magic Guarri	256	Thorn Acacia	312	Cape Ash	274	*Red Milkwood	156
*Red Thorn Acacia	260	Buffalo-thorn	292	Kooboo-berry	116	Red Thorn Acacia	260
Sickle Bush	264	Marula	304	Natal Mahogany	278	*Red-leaved	
*Dwarf Boer-bean	340	Umbrella Thorn		Tassel Berry	124	Rock Fig	368
*Fire-thorn Karree	328	Acacia	352	Black Monkey		Red-stem Corkwood	94
*Horsewood	220	Velvet Bushwillow	308	Orange	146	*Resin Tree	21
*Natal Gardenia	138	Black Monkey		Black Monkey		*Rock Cabbage Tree	92
*River Climbing Thorn		Orange	146	Thorn Acacia	312	Rubber Euphorbia	84
Acacia	27	Brack Thorn Acacia	358	Brack Thorn Acacia	358	Scented Thorn	
Scented Thorn		Common Cabbage		*Broad-leaved Coral		Acacia	316
Acacia	316	Tree	90	Tree	212	Sickle Bush	264
		Coral Tree	210	Broom Cluster Fig	182	Small Knobwood	218
		Crow-berry Karree	326	Buffalo-thorn	292	*Small-leaved	
		Hook Thorn Acacia	330	Camphor Bush	252	Guarri	258, 272
		*Horsewood	220	Cape Beech	206	Sneezewood	238
		Knob Thorn Acacia	296	*Cape Chestnut	45, 69	Spike-thorn	334
		Large-leaved Albizia	300	*Cape Gardenia	138	*Spiny Gardenia	138
		Paperbark Acacia	348	Coast Silver Oak	150	*Sweet Thorn Acacia	352
		Red Bushwillow	120	Common Cabbage		Tamboti	370
		Red Thorn Acacia	260	Tree	90	Tinderwood	128
		Red-stem Corkwood	94	Common Poison		*Transvaal Gardenia	138
		*Rock Cabbage Tree	92	Bush	186	Tree Euphorbia	86
		Scented Thorn		Coral Tree	210	Umbrella Thorn	
		Acacia	316	Cross-berry Raisin	104	Acacia	320
		Sickle Bush	264	Crow-berry Karree	326	Velvet Bushwillow	308
		Sneezewood	238	*Dwarf Boer-bean	340	Water Berry	172
		Spike-thorn	334	*Dwarf Coral Tree	22	Weeping Boer-bean	338
		Sweet Thorn Acacia	352	*False Horsewood	220	Weeping Wattle	332
		Weeping Boer-bean	338	*Fire-thorn Karree	328	White Gardenia	136
		White Milkwood	342	Flame Thorn Acacia	108	White Ironwood	242
		Wild Pear	140	Forest Karree	230	White Milkwood	342
				*Green Monkey		White Pear	198
				Orange	148	*White Stinkwood	13
				*Green-stem		Wild Medlar	176
				Corkwood	96	Wild Olive	286
				Hook Thorn Acacia	330	Wild Pear	140
				*Horsewood	220		
				Knob Thorn Acacia	296		
				Large-leaved			
				Albizia	300		
				Magic Guarri	256		
				*Mangosteen	52		
				Marula	304		
				Mitzeeri	214		
				*Natal Fig	184, 368		
				*Natal Guarri	258, 272		
				Paperbark Acacia	348		
				Pigeonwood	194		
				Red Beech	234		
				Red Bushwillow	120		

Ecozone Tree List

This is the list of trees you are most likely to find in each Habitat. The trees you should look for first are shown at the top of the list in the darker colour.

* This list includes Look-alike trees, trees from the Forest Trail (pages 60 - 69), trees in the Distinctive Striking Features section (pages 44 - 59), and trees identified in the introductory pages.

Dune Forest

Tree	Page
Coast Silver Oak	150
Coastal Red Milkwood	154
Black Monkey Orange	146
Broom Cluster Fig	182
Buffalo-thorn	292
Bush Guarri	270
Cape Ash	274
Cape Beech	206
Climbing Flat-bean	100
* Coast Coral Tree	212
* Common Guarri	270
Common Poison Bush	186
Coral Tree	210
Cross-berry Raisin	104
* Dwarf Coral Tree	22
Flat-crown Albizia	190
Forest Karree	230
* Forest Mahogany	28
* Forest Raisin	204
Giant-leaved Fig	76
* Green Monkey Orange	148
* Horsewood	220
Kooboo-berry	116
Large-leaved Dragon Tree	80
Marula	304
Natal Banana	82
* Natal Fig	184, 368
* Natal Forest Cabbage Tree	92
* Natal Guarri	258, 272
Natal Mahogany	278
Pigeonwood	194
Red Beech	234
* Red Milkwood	156
* Red-leaved Rock Fig	368
Small Knobwood	218
* Small-leaved Guarri	258, 272
Spike-thorn	334
Sweet Thorn Acacia	352
Sycamore Cluster Fig	366
Thorny Elm	222
Thorny Rope	226
Umzimbeet	132
Water Berry	172
Weeping Boer-bean	338
White Ironwood	242
White Milkwood	342
White Pear	198
* White Stinkwood	13
Wild Medlar	176
Wild Plum	246

Low-lying Forest

Tree	Page	Tree	Page
Broom Cluster Fig	182	* Natal Forest Cabbage Tree	92
Flat-crown Albizia	190	* Natal Guarri	258, 272
Pigeonwood	194	Natal Mahogany	278
Thorny Rope	226	* Outeniqua Yellowwood	16
White Milkwood	342	Paperbark Acacia	348
White Pear	198	Powder Puff Tree	168
Black Monkey Orange	146	* Real Yellowwood	16
Black Monkey Thorn Acacia	312	Red Beech	234
Brack Thorn Acacia	358	Red Ivory	282
* Broad-leaved Coral Tree	212	* Red Milkwood	156
Buffalo-thorn	292	* Red-leaved Rock Fig	368
Bush Guarri	270	Red-stem Corkwood	94
Camphor Bush	252	* Resin Tree	21
Cape Ash	274	* River Climbing Thorn Acacia	110, 332
Cape Beech	206	Rubber Euphorbia	84
* Cape Gardenia	138	Scented Thorn Acacia	316
Climbing Flat-bean	100	Sickle Bush	264
* Coast Coral Tree	212	Small Knobwood	218
Coast Silver Oak	150	* Small-leaved Guarri	258, 272
Coastal Red Milkwood	154	Sneezewood	238
Common Cabbage Tree	90	Spike-thorn	334
Common Poison Bush	186	* Spiny Gardenia	138
* Common Wild Fig	184, 368	Sweet Thorn Acacia	352
Coral Tree	210	Tamboti	370
Cross-berry Raisin	104	Tassel Berry	124
Crow-berry Karree	326	Thorny Elm	222
Date Palm	72	Tinderwood	128
* Dwarf Coral Tree	22	* Toad Tree	62
* False Cabbage Tree	29	Tree Euphorbia	86
* False Horsewood	220	Umbrella Thorn Acacia	320
Flame Thorn Acacia	108	Umzimbeet	132
Forest Karree	230	Velvet Bushwillow	308
* Forest Knobwood	220	Water Berry	172
* Forest Mahogany	28	Weeping Boer-bean	338
* Forest Raisin	204	White Gardenia	136
Giant-leaved Fig	76	White Ironwood	242
Green Monkey Orange	148	* White Stinkwood	13
* Green-stem Corkwood	96	Wild Medlar	176
* Horsewood	220	Wild Mulberry	202
Kooboo-berry	116	Wild Olive	286
Large-leaved Albizia	300	Wild Plum	246
Large-leaved Dragon Tree	80		
Magic Guarri	256		
* Mangosteen	52		
Marula	304		
Mitzeeri	214		
Natal Banana	82		
* Natal Fig	184, 368		

Sand Forest

Tree	Page
Black Monkey Orange	146
Date Palm	72
Fever Tree Acacia	74
Lala Palm	78
Sneezewood	238
Black Monkey Thorn Acacia	312
Brack Thorn Acacia	358
Buffalo-thorn	292
Bush Guarri	270
Camphor Bush	252
Coast Silver Oak	150
* Dwarf Coral Tree	22
Flat-crown Albizia	190
* Green Monkey Orange	148
* Green Thorn	224
* Green-stem Corkwood	96
Knob Thorn Acacia	296
Kooboo-berry	116
* Lebombo Wattle	1
Magic Guarri	256
* Mangosteen	52
Marula	304
* Natal Gardenia	138
* Natal Guarri	258, 272
Natal Mahogany	278
Red Ivory	282
Red Thorn Acacia	260
Red-stem Corkwood	94
* Resin Tree	21
* River Climbing Thorn Acacia	110, 332
Rubber Euphorbia	84
Sickle Bush	264
* Silver Cluster-leaf	25
* Small-leaved Guarri	258, 272
* Spiny Gardenia	138
Sycamore Cluster Fig	366
Tamboti	370
* Toad Tree	62
Tree Euphorbia	86
Umbrella Thorn Acacia	320
Velvet Bushwillow	308
Weeping Boer-bean	338
White Gardenia	136
White Milkwood	342
Wild Medlar	176
Wild Pear	140

Scarp Forest

Waterlogged Grassland

Mangrove Forest

Swamp Forest

Moist Upper Grassland

How to meet a tree

CREATE A SEARCH IMAGE

Finding a tree that you do not know, is like looking for a stranger in a crowded room. You need to have a clear Search Image of certain Striking Features that you can visualise easily. For example, when looking for a specific person, you may think of a grey-haired, old man, smoking a pipe. Most trees covered in this book have a specific form and look about them that will help you find them.

Look at a number of different trees carefully and you will see many patterns. The fascinating part is that most species have their own pattern so strongly encoded that it is repeated to a greater or lesser degree in each individual tree. As you learn these patterns of growth you will learn to recognise many trees at a glance.

Sappi Tree Spotting descibes these patterns in this order:

- How main branches split off the trunk/stem.
- How branchlets split off the branches, splitting into twigs.
- Leaf-stems are the short attachment between the leaf and twig, or in a few trees between the leaf and branchlet.

Main branches always leave the main trunk (or stem) in a generally upward or horizontal direction. However, branchlets and twigs can tend to be in an upward, horizontal or downward pattern, or they can be a mixture.

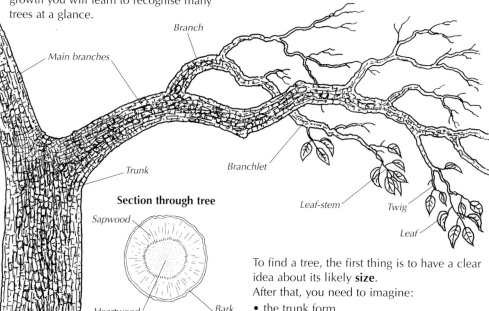

Branch

Main branches

Trunk

Branchlet

Section through tree

Sapwood

Leaf-stem

Twig

Leaf

Heartwood

Bark

Thorns and spines
They are both sharp.
Thorns are protuberances not covered in bark. **Spines** are bark-covered twigs that may carry leaves.

To find a tree, the first thing is to have a clear idea about its likely **size**.
After that, you need to imagine:
- the trunk form
- how this trunk splits up into branches, branchlets and twigs
- the form and density of the canopy

Finally the shape, size and colour of the leaves, flowers, fruit or pods will help you with a positive identification.

On the following pages you will find the terms used in **Sappi Tree Spotting**. These will help you to create your Search Images.

TRUNKS AND STEMS

"Trunk" is used for larger trees and "stems" for smaller and multi-stemmed trees.

Multi-stemmed
eg. Magic Guarri
- p. 256

**Single-trunked,
low-branching**
eg. Spike-thorn
- p. 334

**Single-trunked,
high-branching**
eg. White Ironwood
- p. 242

Straight trunk
eg. Wild Plum
- p. 246

Crooked trunk
eg. Velvet
Bushwillow
- p. 308

Fluted trunk
eg. Wild Olive
- p. 286

Buttressed trunk
eg. Giant-leaved Fig
- p. 76

CANOPIES

The canopy is the upper area of a tree, formed by the branches and the leaves.

Round
eg. Natal Mahogany
- p. 278

Semi-circular
eg. Marula
- p. 304

Umbrella
eg. Umbrella Thorn
Acacia - p. 320

Wide spreading
eg. Giant-leaved Fig
- p. 76

V-shaped
eg. Sneezewood
- p. 238

Narrow
eg. Common
Poison Bush
- p. 186

Irregular
eg. Kooboo-
berry
- p. 116

LEAVES

A leaf grows on a leaf-stem that attaches the leaf to the twig or branchlet. It snaps off the twig or branchlet relatively easily at the leaf-bud (auxillary bud). You can often see this bud as a swelling at the base of the leaf-stem.

All leaves are described as **simple** or **compound.**

Sometimes it is not easy to tell the difference between a simple and a compound leaf. Some of the ways are:

- Look for the position of the leaf-bud.
- Compound leaves look organised on their leaf-stem. Most simple leaves that are grouped close together look irregular on the twig.
- The leaflet of a compound leaf tends to tear off the leaf-stem – it does not snap off neatly, the way the leaf itself usually snaps off the twig at the leaf-bud.

Please note this is not true for all species, nor at all times of the year.

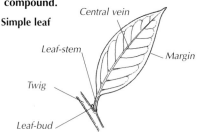

Simple leaf

Central vein

Leaf-stem

Margin

Twig

Leaf-bud

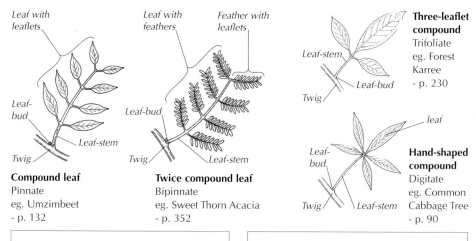

Leaf with leaflets

Leaf-bud

Leaf-stem

Twig

Compound leaf
Pinnate
eg. Umzimbeet
- p. 132

Leaf with feathers

Feather with leaflets

Leaf-bud

Twig

Leaf-stem

Twice compound leaf
Bipinnate
eg. Sweet Thorn Acacia
- p. 352

Leaf-stem

Leaf-bud

Twig

Three-leaflet compound
Trifoliate
eg. Forest Karree
- p. 230

leaf

Leaf-bud

Twig

Leaf-stem

Hand-shaped compound
Digitate
eg. Common Cabbage Tree
- p. 90

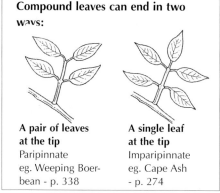

Compound leaves can end in two ways:

A pair of leaves at the tip
Paripinnate
eg. Weeping Boer-bean - p. 338

A single leaf at the tip
Imparipinnate
eg. Cape Ash
- p. 274

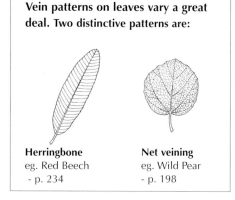

Vein patterns on leaves vary a great deal. Two distinctive patterns are:

Herringbone
eg. Red Beech
- p. 234

Net veining
eg. Wild Pear
- p. 198

LEAF ATTACHMENTS TO TWIGS OR BRANCHLETS

Leaf-stems can attach to the twigs in a number of ways and these tend to be predictable, species by species. Sometimes, however, you will find a variety of attachments on a single tree – this is done simply to confuse you and to make traditional keying methods difficult to follow! Attachments of the leaves to the twig or branchlet can be:

Opposite
eg. River
Bushwillow
- p. 362

Alternate
eg. Buffalo-thorn
- p. 292

Spiral
eg. Wild Plum
- p. 246

Clustered
eg. Black Monkey
Orange
- p. 146

Winged
eg. Cape Ash
- p. 274

LEAF OR LEAFLET SHAPE

There are many varieties of leaf shape. As a basis for all descriptions this book refers to them as:

Round
eg. Wild
Mulberry
- p. 202

Heart-shaped
eg. Wild
Cotton Tree
- p. 88

Narrow elliptic
eg. Large-leaved
Dragon Tree
- p. 80

Broad elliptic
eg. Broom
Cluster Fig
- p. 182

Butterfly
- not in
this book

Needle
- Real
Yellowwood
- p. 16

Triangular leaf
eg. Pigeonwood
- p. 194

LEAF MARGINS

The edge of the leaf can be:

Smooth
eg. Forest Elder
- p. 112

Wavy
eg. Magic Guarri
- p. 256

Toothed
eg. Tamboti
- p. 370

FLOWER PARTS

All flowers are made up of these parts:

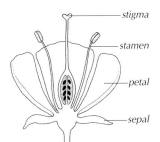

stigma

stamen

petal

sepal

BARK

The bark texture, and/or colour, is often characterisitc of a tree. However, it often differs between trunk and branches, older and younger trunks, and older and younger branches. Thinner and younger branches mostly have smoother and paler bark.

Smooth
eg. White
Pear
- p. 198

Rough
eg. Common
Cabbage Tree
- p. 90

Fissured or grooved
eg. Camphor Bush
- p. 252

Blocky
eg. Tamboti
- p. 370

Loose, peeling
eg. Red-stem
Corkwood
- p. 94

FLOWERS

Plants, including trees, are scientifically classified and named according to their flower shape. Looking carefully at flower shapes can help with family identification, but this is often technical and not easy to see.

Most families, however, share general flower shapes (pages 44-47). Some flowers have a unique shape, eg. Natal Banana, or are inconspicuous, eg. Buffalo-thorn. These are described in detail in the specific texts.

Ball
eg. Sweet Thorn
Acacia - p. 352

Spike
eg. Black Monkey
Acacia Thorn
- p. 312

Pea
eg. Umzimbeet
- p. 132

Trumpet
eg. White
Gardenia
- p. 136

Star
eg. Cross-berry
Raisin
- p. 104

Protea
- not in this
book

Pincushion
eg. Flat-crown
Albizia
- p. 190

FRUIT

Fruit has a fleshy pulp covering the seed/s. The pulp may be oily, watery or dry, and must be removed before the seeds can germinate. Birds and animals are attracted to the fruit and distribute the seeds.

Berry – small, single
eg. Water Berry - p. 172

Grape – small, in bunches
eg. Forest Karree - p. 230

Plum – larger, single
eg. Wild Plum
- p. 246

PODS

Pods are hard envelopes covering a seed, or more often, several seeds. They are members of the Thorn-tree, Flamboyant and Pea families, previously combined in the Legume family. Other pods have seeds with wings, such as those of the Bushwillow family.

Flat bean
eg. Black Monkey
Thorn Acacia
- p. 312

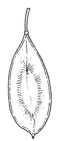

Broad bean
eg. Weeping
Boer-bean
- p. 338

Bumpy bean
eg. Coral Tree
- p. 210

Coiled
eg. Umbrella Thorn
Acacia
- p. 320

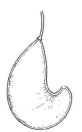

Sickle/kidney
- not in this book

Capsule
eg. Sneezewood
- p. 238

Two-winged
eg. Silver Cluster-leaf
- p. 25

Four-winged
eg. Velvet Bushwillow
- p. 308

Trees greet you

DISTINCTIVE STRIKING FEATURES

This section of the book summarises the most distinctive of the Striking Features of each tree. When a flower, fruit, pod, leaf or bark jumps out and asks to be recognised, you simply look up the relevant page here. Page numbers of each tree are given to encourage you to look up the other Striking Features of the tree. This will enable you to recognise the tree in other areas, at other times of the year too.

Many trees have features which are distinctive. New leaves of fig trees are often red throughout the year.

Distinctive Striking Features

The following pages show, flowers, fruit, pods and leaves that are all very striking or that are so distinctive you can often identify these trees on this information alone. You can use these pages as a quick reference – but it is wise to turn to the full tree description to be sure.

UNIQUE FLOWERS (50% of life-size)

Coral Tree
- p. 210

Broad-leaved
Coral Tree
- p 212

Dwarf Coral
- p 22

Coast Coral
- p 212

Weeping
Boer-bean
- p. 338

Dwarf Boer-bean
- p 340

Natal Banana
- p. 82

Wild Cotton Tree
- p. 88

STAR, PINCUSHION & TRUMPET FLOWERS

Cape Chestnut
- p. 69
(90% of life-size)

Cross-berry
Raisin
- p. 104
(90% of life-size)

Wild Pear
- p. 140
(life-size)

Flat Crown Albizia
- p. 190
(60% of
life-size)

Powder-puff Tree
- p. 168
(10% of life-size)

White Gardenia
- p. 136
(50% of life-size)

FLOWERS IN SPRAYS & CLUSTERS

Water Berry
- p. 172
(70% of life-size)

Forest Elder
- p. 112
(60% of life-size)

Tinderwood
- p. 128
(50% of life-size)

False Olive Sage
- p 114, 228
(40% of life-size)

False Cabbage Tree
- p 29
(30% of life-size)

Common Poison
Bush - p. 186
(25% of life-size)

FLOWERS IN BALLS & SPIKES

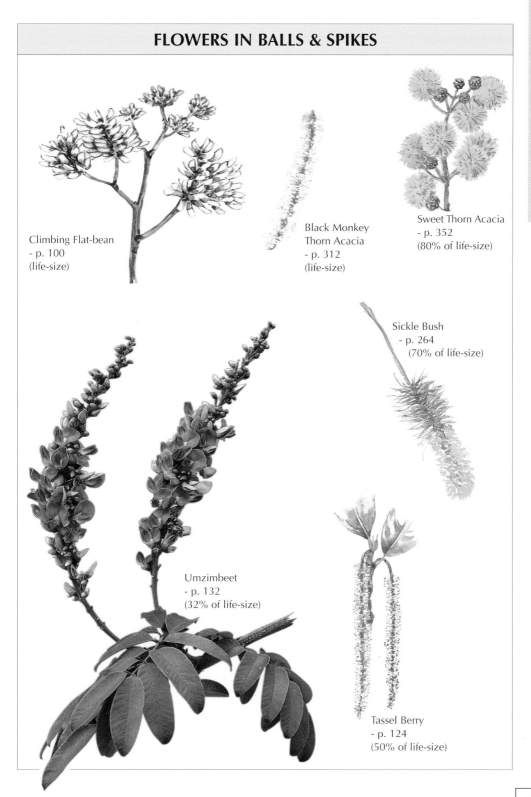

Climbing Flat-bean
- p. 100
(life-size)

Black Monkey
Thorn Acacia
- p. 312
(life-size)

Sweet Thorn Acacia
- p. 352
(80% of life-size)

Sickle Bush
- p. 264
(70% of life-size)

Umzimbeet
- p. 132
(32% of life-size)

Tassel Berry
- p. 124
(50% of life-size)

UNIQUE FRUIT

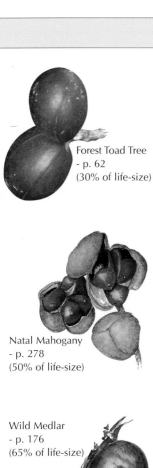

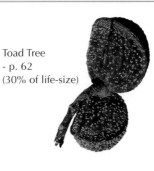

Toad Tree
- p. 62
(30% of life-size)

Cape Chestnut
- p 69
(50% of life-size)

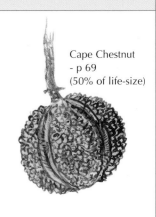

Forest Toad Tree
- p. 62
(30% of life-size)

White Gardenia
- p. 136
(50% of life-size)

Natal Mahogany
- p. 278
(50% of life-size)

Transvaal Gardenia
- p 138
(50% of life-size)

Wild Medlar
- p. 176
(65% of life-size)

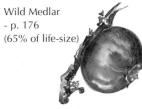

Thorny Gardenia
- p. 138
(75% of life-size)

Natal Gardenia
- p 138
(45% of life-size)

Black and Green Monkey Orange
- p 146, 148
(45% of life-size)

Cape Gardenia
- p. 138
(30% of life-size)

UNIQUE & GRAPE-LIKE FRUIT (50% of life-size)

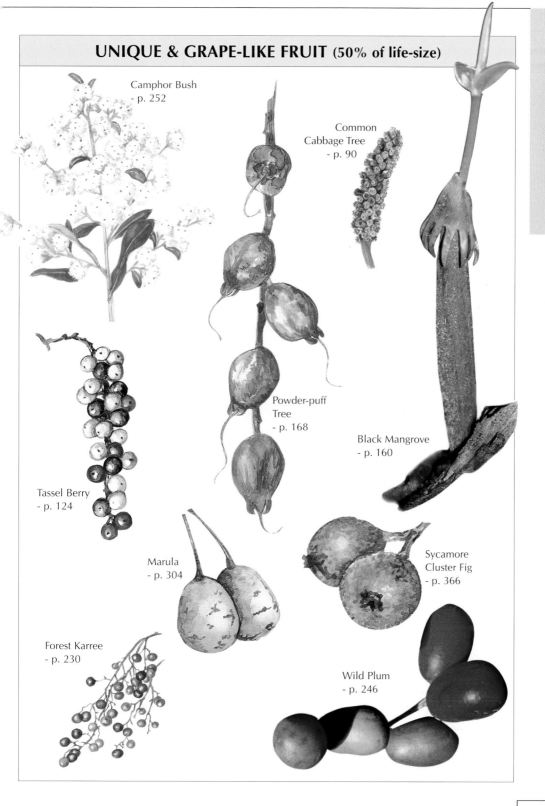

Camphor Bush
- p. 252

Common
Cabbage Tree
- p. 90

Powder-puff
Tree
- p. 168

Black Mangrove
- p. 160

Tassel Berry
- p. 124

Marula
- p. 304

Sycamore
Cluster Fig
- p. 366

Forest Karree
- p. 230

Wild Plum
- p. 246

49

BERRIES (60% of life-size)

Common Poison Bush
- p. 186

Tinderwood
- p. 128

Water Berry
- p. 172

Coastal Red
Milkwood
- p. 154

Buffalo-thorn
- p. 292

Cape Ash
- p. 274

White Pear
- p. 198

Kooboo-berry
- p. 116

Cross-berry
Raisin
- p. 104

PODS (60% of life-size)

For other distinctive pods, see Twice Compound Leaves, pages 56 - 57.

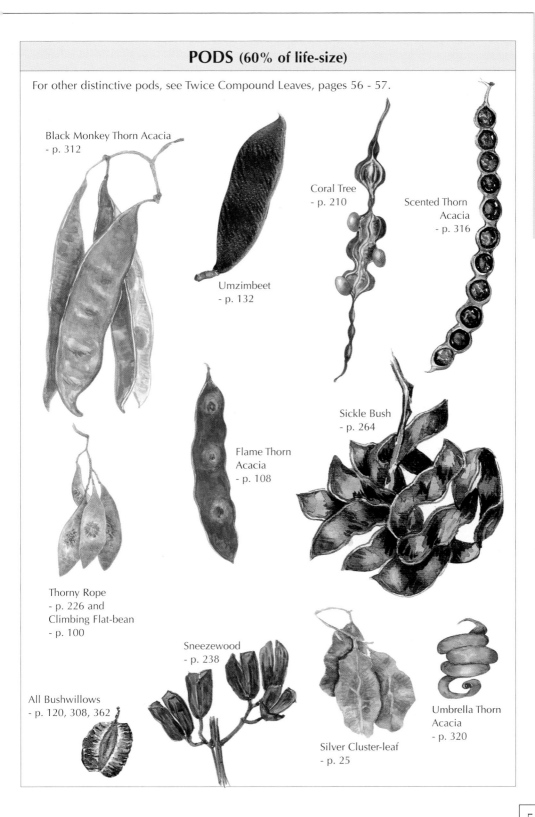

Black Monkey Thorn Acacia
- p. 312

Coral Tree
- p. 210

Scented Thorn
Acacia
- p. 316

Umzimbeet
- p. 132

Sickle Bush
- p. 264

Flame Thorn
Acacia
- p. 108

Thorny Rope
- p. 226 and
Climbing Flat-bean
- p. 100

Sneezewood
- p. 238

All Bushwillows
- p. 120, 308, 362

Umbrella Thorn
Acacia
- p. 320

Silver Cluster-leaf
- p. 25

LARGE, SIMPLE LEAVES (20% of life-size)

Wild Medlar
- p. 176

Wild Poplar
- p. 27

Powder-puff Tree
- p. 168

Wild Cotton Tree
- p. 88

Giant-leaved Fig
- p. 76

PALE-VEINED & SIMPLE LEAVES

NEEDLE

Mangosteen
(45% of life size)

White Milkwood
- p. 342
(45% of life size)

Common Wild Fig
- p 184, 368
(20% of life-size)

Outeniqua Yellowwood
- p 16
(20% of life-size)

White Pear
- p. 198
(65% of life-size)

Water Berry
- p. 172
(45% of life-size)

Natal Fig
- p 184, 368
(30% of life-size)

Real Yellowwood
- p 16
(20% of life-size)

HERRINGBONE & THREE-VEINED SIMPLE LEAVES (50% of life-size)

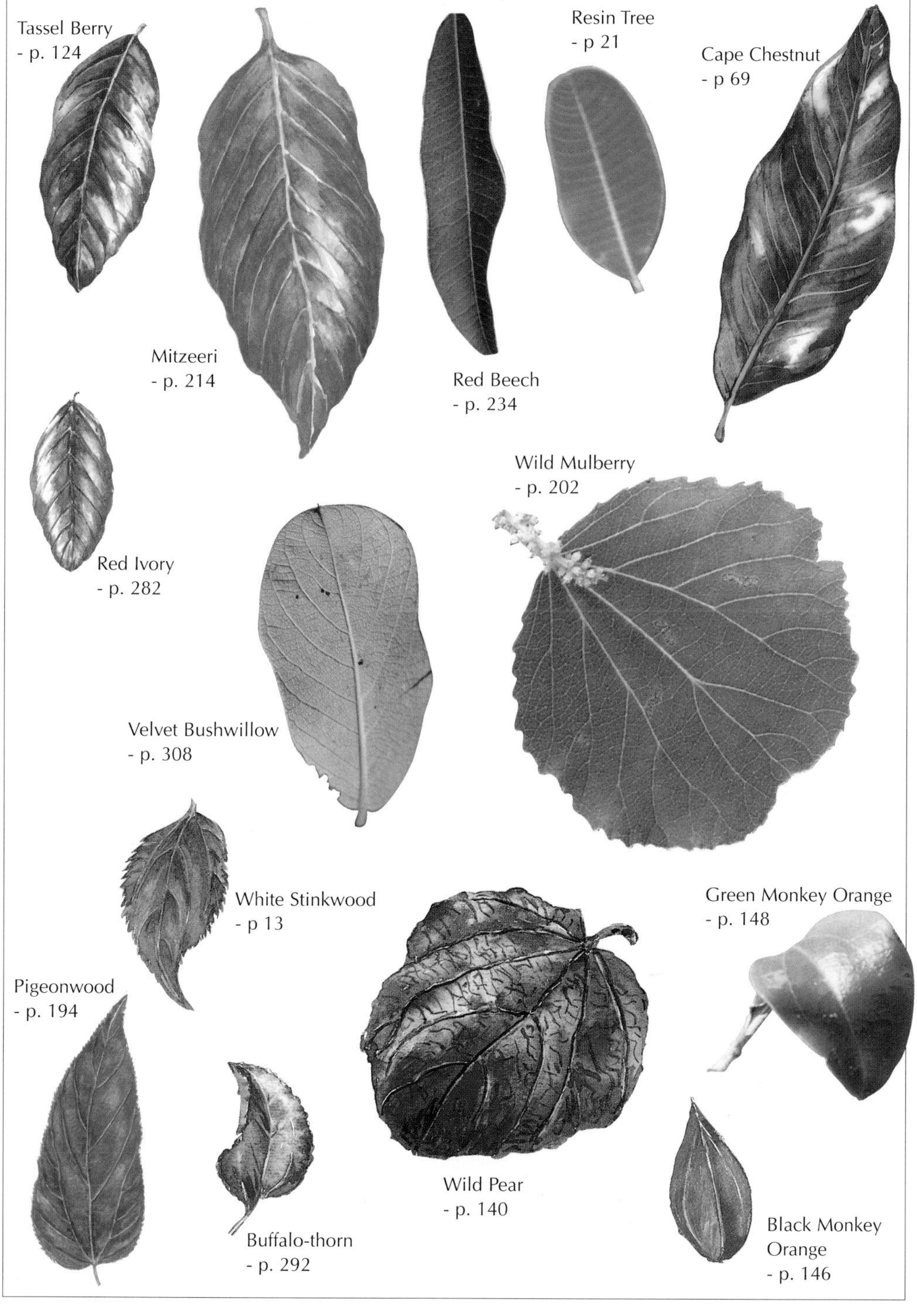

Tassel Berry
- p. 124

Resin Tree
- p 21

Cape Chestnut
- p 69

Mitzeeri
- p. 214

Red Beech
- p. 234

Red Ivory
- p. 282

Wild Mulberry
- p. 202

Velvet Bushwillow
- p. 308

White Stinkwood
- p 13

Green Monkey Orange
- p. 148

Pigeonwood
- p. 194

Wild Pear
- p. 140

Buffalo-thorn
- p. 292

Black Monkey
Orange
- p. 146

BI-COLOURED, SIMPLE LEAVES (40% of life-size)

False Olive Sage
- p. 114

Coast Silver Oak
- p. 150

Cape Beech
- p. 206

Camphor
Bush
- p. 252

Wild Olive
- p. 286

THREE-LEAFLET LEAVES (40% of life-size)

Red-stem
Corkwood
- p. 94

Crow-berry Karree
- p. 326

Green-stem Corkwood
- p 96

White Ironwood
- p. 242

Broad-leaved
Coral Tree
- p. 212

Coral Tree
- p. 210

Dwarf Coral
Tree - p 22

ONCE COMPOUND LEAVES (30% of life-size)

Forest
Knobwood
- p 220

Weeping
Boer-bean
- p. 338

Small
Knobwood
- p. 218

Sneezewood
- p. 238

Wild Plum
- p. 246

Horsewood
- p 220

Cape Ash
- p. 274

Natal Mahogany
- p. 278

False Horsewood
- p 67

Thorny Rope
- p. 226

Marula
- p. 304

Forest Mahogany
- p 280

Climbing Flat-bean
- p. 100

Umzimbeet
- p. 132

TWICE COMPOUND LEAVES (25% of life-size)

Many other compound leaves look very similar and can often be identified by the accompanying flowers and pods.

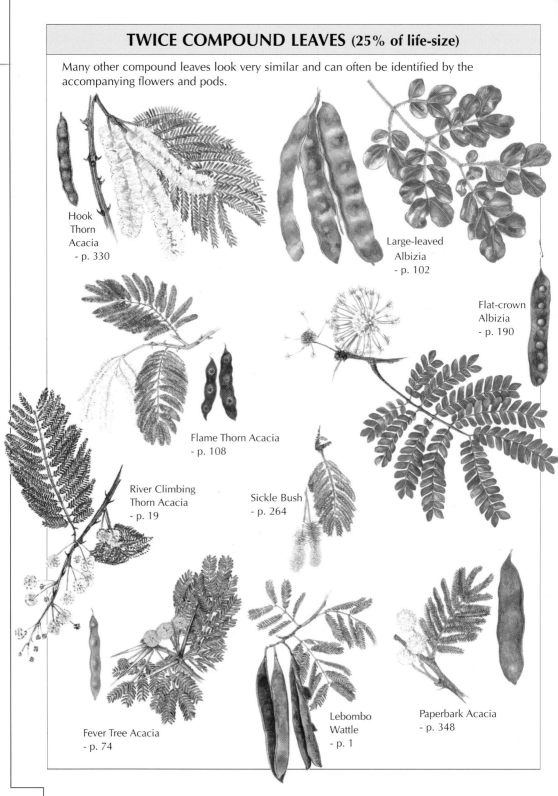

Hook
Thorn
Acacia
 - p. 330

Large-leaved
Albizia
 - p. 102

Flat-crown
Albizia
 - p. 190

Flame Thorn Acacia
 - p. 108

River Climbing
Thorn Acacia
 - p. 19

Sickle Bush
 - p. 264

Fever Tree Acacia
 - p. 74

Lebombo
Wattle
 - p. 1

Paperbark Acacia
 - p. 348

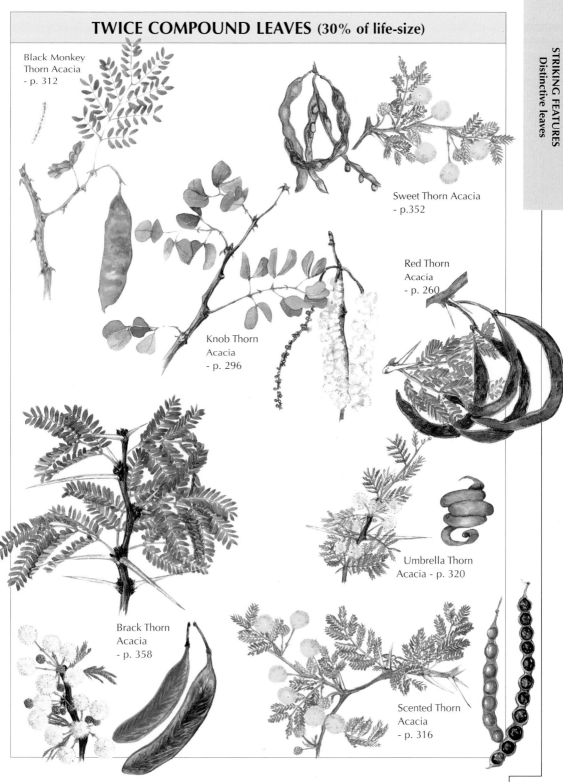

TWICE COMPOUND LEAVES (30% of life-size)

Black Monkey
Thorn Acacia
- p. 312

Sweet Thorn Acacia
- p.352

Red Thorn
Acacia
- p. 260

Knob Thorn
Acacia
- p. 296

Umbrella Thorn
Acacia - p. 320

Brack Thorn
Acacia
- p. 358

Scented Thorn
Acacia
- p. 316

57

SPIRALS & CLUSTERS (15% of life-size)

Wild Plum
- p. 246

Cape Ash
- p. 274

Red Beech
- p. 234

Black Monkey Orange
- p. 146

Common
Poison Bush
- p. 186

Broad-leaved
Resin Tree
- p 21

Bush Guarri
- p. 270

Water Berry
- p. 172

SIMPLE AUTUMN LEAVES

Red Bushwillow
- p. 120
(50% of life-size)

Velvet Bushwillow
- p. 308
(50% of life-size)

Tamboti
- p. 370
(50% of life-size)

Wild Poplar
- p 27
(40% of
life-size)

Red Beech
- p. 234
(40% of life-size)

River Bushwillow
- p. 362
(40% of life-size)

ASYMMETRICAL LEAVES (40% of life-size)

Wild Plum
- p. 246

Sneezewood
- p. 238

Cape Ash
- p. 274
(20% of
life-size)

Horsewood
- p 220

Weeping
Boer-bean
- p. 338

Pigeonwood
- p. 194

COMPOUND AUTUMN LEAVES

Coral Tree
- p. 210
(30% of life-size)

Sneezewood
- p. 238
(40% of life-size)

Wild Plum
- p. 246
(30% of life-size)

STRIKING FEATURES
Distinctive leaves

Forest trail

The trees covered here are specifically of the Scarp and Low-lying forests of the Coast. They do not include trees more likely to be found in Riverine, Dune, Sand, Swamp and Mangrove forests. Trees that thrive in Low-lying and Scarp forests are so tall, and grow so close together, with their canopies intertwined, that it is difficult to see the leaves, fruit or flowers. It is often easier to get to know these trees by looking at their bark, rather than the whole tree.

This Forest Trail has been designed to find the trees by bark and leaves, and by a short description of a main feature. Most of the trees are covered in full detail further on in the book. A few are shown here only, or here and in the Distinctive Striking Features section, pages 44 - 59.

All bark tends to be smoother while the tree is young, and in dense forest they are often also paler than in the adult tree. This adds to the visual delight as you are walking, but makes the identification of trees with "smooth, pale bark" extremely complex. Novices should promise themselves that they will return at some later date, when they know more! Lichen on the bark of trees in forests adds to the confusion as it grows in different colours and textures. The lichen also adds to the appeal of forests, but usually cannot be used to help with identification as it is not associated with specific trees.

Most bark, however, does have very distinctive characteristics. Spend a little time familiarising yourself with the classification of the Forest Trail – Knobs and Thorns, Lengthways Grooved, Rough etc. When you find bark that seems to fit one of the categories, look at the lower leaves, or leaves on the ground near the tree. Often, leaf detail can also be seen with binoculars. Be aware that immature leaves sometimes differ from the older ones, eg. Thorny Elm, and that leaves on long, straight, coppice shoots are sometimes not characteristic of the tree. You could be lucky and find a pod, fruit or flower, even on the forest floor. If so, be sure it belongs to your tree, and not the one next door! Please note that the pictures of leaves next to the bark, are not in proportion to one another.

As we move into the twenty-first century, the forests of South Africa are few and far between, and their value cannot be over-estimated. Enjoy them, treasure them, boast about them, and return to them again, to find that in every season of every year, they offer new experiences.

Thorny Rope (no. 231) - p. 226. Long thorns clumped on swellings, on a dark trunk. Leaf: 15 - 80 mm

Thorny Elm (no. 43) - p. 222. When folded leaves crack as if varnished; thorny young stems; sharp, hair-like spine at leaf-tip. Leaf: 20 - 150 mm

Small Knobwood (no. 253) - p. 218. Spiral arrangement of compound leaves; leaflets with 4 - 8 pairs of side veins; citrus smell when crushed. Leaf: 40 - 200 mm

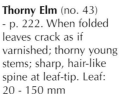

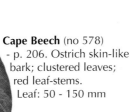

Forest Knobwood (no 254) - p. 220. Leaflets of compound leaves have 16 - 20 pairs of side veins, and a wavy margin; citrus smell when crushed. Leaf: 50 - 300 mm

Cape Beech (no 578) - p. 206. Ostrich skin-like bark; clustered leaves; red leaf-stems. Leaf: 50 - 150 mm

Coral Tree (no 245) - p. 210. Thorns on trunk and branches; 3-leaved compound leaves; red and black seeds in pods. Leaf: 60 - 220 mm

61

Common Cabbage Tree
(no 564) - p. 90.
Unique leaf shape.
Leaf: 200 - 700 mm

Large-leaved Albizia (no 158) - p. 300.
Twice compound leaves, with large, roundish
leaflets and brown, broad bean pods.
Leaf: 100 - 350 mm

Toad Trees
Long elliptic, simple leaves.
Leaf: 90 - 200 mm
Toad Tree: (no 644)
Fruit dark with pale spots.
Forest Toad Tree: (no 645)
Fruit smooth and green.

Coast Silver Oak (no 724)
- p. 150. Silvery-blue, bi-coloured
leaves, with a toothed margin.
Leaf: 25 - 120 mm

Camphor Bush (no 733) - p. 252.
Cottonwool-ball-like fruit and bi-
coloured leaves; all parts smell of
camphor. Leaf: 20 - 150 mm

Umbrella Thorn Acacia
(no 188) - p. 320.
Very tiny, twice compound
leaflets; straight and hooked
thorns; characteristic pods.
Leaf: 20 - 30 mm

Brack Thorn Acacia (no 183.1)
- p. 358. Dark, prickly, large
cushions at base of thorns and
leaves. Leaf: 45 - 90 mm

Scented Thorn Acacia (no 179)
- p. 316. Necklace-like pods; twice
compound leaves;
ball-flowers.
Leaf: 40 - 50 mm

Tinderwood (no 667) - p. 128.
Simple, downward arched
leaves, in whorls of three;
white marks on pale grey bark
of branchlets. Leaf: 20 - 250 mm

**Black Monkey Thorn
Acacia** (no 161) - p. 312.
Deeply fissured bark, with
yellowish under-bark and
pointed, flat bean pods.
Leaf: 25 - 70 mm

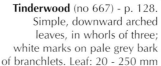

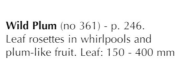

Wild Plum (no 361) - p. 246.
Leaf rosettes in whirlpools and
plum-like fruit. Leaf: 150 - 400 mm

Marula (no 360) - p. 304. Compound leaves with pointed leaflets; characteristic plum-like fruit; twigs end as stubby fingers. Leaf: 100 - 150 mm

Mitzeeri (no 324) - p. 214. Knob-like protrusions on branchlets and twigs and large, simple leaves with herringbone veins. Leaf: 60 - 180 mm

Weeping Boer-bean (no 202) - p. 338. Dark-brown, broad bean pods, and compound leaves with paired leaflets at the tip. Leaf: 110 - 180 mm

Forest Karree (no 380) - p. 230. Large 3-leaflet compound leaves with reddish leaf-stem, delicate, long flower-sprays. Leaf: 130 - 200 mm

Red Ivory (no 450) - p. 282. Roundish, shiny, simple leaves with herring-bone veins. Leaf: 25 - 60 mm

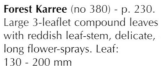

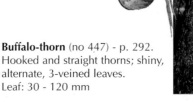

Buffalo-thorn (no 447) - p. 292. Hooked and straight thorns; shiny, alternate, 3-veined leaves. Leaf: 30 - 120 mm

Tamboti (no 341) - p. 370. Small, simple, alternate leaves with a toothed margin; dark, blocky bark. Leaf: 30 - 80 mm

Velvet Bushwillow (no 537) - p. 308. Herringbone veins on large, roundish, velvety leaves; four-winged pods. Leaf: 60 - 100 mm

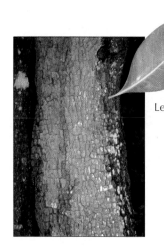

White Milkwood (no 579) - p. 342. Single, pale central vein in dark, simple, leaves; pale, blocky bark. Leaf: 40 - 150 mm

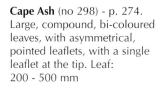

Cape Ash (no 298) - p. 274. Large, compound, bi-coloured leaves, with asymmetrical, pointed leaflets, with a single leaflet at the tip. Leaf: 200 - 500 mm

Natal Mahogany (no 301) - p. 278. Conspicuous, shiny leaflets have a rounded tip, and become smaller towards leaf-base; more common in the north. Leaf: 350 - 500 mm

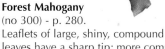

Forest Mahogany (no 300) - p. 280. Leaflets of large, shiny, compound leaves have a sharp tip; more common south of Stanger. Leaf: 400 - 700 mm

65

Red-stem Corkwood (no 277) - p. 94.
Compound leaves have 5 leaflets and no
spines on trunk or branches; bark sheds
reddish flakes.
Leaf: 70 - 200 mm

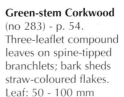

Green-stem Corkwood
(no 283) - p. 54.
Three-leaflet compound
leaves on spine-tipped
branchlets; bark sheds
straw-coloured flakes.
Leaf: 50 - 100 mm

Umzimbeet (no 227) - p. 132.
Characteristic purple flower-spikes,
velvety pods and compound leaves.
Leaf: 130 - 250 mm

Wild Mulberry
(no 503) - p. 202.
Smallish tree with striking,
roundish leaves with 5 - 9
veins radiating from the base.
Leaf: 50 - 200 mm

Real Yellowwood (no 18) - p. 16.
Long, thin, dark green leaves
spirally arranged at tips of
branchlets. Bark flakes in long
strips. Leaf: 15 - 100 mm

Outeniqua Yellowwood (no 16)
- p. 16. Leaves thin and small, often
sickle-shaped, and blue-grey. Bark
flakes in large, irregular to circular
strips. Leaf: 60 - 100 mm

Bush Guarri (no 600) - p. 270.
Blue-green leaves form dense
star-like clusters towards ends
of twigs. Leaf: 30 - 110 mm

Water Berry (no 555) - p. 172.
Blue-green leaves with distinct,
yellow central veins form
rosettes. Leaf: 30 - 100 mm

Horsewood (no 265) - p. 220.
Clusters of compound leaves,
with asymmetrical leaflets;
offensive aniseed smell
when crushed.
Leaf: 200 - 300 mm

False Horsewood (no 438)
- p. 220. Compound leaves
with alternately winged leaf-
stems, and toothed leaflets.
Leaf: 40 - 200 mm

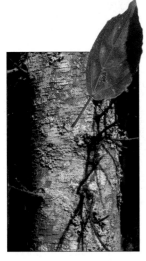

Broom Cluster Fig
(no 50) - p. 182.
Clusters of figs hang
from long, thick,
broom-like stalks.
Leaf: 80 - 200 mm

Flat-crown Albizia (no 148)
- p. 190. Distinct flat canopy; twice
compound leaves with square
leaflets and diagonal central veins.
Leaf: 100 - 400 mm

Green Monkey Orange (no 629)
- p. 148. Single, shiny, alternate leaves on spiny twigs and branchlets; huge, orange-like, green to yellow fruit. Leaf: 15 - 90 mm

Black Monkey Orange (no 626)
- p. 146. Leathery, dark green leaves in clusters, on short, stubby branchlets; huge, orange-like green to yellow fruit. Leaf: 20 - 90 mm

Common Poison Bush (no 639)
- p. 186. Clustered, simple, opposite, leathery leaves with sharp thorn-like tip; red to black berries. Leaf: 50 - 100 mm

Pigeonwood (no 42) - p. 194. Triangular leaf with completely toothed edge and asymmetrical base. Leaf: 60 - 200 mm

Natal Fig (no 57) - p. 184, 368. Aerial roots and shiny, dark green leaves with a pale central vein. Figs small (10 mm), hairless, stalkless. Leaf: 30 - 80 mm

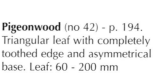

Kooboo-berry (no 410) - p. 116. Red fruit like small apples; simple, blue-green, leathery leaves. Leaf: 20 - 90 mm

Wild Poplar (no 335) - p. 27. Large, heart-shaped, poplar-like leaves and smooth, pale to yellow bark. Leaf: 100 - 150 mm

Cape Chestnut (no 256) - p. 45. Large, simple leaves with herringbone veins, deep pink flowers, plum-like fruitwith a warty skin. Leaf: 50 - 220 mm

Red Beech (no 364) - p. 234. Obvious herringbone veins on long, thin, simple leaves in clusters with red leaves among the foliage. Leaf: 50 - 160 mm

White Pear (no 422) - p. 198. Distinct pale central vein on simple leaves and circular ridges on smooth, pale bark. Leaf: 50 - 150 mm

White Ironwood (no 261) - p. 242. Compound, three-leaflet leaves with distinctly wavy margin and smooth, whitish-grey to pink bark. Leaf: 140 - 200 mm

White Stinkwood (no 39) - p. 13. Tall straight trunk with smooth, pale grey bark and bright green, almost heart-shaped leaves with only upper two-thirds toothed. Leaf: 15 - 100 mm

Trees greet you

UNIQUE TREES

The trees in this section have such unique forms that you do not need to spend time developing comprehensive Search Images of them. It is helpful to page through this section and look at "Where to find this tree easily", for each tree, to see if it is likely to occur in the area where you are tree spotting. Once you know it is there, you are going to find that it greets you!

UNIQUE FAMILY GROUPS

Lala Palms can be found all along the KwaZulu-Natal coast, and here they are growing in a Sand Forest, south of Kosi Bay.

DATE PALM (WILD DATE PALM)

Phoenix reclinata

PALM FAMILY **ARECACEAE**	**SA Tree Number 22**

AFRIKAANS Wildedadelboom, Wildekoffie **N. SOTHO** Mopalamo **SISWATI** liLala **TSONGA** Ncindzu **VENDA** Mutshevho **XHOSA** iSundu **ZULU** iSundu

The term **reclinata** means bent down or backwards, and refers to the shape of the leaves.

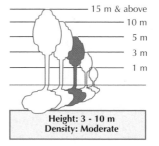

Where you'll find this tree easily

Date Palms are normally found in groups and usually grow near water.

🍃 They are easiest to find in river beds and Along Rivers (A).

🍃 They are also common in the Sand, Swamp, Scarp and Low-lying forests, and Waterlogged Grassland of the Coast (C).

A	B
C	D

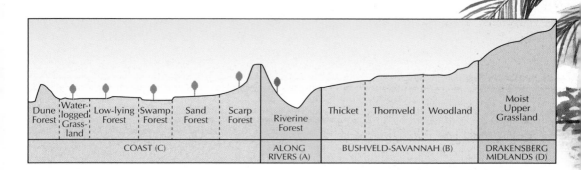

Dune Forest	Water-logged Grass-land	Low-lying Forest	Swamp Forest	Sand Forest	Scarp Forest	Riverine Forest	Thicket	Thornveld	Woodland	Moist Upper Grassland
COAST (C)						ALONG RIVERS (A)	BUSHVELD-SAVANNAH (B)			DRAKENSBERG MIDLANDS (D)

Striking features

- Massive, fern-like leaves grow directly from the top of stems, or from very low down in younger, smaller trees.

- It can be multi- or single-stemmed, with no stems visible between the leaves.

- The grape-like, orange-brown, fleshy fruit grows in bunches on long stalks.

- It can be a taller, trunked palm, with low-branching stems and leaves around its base.

15 m & above
10 m
5 m
3 m
1 m

Height: 3 - 10 m
Density: Moderate

Male flower

Female flower

Fruit

FEVER TREE ACACIA

Acacia xanthophloea

THORN-TREE FAMILY
MIMOSACEAE

SA Tree Number 189

AFRIKAANS Koorsboom, Geeldoringboom **N. SOTHO** Mosehla **TSONGA** Nkelenga
TSWANA More o mosetlha **VENDA** Muunga-gwena **ZULU** umHlosinga, umHlofunga, umDlovune

The term **xanthophloea** comes from the Greek "xanthos" which refers to the yellow colour of the bark.

Where you'll find this tree easily

Fever Tree Acacias often form small groups around wet areas.

🌱 They are easiest to find Along Rivers (A), especially in the Sand Forest of the Coast (C).

🌱 They can also be found in some of the Swamp Forests of the Coast (C).

A	B
C	D

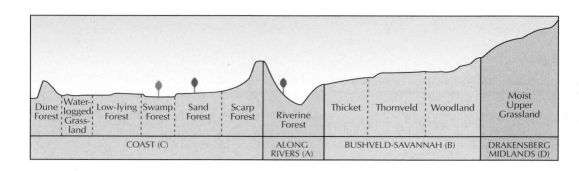

| | COAST (C) | | | | ALONG RIVERS (A) | BUSHVELD-SAVANNAH (B) | | DRAKENSBERG MIDLANDS (D) |

Dune Forest | Water-logged Grassland | Low-lying Forest | Swamp Forest | Sand Forest | Scarp Forest | Riverine Forest | Thicket | Thornveld | Woodland | Moist Upper Grassland

Striking features

- **Distinctive, smooth, yellow-green bark peels off the trunk and branches in paper-thin layers, and is covered in a yellow powder.**

- It is a single-stemmed thorn tree that branches upwards to form a moderate, spreading canopy.

- The yellow-green leaves are twice compound and delicate.

- The flower-balls are yellow and bloom from August to November.

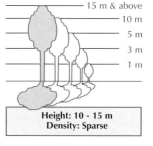

15 m & above
10 m
5 m
3 m
1 m

Height: 10 - 15 m
Density: Sparse

Leaves & flowers

Pods

GIANT-LEAVED FIG

Ficus lutea

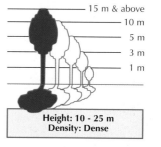

MULBERRY FAMILY MORACEAE	SA Tree Number 61

AFRIKAANS Reuseblaarvy **XHOSA** umThombe, uluZi **ZULU** umVubu omkhulu

Where you'll find this tree easily

The Giant-leaved Fig grows singly among other
species of trees.

🌱 It is easiest to find in the Low-lying and Swamp forests
of the Coast (C).

🌱 It can also be found in the Dune Forest of the Coast (C).

A	B
C	D

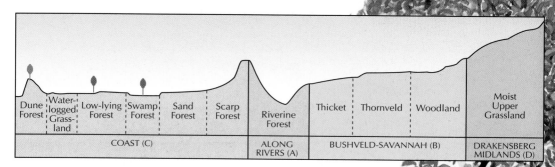

Dune Forest	Water-logged Grass-land	Low-lying Forest	Swamp Forest	Sand Forest	Scarp Forest	Riverine Forest	Thicket	Thornveld	Woodland	Moist Upper Grassland
COAST (C)						ALONG RIVERS (A)	BUSHVELD-SAVANNAH (B)			DRAKENSBERG MIDLANDS (D)

Striking features

• This single-stemmed tree has a thick, buttressed trunk
and smooth, dark-grey bark.

• **The dark green leaves are huge and leathery and
resemble those of the exotic ornamental house plant,
the Rubber Plant.**

• The yellowish central vein and 6 - 8 pairs of side veins
are pale but clearly visible, forming loops along the
leaf-margin.

• **The furry, yellow, fleshy fruit has no stalk and grows at
the ends of branchlets in the angles formed by the
leaf-stem.**

• The branches often hang so low down that the foliage
hides the trunk.

• New leaves have a reddish-bronze tinge and stand
out among the foliage in early spring.

15 m & above
10 m
5 m
3 m
1 m

**Height: 10 - 25 m
Density: Dense**

Leaf

Fruit

LALA PALM

Hyphaene coriacea

PALM FAMILY
ARECACEAE

SA Tree Number 23

AFRIKAANS Lalapalm **SISWATI** iLala **TSONGA** Nala **VENDA** Mulala **ZULU** iLala

Where you'll find this tree easily

The Lala Palm normally grows in spread-out groups.
It is often the dominant tree on deep, nutrient-poor,
sandy and clay soils.

⚲ It is easiest to find in the Sand Forest of the Coast (C).

⚲ It can also be found Along Rivers (A), as well as in
the Swamp Forest and Waterlogged Grassland of the
Coast (C).

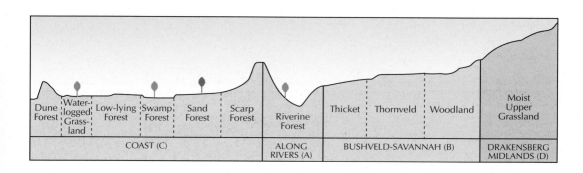

Striking features

• This is a typical palm tree.

• **It has huge, hand-shaped leaves growing from the top
of the trunk.**

• **Mature trunks are tall, smooth and bare; shorter and
immature trunks are wrapped with the dry remains of
old leaf-stems.**

• **The fruit is a large, dry, dark brown, shiny ball that is
present throughout the year.**

• There are hooked thorns along the long leaf-stems.

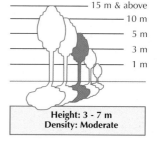

Height: 3 - 7 m
Density: Moderate

Female flowers   **Male flowers**   **Fruit**

LARGE-LEAVED DRAGON TREE

Dracaena aletriformis

DRAGON TREE FAMILY
DRACAENACEAE

SA Tree Number 30.9

AFRIKAANS Grootblaardrakeboom **N. SOTHO** Photsoloma **VENDA** Tshila-mbila
XHOSA umKhoma-khoma **ZULU** iGonsi-lasehlathini

The term **aletriformis** refers to the shape of the leaves.

Where you'll find this tree easily

This is a conspicuous tree of the forest under-storey.

- It is easiest to find in the Low-lying Forest of the Coast (C).
- It can also be found in most of the other Coastal forests (C) and Along Rivers (A).

A	B
C	D

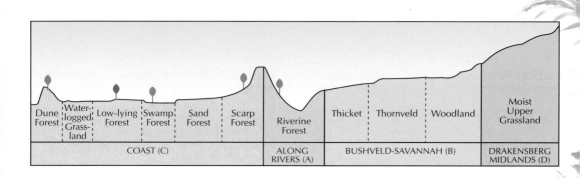

Dune Forest	Water-logged Grass-land	Low-lying Forest	Swamp Forest	Sand Forest	Scarp Forest	Riverine Forest	Thicket	Thornveld	Woodland	Moist Upper Grassland
COAST (C)						ALONG RIVERS (A)	BUSHVELD-SAVANNAH (B)			DRAKENSBERG MIDLANDS (D)

Striking features

- This is a small, single-stemmed tree that may branch low down to form a few similar-sized stems.
- **Many long, drooping, pointed, dark green leaves grow at the end of the single trunk.**
- The straight stems are smooth and light brown, with distinct rings of old leaf-scars.
- Even though the leaves look thick and leathery, they are soft and pliable and move easily in the wind.

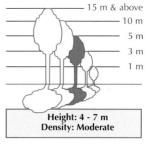

15 m & above
10 m
5 m
3 m
1 m

Height: 4 - 7 m
Density: Moderate

Flower

Fruit

81

NATAL BANANA (NATAL WILD BANANA)

Strelitzia nicolai

CRANE-FLOWER FAMILY
STRELITZIACEAE

SA Tree Number 34

AFRIKAANS Natalse Wildepiesang, Witpiesang **XHOSA** iKhamanga **ZULU** isiGude, isiGceba

The term **nicolai** refers to the Emperor Nicholas of Russia.

Where you'll find this tree easily

This tree is a feature of the KwaZulu-Natal coast.

🌳 It can easily be found in the Low-lying Forest of the Coast (C).

🌳 It can also be found in the Dune, Swamp and Scarp forests of the Coast (C), and Along Rivers (A).

A	B
C	D

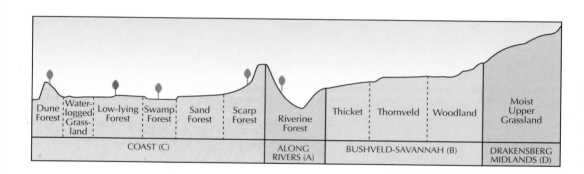

Dune Forest | Water-logged Grassland | Low-lying Forest | Swamp Forest | Sand Forest | Scarp Forest | Riverine Forest | Thicket | Thornveld | Woodland | Moist Upper Grassland

COAST (C) | ALONG RIVERS (A) | BUSHVELD-SAVANNAH (B) | DRAKENSBERG MIDLANDS (D)

Striking features

- It is a single- or multi-stemmed tree with leaves growing from the top of the trunk in one vertical plane to form a characteristic fan-like canopy.
- **The huge leaves, like those of banana trees, break up to resemble giant feathers.**
- The leaf-stalks are long and thick.
- The stem is smooth with elevated rings of old leaf-scars.
- **The flowers resemble the head of a bird, with a white crest and purple beak.**

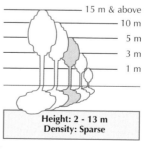

15 m & above
10 m
5 m
3 m
1 m

Height: 2 - 13 m
Density: Sparse

82

Flower

RUBBER EUPHORBIA

Euphorbia tirucalli

EUPHORBIA FAMILY **EUPHORBIACEAE**	**SA Tree Number 355**

AFRIKAANS Kraalmelkbos, Kraalnaboom   **N. SOTHO** Motlalamela   **TSONGA** Mahumbana
VENDA Muṱungu   **XHOSA** umHlontlo   **ZULU** umSululu

The term **tirucalli** refers to the place in India, Tira-Calli, to which the tree was exported early in the twentieth century.

Where you'll find this tree easily

The Rubber Euphorbia grows on rocky outcrops and is often seen around old kraal sites.

- It is easiest to find in the Woodland of the Bushveld-Savannah (B).
- It is also found in the Moist Upper Grassland of the Drakensberg Midlands (D), and the Low-lying and Sand forests of the Coast (C).

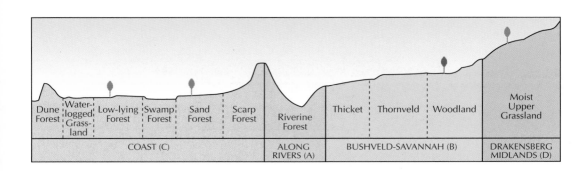

Dune Forest / Water-logged Grass-land / Low-lying Forest / Swamp Forest / Sand Forest / Scarp Forest	Riverine Forest	Thicket / Thornveld / Woodland	Moist Upper Grassland
COAST (C)	ALONG RIVERS (A)	BUSHVELD-SAVANNAH (B)	DRAKENSBERG MIDLANDS (D)

Striking features

- This is an evergreen tree without obvious leaves.
- **It is a single-stemmed tree and branches low down into many thin succulent branches to form a sparse, irregular canopy.**
- **The branches are green, thin and spindly and stand out like many fingers.**
- The small, yellow flowers grow on the tips of the branches from June to September.
- The tree contains a poisonous, milky latex.

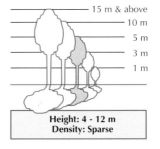

15 m & above
10 m
5 m
3 m
1 m

Height: 4 - 12 m
Density: Sparse

Flower

Fruit

TREE EUPHORBIA (COMMON TREE EUPHORBIA)

Euphorbia ingens

EUPHORBIA FAMILY **EUPHORBIACEAE**	**SA Tree Number 351**

AFRIKAANS Gewone Naboom, Noorsdoring **N. SOTHO** Mohlohlo-kgomo, Mokgoto **SISWATI** iShupa **TSONGA** Nkondze **TSWANA** Monkgôpô **VENDA** Mukonde **ZULU** umHlonhlo, umPhapha

The term **ingens** means large and refers to the size of the tree.

Where you'll find this tree easily

The Tree Euphorbia is fairly widespread in the low-lying areas of KwaZulu-Natal, where it prefers well-drained soils.

- It is easiest to find in Sand and Low-lying forests of the Coast (C).
- It also occurs on Rocky Outcrops and Termite Mounds of the Bushveld-Savannah (B).

A	B
C	D

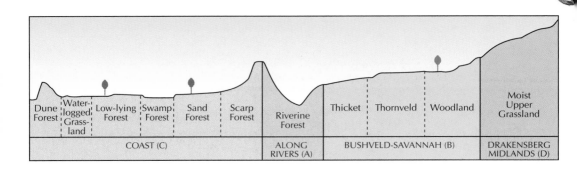

Dune Forest	Water-logged Grass-land	Low-lying Forest	Swamp Forest	Sand Forest	Scarp Forest	Riverine Forest	Thicket	Thornveld	Woodland	Moist Upper Grassland
COAST (C)						ALONG RIVERS (A)	BUSHVELD-SAVANNAH (B)			DRAKENSBERG MIDLANDS (D)

Striking features

- **This is an evergreen tree with no obvious leaves.**
- The trunk is short, with coarse bark.
- **The thick, straight, green branches have constricted, angular segments.**
- The tree branches low down, splitting again repeatedly to form a densely branched, rounded canopy.
- There are sometimes very short, paired spines on the edges of the branches which contain an irritant, milky latex.

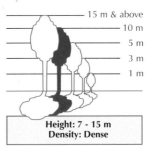

15 m & above
10 m
5 m
3 m
1 m

Height: 7 - 15 m
Density: Dense

86

Flowers

Fruit

WILD COTTON TREE

Hibiscus tiliacea

COTTON FAMILY
MALVACEAE

SA Tree Number 464

AFRIKAANS Kuskatoenboom, Wildekatoenboom **XHOSA** umLolwa **ZULU** uLola

The term **tiliaceus** refers to the similarity of this tree and those of the genus *Tilia*, which is the ancient name for the Lime Tree.

Where you'll find this tree easily

The Wild Cotton Tree usually forms large uniform stands.

🍶 It is most easily found in the Swamp Forest of the Coast (C).

🍶 Because the seeds are distributed by the sea, it also occurs in India, on the Indian Ocean islands, as well as many Pacific Ocean islands.

A	B
C	D

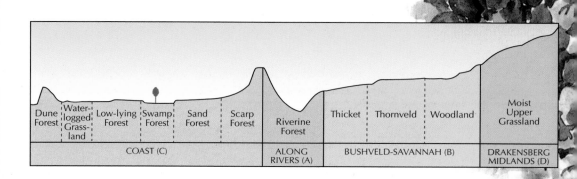

Dune Forest	Water-logged Grass-land	Low-lying Forest	Swamp Forest	Sand Forest	Scarp Forest	Riverine Forest	Thicket	Thornveld	Woodland	Moist Upper Grassland
COAST (C)						ALONG RIVERS (A)	BUSHVELD-SAVANNAH (B)			DRAKENSBERG MIDLANDS (D)

Striking features

- This multi-stemmed tree branches low down into many thick branches to form a dense, leafy canopy that hides the main trunk and branches.

- The bark is smooth and grey-brown and is covered in small, raised dots.

- **The huge leaves are heart-shaped and leathery, olive-green above and velvety white underneath.**

- **The flowers are huge, yellow cups with a purple centre, that turn a deep apricot with age.**

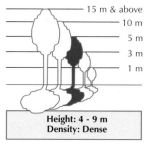

15 m & above
10 m
5 m
3 m
1 m

Height: 4 - 9 m
Density: Dense

Flower

COMMON CABBAGE TREE

Cussonia spicata

CABBAGE TREE FAMILY ARALIACEAE	SA Tree Number 564

AFRIKAANS Gewone Kiepersol, Laeveld Kiepersol   **N. SOTHO** Motšhetšhe   **SISWATI** umSenge, umSenga **TSONGA** Musenje   **TSWANA** Mosêtsê   **VENDA** Musenzhe   **XHOSA** umBoza, umSingomzane **ZULU** umSenge

The term **spicata** refers to the flowers that grow in spikes.

Where you'll find this tree easily

The Common Cabbage Tree grows singly among other species of trees.

🌱 It is easiest to find on Rocky Outcrops in the Thornveld and Woodland of the Bushveld-Savannah (B) and the Moist Upper Grassland of the Drakensberg Midlands (D).

🌱 It can also be found in the Low-lying and Scarp forests of the Coast (C), and Along Rivers (A).

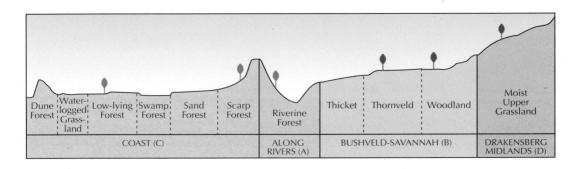

| COAST (C) | ALONG RIVERS (A) | BUSHVELD-SAVANNAH (B) | DRAKENSBERG MIDLANDS (D) |

Striking features

- This is a single-stemmed tree with a grey, corky bark that branches fairly high up into many large, crooked branches to form a dense, round canopy.

- **The compound, hand-shaped leaves are large and blue-grey-green, with very long leaf-stems.**

- The leaves are spirally arranged at the tips of thick branchlets.

- **The distinctively shaped leaflets have a toothed margin and are deeply indented, often very close to the central vein to form 2 - 3 lobes.**

- Up to nine leaflets come from a single point at the tip of the leaf-stem.

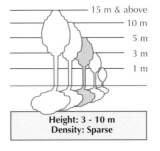

15 m & above
10 m
5 m
3 m
1 m

Height: 3 - 10 m
Density: Sparse

COMMON CABBAGE TREE

Cussonia spicata

Links with animals

Black Rhino eat bark and roots. Baboons and Bushpigs eat bark and roots in times of scarcity. Several species of Charaxes butterflies are attracted to the ripe fruits. Leaves are browsed by domestic stock and game, including Elephant and Kudu. Barbets eat the fruit. Flowers and fruit are eaten by Sombre and Black-eyed Bulbuls, Knysna Lourie, Speckled Mousebird and Redwinged Starling.

Human uses

The roots are eaten in emergencies when water and food are scarce. The caterpillars which breed on the tree are edible and considered a delicacy. Roots, flowers and flower-stalks are used to treat malaria, biliousness and venereal diseases.

Gardening

This is a fast-growing Cabbage Tree but is tender to frost. It has an invasive root system and should not be planted close to buildings or paving.

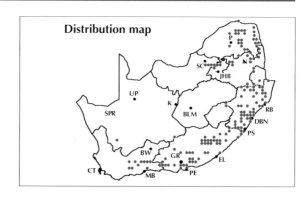

Distribution map

Rare wood; perishable; does not take paint and varnish readily; little difference in colour between heart- and sapwood; straight grain; can be sawn cleanly despite its softness.

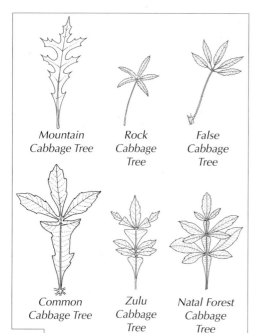

Mountain Cabbage Tree   *Rock Cabbage Tree*   *False Cabbage Tree*

Common Cabbage Tree   *Zulu Cabbage Tree*   *Natal Forest Cabbage Tree*

Look-alike trees

The other Cabbage Trees have a very similar growth form, and attention must be given to the leaves to be sure of the species.

Zulu Cabbage Tree *(Cussonia zuluensis)* has twice compound leaves with deeply divided margins and side leaflets. The leaves are glossy, dark green above and dull underneath.

Rock Cabbage Tree *(Cussonia natalensis)* has simple palmate leaves with 3 - 5 clearly demarcated lobes, with a shiny sheen and a conspicuous central vein in each lobe.

The Mountain Cabbage Tree *(Cussonia paniculata)* has compound leaves with a serrated, deeply cut margin but never cutting to the central vein. See **Sappi Tree Spotting Highveld.**

The False Cabbage Tree *(Schefflera umbellifera)*, page 29, has a smoother bark, is normally more branched and the leaves are hand-shaped, compound, with a very wavy, sometimes toothed margin.

The Natal Forest Cabbage Tree *(Cussonia sphaerocephala)* has a distinct rounded canopy, and twice compound leaves with a winged leaf-stem.

GROWTH DETAILS

This is a single-stemmed tree that branches into many large branches. The large, hand-shaped leaves are spirally arranged at the tips of the large branches. The canopy is dense and may be round or irregular.

Leaves The hand-shaped, compound leaves are spirally arranged at the tips of the large branches. There are 5 - 9 leaflets that are deeply lobed, cutting close to the central vein. They are shiny, blue-grey to grey-green and may be dark green. The central vein is conspicuous and the margin is normally toothed. The tips of the leaflets gradually taper to a point and the base is narrow. The leaf-stem is sturdy and long. (Leaf: 200 - 1 000 mm; leaf-stem 300 - 500 mm)

Flowers The small, greenish-yellow flowers are densely packed in 8 - 12 candelabra-like spikes on much-branched stalks at the end of the branchlets and twigs (April to June). (Spike: 50 - 150 x 15 - 40 mm)

Fruit The grape-like fruit is crowded on the spikes, and purple when ripe, from October to December. (Spike: 60 mm; fruit: 6 mm)

Bark The bark is light brown and corky, becoming darker and fissured with age. There are scars from old leaves on the branches.

Seasonal changes

Deciduous, may be evergreen. This tree can be identified by its growth form throughout the year.

	Oct	Nov	Dec	Jan	Feb	Mar	Apr	May	Jun	Jul	Aug	Sep
Leaf	▓	▓	▓	▓	▓	▓	▓	▓	▓			▓
Flower							▓	▓	▓			
Fruit/Pod	▓	▓	▓								▓	▓

93

RED-STEM CORKWOOD

Commiphora harveyi

**MYRRH FAMILY
BURSERACEAE**

SA Tree Number 277

AFRIKAANS Bruinkanniedood, Rooistamkanniedood **XHOSA** umHlunguthi
ZULU iMinyela, iHlunguthi, umuMbu

The term **harveyi** honours the well-known Irish botanist WH Harvey who worked in South Africa from 1811 to 1866.

Where you'll find this tree easily

The Red-stem Corkwood grows singly among other species of trees.

🌱 It is easiest to find on Rocky Outcrops of the Bushveld-Savannah (B).

🌱 It can also be found in Low-lying, Sand and Scarp forests of the Coast (C), and Along Rivers (A).

A	B
C	D

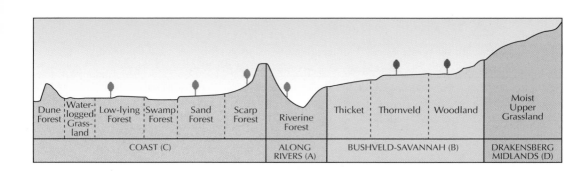

Dune Forest	Water-logged Grass-land	Low-lying Forest	Swamp Forest	Sand Forest	Scarp Forest	Riverine Forest	Thicket	Thornveld	Woodland	Moist Upper Grassland
COAST (C)						ALONG RIVERS (A)	BUSHVELD-SAVANNAH (B)			DRAKENSBERG MIDLANDS (D)

Striking features

- This is a single- or multi-stemmed tree and forms a few large branches that divide into rigid, thin branchlets and twigs.

- **The shiny, dark green bark is smooth and peels in large, coppery-bronze, paper-like flakes.**

- **The compound leaves have 2 - 3 pairs of leaflets with a single leaflet at the tip, and are dark green with a toothed margin.**

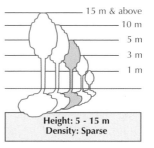

15 m & above
10 m
5 m
3 m
1 m

**Height: 5 - 15 m
Density: Sparse**

RED-STEM CORKWOOD

Commiphora harveyi

Links with animals

Klipspringers eat the leaves and Elephant seek the root and bark. The fleshy fruit is eaten by Monkeys and birds.

Human uses

The wood can be sanded down very smoothly to produce soft, white spoons, small stools and other small articles. The wood is carved into a mould for Zulu beer-strainer baskets. It is also used as fencing posts. The very soft centre can be eaten to stave off hunger pangs.

Gardening

This tree can be cultivated from seed or cuttings. It grows relatively fast, but is sensitive to frost. It often grows from pole cuttings. It is suitable as a bonsai tree.

Look-alike tree
The Green-stem Corkwood (*Commiphora neglecta*), page 66, occurs in similar areas and its bark is green, but it peels with light brown, papery flakes, and its leaves have three leaflets and a smooth margin.

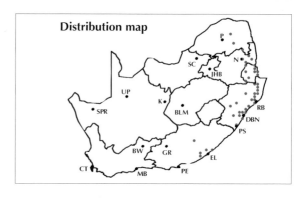

Distribution map

Striking light brown year-rings; soft wood; rough texture but sanding results in a smooth finish.

Green-stem Corkwood

Red-stem Corkwood

This is a single- or multi-stemmed tree with only a few large branches. The thick branches divide into very thin branchlets, with the leaves coming off towards the ends of the twigs to produce a fine, sparse canopy. It is one of the few cork-woods that does not have spines.

Flowers   The small, greenish, trumpet-shaped flowers appear with the new leaves in spring. They grow in tight bundles in the angle between the leaf and branchlet (October to December). (5 mm)

Leaves   The compound leaves are opposite and have long, slender leaf-stalks that are purple-red when young. There are 2 - 3 pairs of leaflets with a larger one at the tip. The elliptical leaflets have a slightly toothed margin, a broad base and sharp tip. They are shiny, bright green above and have a yellow, raised central vein visible on both surfaces. The leaflets may be slightly hairy. Leaves have a resinous smell when crushed and turn yellow before they drop in autumn. (Leaf: 70 - 200 mm; leaflet: 50 - 70 x 25 - 35 mm)

Fruit   The berry-like fruit ripens to a pinkish-red from November to March. The fruit splits open when ripe to expose a seed covered by four pale red or yellow, fleshy fingers. (10 - 15 mm)

Bark   The trunk is a shiny, dark green and peels in coppery-bronze, papery flakes. The twigs are pale grey and marked by old leaf-scars.

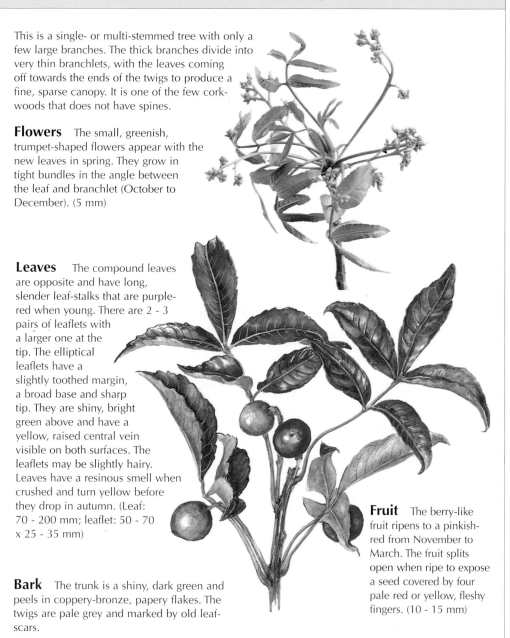

Seasonal Changes
Deciduous. The leaves turn yellow before they fall in autumn. This tree can be identified by its bark throughout the year.

	Oct	Nov	Dec	Jan	Feb	Mar	Apr	May	Jun	Jul	Aug	Sep
Leaf												
Flower												
Fruit/Pod												

97

Trees greet you

SEASONALLY STRIKING TREES

These trees are particularly easy to find in certain seasons, and, on the whole, are more difficult to spot without their seasonal garb. Read through this section and check the Seasonal Grid for each tree. Also check "Where you'll find this tree easily" to be sure it occurs in the area you are tree spotting. Once you know which trees are seasonally striking, in your area, you will have difficulty missing them!

The fruit of the Kooboo-berry weighs down the branches, and calls out to be recognised.

CLIMBING FLAT-BEAN
Dalbergia obovata

PEA FAMILY
FABACEAE

SA Tree Number 235

AFRIKAANS Bobbejaantou, Rankplatboontjie **XHOSA** umZungulu **ZULU** uPhandlazi, umZungulu

The term **obovata** refers to the obovate or oval leaflets.

Where you'll find this tree easily

The Climbing Flat-bean is widespread in forests and along forest margins.

🌡 It is easiest to find in the Low-lying Forest of the Coast (C).

🌡 It can also be found in the Dune and Swamp forests of the Coast (C), as well as Along Rivers (A).

A	B
C	D

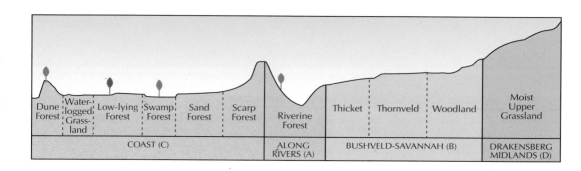

Dune Forest	Water-logged Grass-land	Low-lying Forest	Swamp Forest	Sand Forest	Scarp Forest	Riverine Forest	Thicket	Thornveld	Woodland	Moist Upper Grassland
COAST (C)						ALONG RIVERS (A)	BUSHVELD-SAVANNAH (B)			DRAKENSBERG MIDLANDS (D)

Striking features

- This can be a small tree, or a low-growing, spreading climber, often leaning on other vegetation.
- The dark grey bark is smooth and the stem divides into many small branchlets and twigs to form a moderate canopy with a dense mat of intertwined branchlets.
- **The twigs form tight curls around the surrounding vegetation for support.**
- **The winged pods, with one central seed, grow in profusion from February to April and remain on the tree in bunches for long periods.**
- The leaves are shiny, dark green, compound, with alternate leaflets and one at the tip.

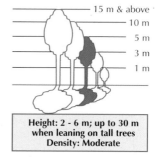

15 m & above
10 m
5 m
3 m
1 m

**Height: 2 - 6 m; up to 30 m when leaning on tall trees
Density: Moderate**

CLIMBING FLAT-BEAN

Dalbergia obovata

Links with animals

The leaves are heavily browsed by game, cattle and goats. Insects are attracted to flowers, and the caterpillar of the Common Sailor Butterfly *(Neptis laeta)* feeds on the tree.

Human uses

The wood is heavy with a reddish colour. It is used for stools, walking sticks and small domestic items. The stems are used to make the framework of fishing baskets and for woven hut walls. The bark can be used to make rope, and the ashes of the bark are mixed with snuff. It was used to treat sore mouths in babies.

Gardening

This tree makes a dense, impenetrable hedge, and can be grown from seed.

Distribution map

This is a low-growing, multi-stemmed tree or climber. The branchlets often lean on other vegetation and may cover it, often killing the trees they cover. The stems divide into many small branchlets and twigs to form a moderate canopy with a dense mat of intertwined branchlets.

Leaves   Compound leaves have 5 - 10 alternate leaflets with a single one at the tip. Leaflets are broadly elliptic, tapering to a rounded tip and base. The leaf is dark green and shiny above, and blue-grey with the central vein raised on the under-surface. The side veins are delicate but clearly visible with a herring-bone pattern that curves towards the leaf margin. The leaf margin may be wavy. (Leaf: 60 - 200 mm; leaflet: 40 - 60 x 20 - 30 mm)

Flowers   The small, creamy-white to yellow, pea-like flowers grow in conspicuous, branched sprays in the angles of the leaves, and towards the ends of the twigs (October to November). (Spray: 60 - 100 mm; individual: 3 x 5 mm)

Pods   The broad bean pods have a single seed in the centre of the papery wing. The pods are elliptic with a tapering tip and base, and the wings are conspicuously veined. The pods grow in large obvious clusters towards the ends of twigs and ripen from February to April, but may be seen for long periods after this, hanging in large bunches. (50 - 90 x 12 -18 mm)

Bark   The dark grey bark is smooth. The twigs form intricate, tight curls around the surrounding vegetation for support. These curls can be seen clearly on the branchlets where the original vegetation has disappeared.

Seasonal changes
Deciduous. This tree can be identified by its pods for a long period after the leaves have dropped.

	Oct	Nov	Dec	Jan	Feb	Mar	Apr	May	Jun	Jul	Aug	Sep
Leaf												
Flower												
Fruit/Pod												

103

CROSS-BERRY RAISIN (CROSS-BERRY)

Grewia occidentalis

LINDEN FAMILY
TILIACEAE

SA Tree Number 463

AFRIKAANS Assegaaihout, Kruisbessie **N. SOTHO** Motshwarabadikana, Mogwane **SISWATI** umSipane
S. SOTHO Molutu **TSONGA** Nsihana **TSWANA** Mokukutu **VENDA** Mulembu **XHOSA** umNqabaza
ZULU iLalanyathi, iKlolo

The term **occidentalis** means of the west.

Where you'll find this tree easily

The Cross-berry Raisin is a small tree or climber that
grows singly in protected positions among other species
of trees.

🌶 It is easiest to find on the edge of Low-lying, Dune and
Scarp forests of the Coast (C).

🌶 It is also found in the Rocky Outcrops in the Woodland
of the Bushveld-Savannah (B) and Along Rivers (A).

A	B
C	D

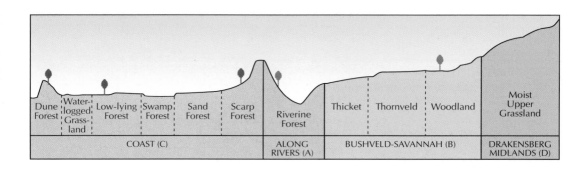

Dune Forest	Water-logged Grass-land	Low-lying Forest	Swamp Forest	Sand Forest	Scarp Forest	Riverine Forest	Thicket	Thornveld	Woodland	Moist Upper Grassland
COAST (C)						ALONG RIVERS (A)	BUSHVELD-SAVANNAH (B)			DRAKENSBERG MIDLANDS (D)

Striking features

- This is a multi-stemmed, small tree or climber with
  branches forming thin, downward-curving bows.
- Leaves grow in a flat plane facing the light.
- It normally leans on other trees and is shaped by them.
- **The characteristic flowers are purple-pink and star-like.**
- **The dry berries are four-lobed and square, giving it
  the name Cross-berry.**

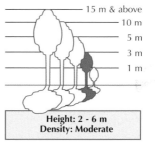

15 m & above
10 m
5 m
3 m
1 m

Height: 2 - 6 m
Density: Moderate

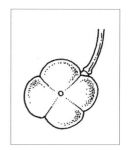

CROSS-BERRY RAISIN (CROSS-BERRY)

Grewia occidentalis

Links with animals

The leaves are eaten by cattle and a wide variety of antelope. The fruit is eaten by birds such as the Speckled Mousebird.

Human uses

The wood was used to make bows and spear shafts. Pounded bark, used regularly as shampoo, was believed to prevent hair from turning grey. Bruised and soaked bark was used to dress wounds. Parts of the plant were used to treat impotency and sterility, and root extracts were used to help in childbirth. This shrub is still used in traditional medicine today.

Gardening

This is an attractive garden plant with seeds that germinate easily. It grows fast in good soil and in well-watered gardens. It is frost- and drought-resistant.

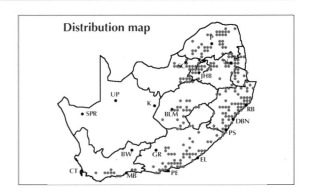

Distribution map

Heavy wood; suitable for turning; heartwood darker than sapwood; fine grain.

GROWTH DETAILS

This is a multi-stemmed, small tree or climber. The branches and branchlets are long and slender and hang in downward-curving bows. The leaves grow in a flat plane facing the light. This tree may grow alone, but is often a semi-climber supported by other trees and bushes.

Leaves   Simple, alternate leaves may vary in size and in form, from narrow to broadly elliptic. They are usually held in a horizontal plane towards the light, have a slender tapering tip and an irregularly toothed margin. The leaves are shiny, deep green, paler underneath, and may be slightly hairy on both surfaces. (Leaf: 20 - 80 x 13 - 40 mm)

Flowers   The small, conspicuous, star-shaped flowers are purple-pink and grow in clusters of 1 - 3 amongst the leaves. They may be present throughout the year, but the peak flowering season is in spring and early summer (October to January). (25 - 35 mm)

Fruit   The berry-like, dry fruit is four-lobed and may be seen on the tree for long periods. It is sometimes covered by hairs and turns reddish-brown to light purple when ripe from January to May. (25 - 35 mm)

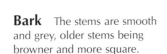

Seasonal changes

Usually deciduous, but may be evergreen under favourable circumstances. It is only really easy to identify while there are fruit or flowers present, which may be for the whole year in protected areas.

Bark   The stems are smooth and grey, older stems being browner and more square.

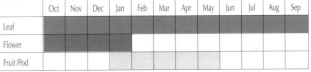

	Oct	Nov	Dec	Jan	Feb	Mar	Apr	May	Jun	Jul	Aug	Sep
Leaf												
Flower												
Fruit/Pod												

FLAME THORN ACACIA

Acacia ataxacantha

THORN-TREE FAMILY **MIMOSACEAE**	**SA Tree Number 160**

AFRIKAANS Rank-wag-'n-bietjie, Vlamdoring **N. SOTHO** Mologa, Mogaletlwa **TSONGA** Nuko
TSWANA Mogôkatau **VENDA** Muluwa **ZULU** umThathawe

The term **ataxacantha** is based on the Greek word meaning "irregular thorns".

Where you'll find this tree easily

This scrambling tree or climber grows in groups.

🌱 It is easiest to find Along Rivers (A).

🌱 It is also found in the Woodland of the Bushveld-Savannah (B), and Low-lying Forest of the Coast (C).

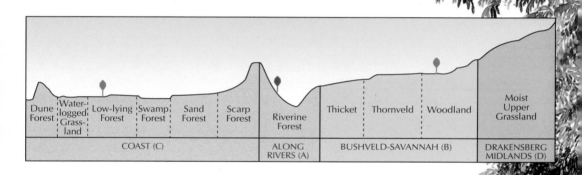

Dune Forest	Water-logged Grassland	Low-lying Forest	Swamp Forest	Sand Forest	Scarp Forest	Riverine Forest	Thicket	Thornveld	Woodland	Moist Upper Grassland
COAST (C)						ALONG RIVERS (A)	BUSHVELD-SAVANNAH (B)			DRAKENSBERG MIDLANDS (D)

Striking features

- This is a multi-stemmed, scrambling tree or climber with tangled branches that form a moderate, irregular canopy.

- **The hooked thorns are scattered along the branchlets and twigs and form no specific pattern.**

- The twice compound leaves are long and droopy.

- The creamy-yellow, conspicuous flower-spikes grow at the ends of branchlets and twigs.

- **The seed-pods grow in conspicuous bunches and turn purple-red when ripe, which gives this tree its name.**

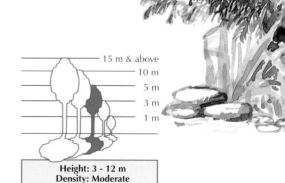

15 m & above
10 m
5 m
3 m
1 m

Height: 3 - 12 m
Density: Moderate

FLAME THORN ACACIA

Acacia ataxacantha

Links with animals

The caterpillars of the *Charaxes ethalion ethalion* butterfly feed on this plant. Birds such as the Redbilled Woodhoopoe or Barthroated Apalis collect insects off the flowers, leaves and tree trunk.

Human uses

The wood can be split into paper-like strips without cracking. These strips are used as weaving material for baskets.

Gardening

The Flame Thorn Acacia is not an appealing garden tree as it has an untidy appearance, although the bright-coloured pods may be attractive in late summer.

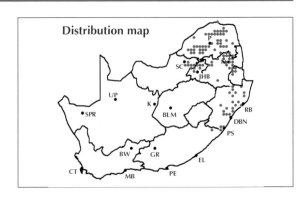

Distribution map

Flame Thorn Acacia – reddish thorns; randomly arranged

River Climbing Thorn Acacia – brown thorns; arranged in rows on dark lines

Look-alike trees

The River Climbing Thorn Acacia *(Acacia schweinfurthii)*, page 19, has a very similar growth form with larger, (up to 190 mm), dark green leaves. Hooked thorns are arranged in rows on dark lines on the pale branchlets. It has creamy-white flower-balls (not spikes), and pale brown (not purple-red) pods.

The Hook Thorn Acacia *(Acacia caffra)*, page 330, also has long, fine, twice compound leaves, but is usually a single-stemmed tree. The hooked thorns are paired, and successive pairs are at right angles to one another. The creamy-white flower-spikes (September to November) are followed by flat bean pods that are chocolate-brown, not purple-red as in the Flame Thorn Acacia.

GROWTH DETAILS

This is a multi-stemmed, scrambling tree that branches low down into many smaller, tangled branches. A moderate, leafy canopy is formed with no visible branches.

Leaves   The pale green, twice compound leaves have small, hooked thorns on the under-surface of the leaf-stem. Each leaf has 7 - 17 feather pairs, with 20 - 45 pairs of tiny leaflets. There are often elevations caused by the stalked glands on the leaf-stem near the base of the leaf. The leaf-buds (stipules) are large and triangular. The leaflets may be slightly hairy. (Leaf: 70 - 140 mm; leaflet: 2 - 5 x 1 mm)

Flowers   Conspicuous, creamy-yellow flower-spikes grow in abundance at the tips of the branchlets and twigs, protruding above the leaves. (September to February). (70 - 100 mm)

Thorns   The small, stout, hooked thorns are purple-brown and are randomly scattered along the branchlets and twigs in no apparent pattern. (5 mm)

Bark   The bark is light brown and smooth in young trees. Older trees have a dark brown bark with lengthways fissures that may become flaky.

Pods   The bunches of flat bean pods are conspicuous as they ripen to purple-red. The pods become dark brown with age and split on the tree when ripe. They remain on the tree for long periods. (December to June). (70 - 100 x 12 - 15 mm)

Seasonal changes

A deciduous tree that can be identified by its growth form and the thorn pattern throughout the year.

	Oct	Nov	Dec	Jan	Feb	Mar	Apr	May	Jun	Jul	Aug	Sep
Leaf												
Flower												
Fruit/Pod												

111

FOREST ELDER

Nuxia floribunda

WILD ELDER FAMILY
LOGANIACEAE

SA Tree Number 634

AFRIKAANS Bosvlier, Wildevlier **N. SOTHO** Motlhabare **VENDA** Mu]a-ṇotshi **XHOSA** isiKhali, iNgqota
ZULU umHlambandlazi

The term **floribunda** refers to the "many flowered" flower-heads.

Where you'll find this tree easily

The Forest Elder grows singly, but where one is found
there will be others in the vicinity.

❦ It is easily recognisable in the Scarp Forest of the
Coast (C), when the tree is covered in white flowers.

❦ It can also be found Along Rivers (A).

A	B
C	D

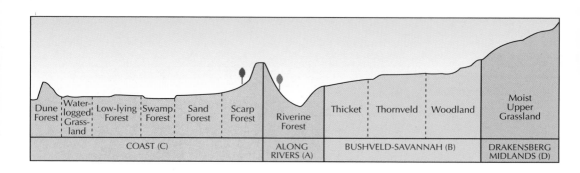

Dune Forest | Water-logged Grass-land | Low-lying Forest | Swamp Forest | Sand Forest | Scarp Forest | Riverine Forest | Thicket | Thornveld | Woodland | Moist Upper Grassland

COAST (C) — ALONG RIVERS (A) — BUSHVELD-SAVANNAH (B) — DRAKENSBERG MIDLANDS (D)

Striking features

- **The trees, covered in white flower-heads, are
  conspicuous from May to September.**

- This is a single-trunked, low-branching tree with a
  dense, rounded canopy.

- The leaves are shiny and arranged in whorls of three.

- **The light green leaves stand out among the darker
  foliage of the other trees when not in flower.**

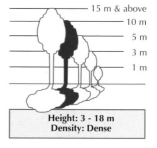

15 m & above
10 m
5 m
3 m
1 m

Height: 3 - 18 m
Density: Dense

FOREST ELDER

Nuxia floribunda

Links with animals

Leaves are eaten by cattle, goats, Kudu, Bushbuck, Nyala, Klipspringer and Red and Grey Duiker. The flowers attract bees and other insects which in turn attract insect-eating birds such as Flycatchers.

Human uses

The wood is used for parquet floors, turnery and furniture, and has a pleasant light colour when polished. The bark is rich in tannin. The leaves were used to help with fevers, coughs, indigestion and to treat convulsions in babies. Parts of the tree were used as a strengthening medicine after the death of one of the kraal members.

Gardening

This is an attractive garden tree and the root system is non-invasive. It can be grown from seed or cuttings and is reasonably fast-growing. It is not frost-resistant and grows best in wetter areas.

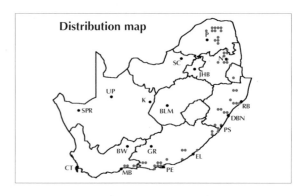

Distribution map

Rare, yellow wood; fine and even texture; straight grain; saws and turns well; takes varnish and paint easily.

Look-alike tree   The flowering tree may be confused with the False Olive Sage *(Buddleja saligna)* that has a more droopy growth form, a fissured and flaking bark, and simple, opposite, narrow elliptic leaves that are dark green above and pale below. See **Sappi Tree Spotting Highveld**.

GROWTH DETAILS

This is a single-trunked, low-branching tree with branches growing upwards, branching into many fine branchlets and twigs to form a dense, round, leafy canopy.

Flowers Conspicuous, sweet-scented, rounded bunches of small, trumpet-shaped flowers grow in dense, rounded heads. They grow at the ends of the branches and twigs and stand out above the leaves. The stamens protrude from the flower tube to give the flowers a soft, delicate appearance (May to September). (Flower head: 70 - 300 mm diameter; individual: 5 x 3 mm)

Leaves The simple, opposite leaves grow in whorls of three. They are shiny, light green above and below, with a smooth or slightly toothed margin. The central vein stands out on the under-surface. Leaves are elliptic with a pointed tip and base and have a long leaf-stem (15 - 45 mm) that is purplish when young. Young leaves are also purplish and those growing on new shoots have a toothed margin. (Leaf: 50 -160 x 15 - 70 mm)

Fruit The fruit is not very easy to see as it is enclosed in a small, oval capsule in the old flower-heads (5 mm) (June to October).

Bark The bark is grey or light brown and smooth when young, becoming slightly fissured and flaky with age. The young twigs are square and have leaf-scars.

Seasonal changes
Evergreen. This tree can be identified by its leaves throughout the year.

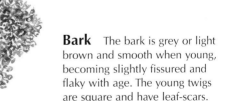

	Oct	Nov	Dec	Jan	Feb	Mar	Apr	May	Jun	Jul	Aug	Sep
Leaf												
Flower												
Fruit/Pod												

115

KOOBOO-BERRY

Mystroxylon aethiopicum (Cassine aethiopica)

SPIKE-THORN FAMILY
CELASTRACEAE

SA Tree Number 410

AFRIKAANS Koeboebessie, Lepelhout **SISWATI** inGulutane **TSONGA** Nqayi **VENDA** Mungugun
XHOSA umGxube **ZULU** umGunguluzane

The term **aethiopicum** means from the country of the black people.

Where you'll find this tree easily

The Kooboo-berry grows singly among other tree species.

- It can easily be found in the Dune, Low-lying, Swamp and Sand forests of the Coast (C).
- It also occurs in the Woodland of the Bushveld-Savannah (B), and Along Rivers (A).

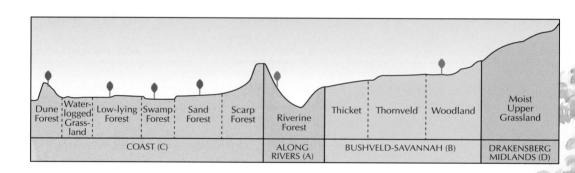

Dune Forest	Water-logged Grass-land	Low-lying Forest	Swamp Forest	Sand Forest	Scarp Forest	Riverine Forest	Thicket	Thornveld	Woodland	Moist Upper Grassland
COAST (C)						ALONG RIVERS (A)	BUSHVELD-SAVANNAH (B)			DRAKENSBERG MIDLANDS (D)

Striking features

- **This is a single- or multi-stemmed tree that branches low down to form a moderate, irregular, blue-green canopy.**

- Long, smooth, grey branches spread outwards, with slender, very pale twigs carrying the leaves in untidy clumps.

- **When ripe, the mass of striking red or yellow, fleshy berries look like tiny, grooved apples (January to June).**

- The simple, elliptic leaves are stiff and leathery, with a finely toothed margin.

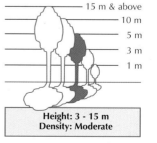

15 m & above
10 m
5 m
3 m
1 m

Height: 3 - 15 m
Density: Moderate

116

117

KOOBOO-BERRY

Mystroxylon aethiopicum (Cassine aethiopica)

Links with animals

The fruit is a favourite with Baboons and Samango and Vervet Monkeys, and is eaten on the ground by Kudu, Nyala, Grey and Red Duiker, Bushpigs and Warthogs. Birds such as Purplecrested Louries, Green Pigeons, Cape Parrots, Blackeyed Bulbuls and Swainson's Francolin eat the fruit with relish. The leaves are not very palatable and only Duiker and Black Rhino eat them.

Human uses

The wood has a fine grain, is tough and hard. It is sometimes used in making carvings and small household articles. The sticks that the Xhosa used to hold above their heads in dancing are traditionally obtained from this tree. A brown dye comes from the bark, which is also used in tanning leather, giving it a characteristic light colour. The bark sap is also used as bird lime. The fruit is sweet and edible. Infusions made from the root bark were taken for dysentery and diarrhoea, while the roots were used for heartburn. It was also used to treat worms in calves. Bark was used in magical charms by the Vhavenda.

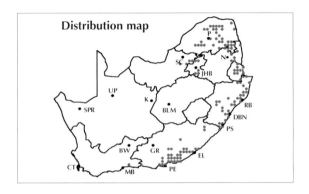

Distribution map

Gardening

This tree is very attractive, especially when laden with fruit, when it will attract many birds. It tolerates mild frost, is very drought-resistant and has a moderate growth rate.

GROWTH DETAILS

This is a single- or multi-stemmed, small tree with a thin stem that branches into many smaller branches to form a moderate, irregular canopy, shaped by the surrounding vegetation.

Leaves   The simple, spiral, elliptic leaves are leathery. They have a finely toothed, sometimes smooth margin and a short leaf-stem. The upper-surface is dark blue-green with a paler under-surface that may be slightly hairy. The central and side veins are yellowish. (20 - 90 x 10 - 60 mm)

Flowers
Inconspicuous, yellow-green, star-shaped, sweet-scented flowers grow in small, dense clusters in the angles of the leaves (October to December). (10 - 13 mm)

Fruit   The striking, berry-like fruit is fleshy and looks like a little, grooved apple. It changes from lemon-yellow to deep pink, scarlet or purple when ripe, and the skin may be wrinkled, smooth, hairy or shiny (January to June). (8 - 25 mm)

Bark   The bark is dark and rough in older trees, but smooth and pale grey in younger trees and on branches. Young twigs are spirally arranged and are very pale grey and smooth but may be hairy.

Seasonal changes
Evergreen. This tree is difficult to identify if it has no fruit.

	Oct	Nov	Dec	Jan	Feb	Mar	Apr	May	Jun	Jul	Aug	Sep
Leaf	■	■	■	■	■	■	■	■	■			■
Flower	■	■										
Fruit/Pod			■	■	■	■	■	■				

RED BUSHWILLOW

Combretum apiculatum

BUSHWILLOW FAMILY **COMBRETACEAE**	**S A Tree Number 532**

AFRIKAANS Rooiboswilg **N. SOTHO** Mohwelere **SISWATI** umBondomyana, inKukutu
TSONGA Xikukutsi **TSWANA** Mofudiri, Mogodiri **VENDA** Musingidzi **ZULU** umBondwe omnyama

The term **apiculatum** refers to the sharp tip of the leaf.

Where you'll find this tree easily

Red Bushwillows grow in groups in sandy or gravelly soils.

🌱 They are easiest to find on the higher lying areas of the
Woodland of the Bushveld-Savannah (B).

🌱 They are also found in the Thornveld of the Bushveld-
Savannah (B).

A	B
C	D

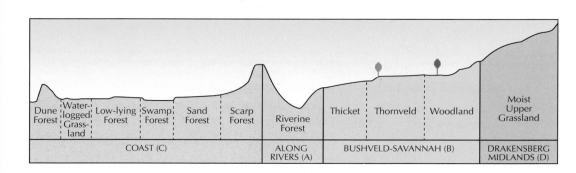

Dune Forest	Water-logged Grass-land	Low-lying Forest	Swamp Forest	Sand Forest	Scarp Forest	Riverine Forest	Thicket	Thornveld	Woodland	Moist Upper Grassland
COAST (C)						ALONG RIVERS (A)	BUSHVELD-SAVANNAH (B)			DRAKENSBERG MIDLANDS (D)

Striking features

- This is a single- or multi-stemmed tree with a short, often curved trunk, and a spreading irregular canopy.

- The long, slender branches hang low down giving the tree a willow-like appearance.

- **The medium-sized, rich yellow-brown, four-winged pods are visible most of the year.**

- **The simple leaves have a sharp, twisted tip.**

- The stands of trees with red, yellow and brown leaves are conspicuous in autumn.

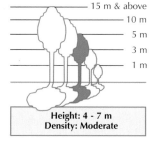

15 m & above
10 m
5 m
3 m
1 m

Height: 4 - 7 m
Density: Moderate

121

RED BUSHWILLOW

Combretum apiculatum

Links with animals
Young or fallen leaves are eaten by Kudu, Bushbuck, Eland, Giraffe and Elephant. The seeds are eaten by Brownheaded Parrots.

Human uses
The wood is used for fence posts and to make furniture. Extracts of the leaves were used for stomach complaints.

Gardening
This is an attractive garden tree, and established trees are frost- and drought-resistant. The tree grows slowly.

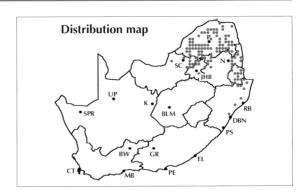

Distribution map

Black heart-wood; yellow sapwood; very hard; durable; suitable for turning.

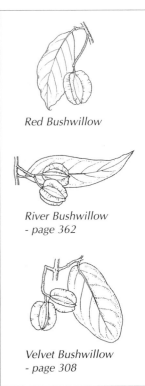

Red Bushwillow

River Bushwillow - page 362

Velvet Bushwillow - page 308

GROWTH DETAILS

This is a single- or multi-stemmed tree with an irregular moderate canopy. The end branches and twigs are thin and tend to droop down.

Leaves   Leaves are simple, opposite, broadly elliptic with a slightly wavy margin. They are shiny yellow-green, and yellow leaves are seen among the green ones for most of the year. The tip of the leaf is sharp and twisted, and the parallel veins are obvious on the upper- and under-surface. (30 - 100 x 20 - 60 mm)

Pods   The characteristic four-winged pods, with a single seed in the centre, hang in large bunches which ripen to a rich yellow-brown (January to May). Pods often stay on the tree until the next flowers appear in August. (20 - 30 mm)

Flowers   The creamy-yellow, sweet-smelling flower-spikes grow in groups of one to four in the angles of the leaves. They are not very conspicuous but give the tree a lemon-yellow tinge in summer when they appear with the new leaves (September to October). (Spike: 70 x 20 mm)

Bark   The bark is grey to blackish, and cracks into irregular blocks that flake off in flat pieces. The bark on the smaller branches and twigs is green to light brown and smooth.

Seasonal changes
Deciduous. This tree is very difficult to find in winter if there are no pods to help with identification.

	Oct	Nov	Dec	Jan	Feb	Mar	Apr	May	Jun	Jul	Aug	Sep
Leaf												
Flower												
Fruit/Pod												

TASSEL BERRY

Antidesma venosum

| EUPHORBIA FAMILY EUPHORBIACEAE | SA Tree Number 318 |

AFRIKAANS Tosselbessie, Voëlsitboom **N. SOTHO** Modulane **SISWATI** imHlalama-hubulu, umHlalanyoni
TSONGA Mphatakhwari **TSWANA** Moingwe **VENDA** Mukwala-kwali, Mupala-khwali
ZULU isiBhangamlotha, umHlabahlungulu

The term **venosum** refers to the conspicuously veined leaves.

Where you'll find this tree easily

The Tassel Berry often grows singly.

🌳 The Tassel Berry is most easily found in the Low-lying Forest of the Coast (C).

🌳 It is also found in the Swamp and Scarp forests of the Coast (C), Along Rivers (A), and in the Woodland of the Bushveld-Savannah (B).

A	B
C	D

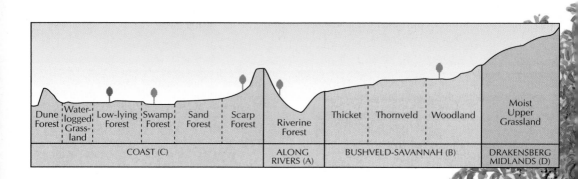

Dune Forest	Water-logged Grass-land	Low-lying Forest	Swamp Forest	Sand Forest	Scarp Forest	Riverine Forest	Thicket	Thornveld	Woodland	Moist Upper Grassland
COAST (C)						ALONG RIVERS (A)	BUSHVELD-SAVANNAH (B)			DRAKENSBERG MIDLANDS (D)

Striking features

- This is a single- or multi-stemmed tree that branches horizontally low down to form a dense, semi-circular, dark green canopy.
- **The flower-spikes hang from the branchlets and look like Christmas decorations.**
- **The small, multi-coloured, fleshy berries hang in long, thin bunches from the branchlets.**
- The simple leaves grow in a relatively flat plane on long, slender branchlets.
- The veins of the leaves are visibly looped along the margin of the dark, velvety leaf.

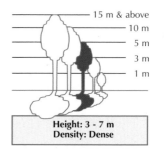

| 15 m & above |
| 10 m |
| 5 m |
| 3 m |
| 1 m |

Height: 3 - 7 m
Density: Dense

125

TASSEL BERRY

Antidesma venosum

Links with animals

The leaves and shoots are occasionally browsed by Kudu, Elephant, Nyala and Bushbuck. The mulberry-tasting fruit is well liked by Impala, Kudu, Nyala, Baboons and Vervet Monkeys. It is also popular with most fruit-eating birds such as the Greenspotted Dove, the Tambourine Dove, the Green Pigeon, Louries, Hornbills, Barbets, Bulbuls and Mousebirds.

Human uses

The fruit is edible and tastes pleasant. Roots are reported to be toxic and were used as fish bait. The tree was known as a cure for dysentery. An infusion made from the roots and leaves was taken for coughs, while root extracts were used in medicines for fertility and menstruation problems. Flaked roots, soaked in bath water, were used to ease body aches.

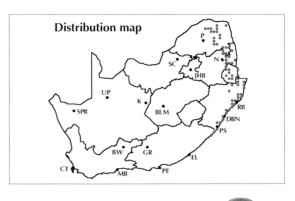

Distribution map

Dark heartwood; yellow sapwood; fine texture; suitable for turning.

Gardening

This is an exceptionally attractive garden tree. Seeds are easily obtainable and germinate readily. Initially it grows quickly, but later slows down. It can resist moderate cold. It does not have an invasive root, and is one of the best trees for attracting birds.

Look-alike tree
The Mitzeeri (*Bridelia micrantha*), page 214, has a very similar growth form and leaves. The leaves of the Mitzeeri are shiny, light green with the veins running only to the margin. Scars of fallen leaves form distinct small knobs that are obvious on bare branchlets. The fruit and flowers of the Mitzeeri grow singly or in pairs in the angles of the leaves.

This is a single- or multi-stemmed tree that branches low down to form a wide-spreading, semi-circular, dense canopy that hangs low down.

Leaves The simple, elliptic leaves grow alternately and have a short leaf-stem and a smooth margin. The upper-surface is smooth and dark green; the under-surface is paler and is often covered by reddish hairs. The central and side veins are distinct on both surfaces, and the side veins form loops along the margin. (Leaf: 25 - 150 x 20 - 100 mm)

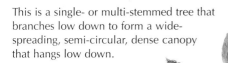

Fruit Trees with bunches of ripe fruit are very striking. The small, fleshy, slightly oval, grape-like berries hang in long, thin bunches from the branchlets. The berries, which take a long time to ripen, ripen at different times and result in a multi-coloured bunch of green, red and purplish-black berries (January to May). (Individual: 8 - 10 mm; bunch 80 - 120 mm)

Bark In older trees the bark is dark brown to black, rough, fissured lengthways, and peels loosely to reveal a reddish-brown under-bark. New branches, branchlets and twigs are smooth, with a light brown bark.

Flowers Small, star-shaped flowers with a strong, sweet smell, form conspicuous strings. Similar-shaped male and female flowers grow on separate trees. The male flowers are yellow-green and the spikes are longer than those of the reddish, female flowers (October to January). (Male spike: 160 mm; female spike: 50 - 80 mm)

Seasonal changes
Evergreen. This tree can be identified throughout the year by looking at the leaf detail and growth form.

	Oct	Nov	Dec	Jan	Feb	Mar	Apr	May	Jun	Jul	Aug	Sep
Leaf												
Flower												
Fruit/Pod												

SEASONALLY STRIKING
Tassel Berry

127

TINDERWOOD

Clerodendrum glabrum

VERBENA FAMILY VERBENACEAE	SA Tree Number 667

AFRIKAANS Tontelhout, Stinkboom **N. SOTHO** Mohlokohloko **TSONGA** Xinhunwelambeva
VENDA Munukha-tshilongwe **XHOSA** umQangazani, umQwaqa **ZULU** umQaqonga

The term **glabrum** refers to the leaves that are mostly without hairs.

Where you'll find this tree easily

The Tinderwood normally grows singly.

🌱 It is easiest to find in the Low-lying and Scarp forests of the Coast (C).

🌱 It may also be found Along Rivers (A), as well as in the Woodland of the Bushveld-Savannah (B), and the Swamp Forest of the Coast (C).

A	B
C	D

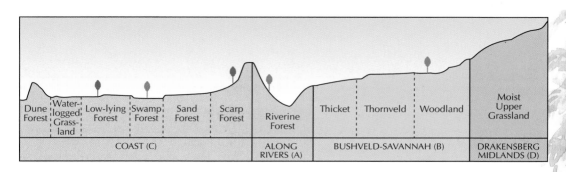

Coast (C)					Along Rivers (A)	Bushveld-Savannah (B)			Drakensberg Midlands (D)
Dune Forest	Water-logged Grassland	Low-lying Forest	Swamp Forest	Sand Forest	Scarp Forest	Riverine Forest	Thicket	Thornveld	Woodland	Moist Upper Grassland

Striking features

- This a multi-stemmed or low-branching, single-stemmed tree, with branches growing upwards to form a V-shaped canopy.

- The leaves grow in whorls of three, and each leaf arches downwards towards the branchlet or twig.

- Leaves are clustered towards the ends of the twigs and branchlets.

- **The compact clusters of white flowers grow at the ends of the twigs and branches, above the leaves, making the tree very conspicuous from November to April.**

- **The straw-coloured, fleshy, berry-like fruit is clustered at the ends of the branchlets and twigs from February to July.**

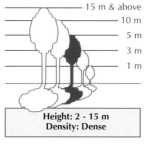

15 m & above
10 m
5 m
3 m
1 m

**Height: 2 - 15 m
Density: Dense**

TINDERWOOD

Clerodendrum glabrum

Links with animals

The flowers attract many insects, especially butterflies. The caterpillars of two butterflies are known to breed on this tree. This is one of the "rain trees" of South Africa – small insects known as Frog-hoppers suck the moisture from the branches. It is then excreted as drops of water that fall to the ground below. The caterpillars of the Natal Bar live in tubes in the stems, formed by ants eating out the pith, and from these they emerge at night to feed on the leaves. The fruit is eaten by White-eyes and Bulbuls.

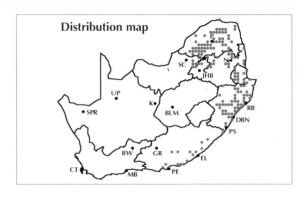

Distribution map

Human uses

The wood was used as firesticks to start fires. Parts of the plant are repellent to beetles, and the leaves are rubbed over the hands and face before collecting honey, to keep bees from attacking. A solution of the leaves was used to treat coughs and colds, aid sleep and avoid bad dreams.

Leaf extracts were used to expel roundworm and threadworm, as a disinfectant and to prevent maggot infection in wounds. The root is a widely known snakebite remedy, used in particular for Mamba bites. Leaves were used to drive away evil spirits.

Gardening

This tree is fast-growing and is an attractive tree for the garden. It may be grown from seed or cuttings. It will flower about one year after planting.

Hard, closely grained wood; suitable for turning; varnishes well.

GROWTH DETAILS

This is a single- or multi-stemmed, often low-branching tree. The branches grow upwards to form a dense, V-shaped canopy. The leaves are clustered towards the tips of the branches and hang down like drooping feathers, creating a soft, rounded effect.

Flowers   Small, white to pinkish, trumpet-shaped flowers have long filaments and are crowded in conspicuous, large, compact heads at the ends of branchlets and twigs in the centre of the leaf-rosettes. They are strong-smelling, and the smell may be offensive or sweet (November to April). (Head: 50 mm; individual: 10 mm)

Leaves   The simple, opposite, broadly elliptic leaves grow in whorls of three or four and are crowded towards the ends of the branchlets and twigs. The leaves have a slightly wavy margin and a tapering tip and base. There is a prominent central vein and the side veins curl at the margin of the leaf. The upper-surface is shiny dark or grey-green and the under-surface is paler and may be covered by short hairs. The leaves have an unpleasant smell when crushed. The leaf size is very variable. (Leaf: 20 - 250 x 10 - 70 mm)

Fruit   The fleshy, berry-like fruit is crowded together in a compact head that stands out above the leaf-rosette. Each "berry" (drupe) is held in a brown, cup-like structure (calyx). The fruit is light yellow when ripe (February to July). (Head: 50 - 80 mm; individual: 10 mm)

Bark   The light brown-grey bark becomes cracked and flaky with age to reveal a pale brown under-bark. The branchlets are light grey and are characteristically covered by distinct white marks (lenticels). Twigs may be hairy when young.

Seasonal changes
Deciduous. This tree is easiest to identify when in flower or fruit.

	Oct	Nov	Dec	Jan	Feb	Mar	Apr	May	Jun	Jul	Aug	Sep
Leaf	■	■	■	■	■	■	■	■				
Flower		■	■	■	■	■	■					
Fruit/Pod												

131

UMZIMBEET

Millettia grandis

PEA FAMILY FABACEAE	SA Tree Number 227

AFRIKAANS Omsambeet **XHOSA** umSimbithi **ZULU** umSimbithi

The term **grandis** means large.

Where you'll find this tree easily

The Umzimbeet grows singly among other trees, and
where one is found, others should be seen in the vicinity.

🌳 It is easiest to find in the Low-lying and Scarp forests of
the Coast (C).

🌳 It can also be found in the Dune Forest of the Coast (C)
and Along Rivers (A).

A	B
C	D

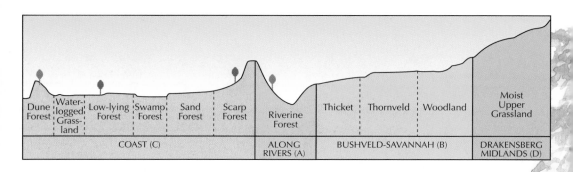

Dune Forest	Water-logged Grass-land	Low-lying Forest	Swamp Forest	Sand Forest	Scarp Forest	Riverine Forest	Thicket	Thornveld	Woodland	Moist Upper Grassland
COAST (C)						ALONG RIVERS (A)	BUSHVELD-SAVANNAH (B)			DRAKENSBERG MIDLANDS (D)

Striking features

- This single- or multi-trunked tree branches low down
  to form a soft, dense, V-shaped canopy.
- **Rusty-brown buds and purple, pea-like flowers grow
  on spikes that stand above the leaves (November to
  March).**
- In older trees, the trunk is often gnarled and the bark is
  grey-brown and flakes off in long, thin strips to show
  pale brown bark underneath.
- The large compound leaves have overlapping, bluish-
  green leaflets that droop. They have a single leaflet at
  the tip.
- **There are obvious, green swellings at the base of each
  leaf and horn-like growths at the base of each leaflet.**

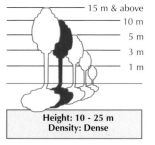

Height: 10 - 25 m
Density: Dense

133

UMZIMBEET

Millettia grandis

Links with animals

Baboons strip and eat the bark. The caterpillars of the Orange Barred Playboy *(Deudorix diocles)* and the Striped Policeman butterfly *(Coeliades forestan)* eat the pods, while the caterpillars of the Pondo Charaxes butterfly *(Charaxes pondoensis)* eat the leaves.

Human uses

The wood is used for furniture, wagon-wheel spokes and axles. Sticks and knobkieries can be made so that one side is white and the other black. Pounded roots were used as fish poison, but fish must be boiled before eating. The seeds ground in milk were used as a cure for roundworm. Roots, mixed with other components, were burnt in a hut to dispel worries.

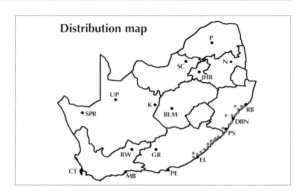

Distribution map

Yellow-brown heartwood; yellow sapwood; straight grain; fine texture; wood has oily feel; extremely heavy and hard timber; difficult to saw and plane.

Gardening

This is a shady, decorative garden tree that flowers when still young. It does not have an aggressive root system and can be grown from fresh seed. It is fairly fast growing and withstands a few degrees of frost.

This can be a single- or multi-trunked tree with a gnarled trunk that branches low down to form a dense V-shaped canopy.

Leaves   The compound leaves are long and droop down. There are 3 to 6 pairs of leaflets with a single leaflet at the tip. The narrow elliptic leaflets are bluish-green above and slightly paler below and have a distinct hairlike tip. On the under-surface of the leaflet, the evenly spaced, parallel side veins stand out and may be covered by fine reddish-brown hairs. There are obvious large, green swellings (stipules) and horn-like growths (stipels) at the base of each leaflet. New leaves stand out against older foliage because they are covered by reddish-brown hairs. (Leaf: 130 - 250 x 100 - 130 mm; leaflet: 20 - 70 x 6 - 20 mm)

Flowers
Conspicuous spikes of rusty-brown buds rise above the leaves in spring to open into purple, pea-like flowers (December to March). (Spike: 110 - 250 mm; individual: 25 x 10 mm)

Pods   The flat bean pods develop on the spikes and grow above the leaves. They are covered in reddish-brown, velvety hairs and split open on the tree when ripe, from February to July. (150 x 40 mm)

Bark   The bark is grey-brown and flakes off in long, thin strips to show light brown bark underneath. The branchlets are covered in light grey spots.

Seasonal changes
Usually deciduous, but may be evergreen under favourable conditions. It is easy to identify as long as it has leaves.

	Oct	Nov	Dec	Jan	Feb	Mar	Apr	May	Jun	Jul	Aug	Sep
Leaf												
Flower												
Fruit/Pod												

135

WHITE GARDENIA

Gardenia thunbergia

GARDENIA FAMILY
RUBIACEAE

SA Tree Number 692

AFRIKAANS Witkatjiepiering, Stompdoring **VENDA** Tshiralala **XHOSA** umKhangazi, iSende
ZULU umValasangweni, umKhangazo

The term **thunbergia** is in honour of Carl Thunberg who was a botanist-traveller in the 18th century.

Where you'll find this tree easily

The White Gardenia is a forest tree that grows singly
among other trees.

🌳 It is easiest to find in the Low-lying and Scarp forests of
the Coast (C).

🌳 It can also be found in the Sand Forest of the Coast (C),
and on Rocky Outcrops in the Woodland of the
Bushveld-Savannah (B).

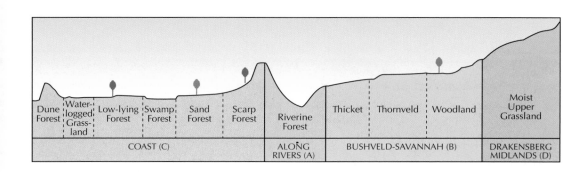

										Moist
Dune Forest	Water-logged Grass-land	Low-lying Forest	Swamp Forest	Sand Forest	Scarp Forest	Riverine Forest	Thicket	Thornveld	Woodland	Upper Grassland
COAST (C)						ALONG RIVERS (A)	BUSHVELD-SAVANNAH (B)			DRAKENSBERG MIDLANDS (D)

Striking features

- It is a single-stemmed, small tree that branches low
  down into numerous small branches to form a
  moderate, V-shaped to rounded canopy.

- The bark is light grey to white and peels in large flakes
  to reveal shiny, slightly greenish under-bark.

- **The creamy-white, sweet-scented, trumpet-shaped**
  flowers form a magnificent display from October to
  February.

- **The large characteristic fruit is present throughout the**
  year. It is hard, woody, pale grey and smooth with
  raised white dots when mature.

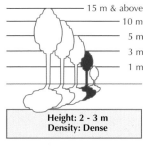

15 m & above
10 m
5 m
3 m
1 m

Height: 2 - 3 m
Density: Dense

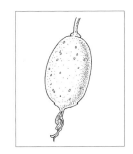

WHITE GARDENIA

Gardenia thunbergia

Links with animals

The dry fruit is eaten by Elephant, Buffalo and larger antelope. The flowers attract bees and moths.

Human uses

The wood was used for making tools, tool handles, knobkieries, clubs, yokes and axles. The trees themselves were planted as gate-posts for cattle kraals. Root extracts were used as an emetic, to treat skin eruptions in leprosy and as an excellent remedy for fevers. The leaf was used to treat syphilis.

Gardening

This is a lovely garden tree. It grows easily from seed or cuttings, is slow growing and fairly hardy. It makes a beautiful bonsai tree.

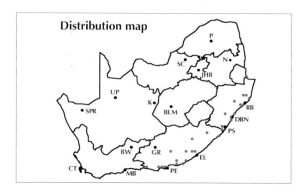

Distribution map

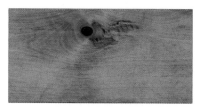

Durable hard wood; yellowish-grey heartwood.

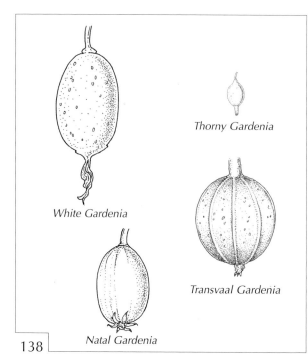

Thorny Gardenia

White Gardenia

Transvaal Gardenia

Natal Gardenia

Look-alike trees   This tree may be confused with the Transvaal Gardenia *(Gardenia volkensii)* in Northern KwaZulu-Natal. The flowers of the Transvaal Gardenia turn yellow within a day after opening and the fruit has thick, prominent ribs.

The Cape Gardenia *(Rothmannia capensis)* has similar flowers but they have sharp-tipped petals; the leaves have very short or no leaf-stalks; the fruit is round and smooth with lines resembling a peeled orange and is soft when ripe.

The Thorny Gardenia *(Hyperacanthus amoenus)* occurs in the Woodland of the Bushveld-Savannah. The white flowers are smaller with fewer petals, the twigs form sharp, prominent spines and the fruit is small and plum-like with the old flower-remains at the tip.

The Natal Gardenia *(Gardenia cornuta)* grows in the Sand Forest of the Coast. The fruit is yellow and oval with curved petals (sepals) at the tip.

GROWTH DETAILS

This is a single- or multi-stemmed tree that branches low down into numerous small branches to form a densely branched, V-shaped to rounded canopy. The rigid branches often form short spines.

Flowers   Conspicuous, sweet-scented, cream-coloured flowers, growing singly at the ends of the branches, appear in profusion from October to February. They are trumpet-shaped and have a long tube that splits into 7 to 9 overlapping petals. (70 - 100 x 60 - 80 mm)

Leaves   The simple, opposite leaves grow in whorls of three to four and are clustered towards the ends of the twigs and branchlets. They are elliptic with a pointed tip, and the base tapers sharply towards the long leaf-stem (25 mm). The upper-surface is shiny, light-green with a slightly paler under-surface. The central vein and side veins are conspicuous, with raised glands visible in the angles formed by the veins. (Leaf: 60 - 10 x 30 - 100 mm)

Fruit   The large, light brown to grey, dry, woody fruit has a smooth skin covered in raised, white dots and may be seen on the tree throughout the year. (70 - 120 x 35 mm)

Bark   The bark is light grey to white and peels in large flakes to expose the shiny, slightly greenish under-bark.

Seasonal changes
Evergreen in protected positions. This tree can be identified by its fruit throughout the year.

	Oct	Nov	Dec	Jan	Feb	Mar	Apr	May	Jun	Jul	Aug	Sep
Leaf												
Flower												
Fruit/Pod												

WILD PEAR (COMMON WILD PEAR)

Dombeya rotundifolia

STAR-CHESTNUT FAMILY
STERCULIACEAE

SA Tree Number 471

AFRIKAANS Drolpeer, Gewone Drolpeer **N. SOTHO** Mokgoba **SISWATI** umBikanyaka, umWane
TSONGA Nsihaphukuma, Xiluvarhi **TSWANA** Mokgofa, Motubane **VENDA** Tshiluvhari
ZULU uNhliziyonkulu

The term **rotundifolia** refers to the round form of the leaf.

Where you'll find this tree easily

The Wild Pear grows singly among other trees, but can
grow in exposed positions.

🌱 It is most conspicuous on drier, rocky slopes of the Moist
Upper Grassland of the Drakensberg Midlands (D).

🌱 It can also be found on the hillsides of the Woodland
and Thornveld of the Bushveld-Savannah (B), as well as
in the Sand Forest of the Coast (C), and Along Rivers (A).

A	B
C	D

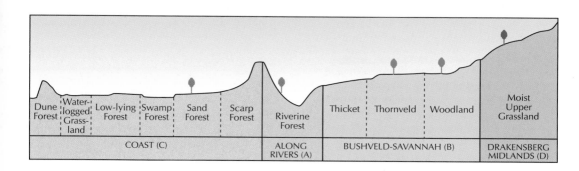

Dune Forest	Water-logged Grass-land	Low-lying Forest	Swamp Forest	Sand Forest	Scarp Forest	Riverine Forest	Thicket	Thornveld	Woodland	Moist Upper Grassland
COAST (C)						ALONG RIVERS (A)	BUSHVELD-SAVANNAH (B)			DRAKENSBERG MIDLANDS (D)

Striking features

- This is a single-stemmed tree with a moderate, irregular
canopy.

- **The star-like, papery flowers are cream-coloured to
pink and cover the whole tree in early spring before
the leaves appear.**

- **The simple, rigid leaves are hairy, rough and
parchment-like, and are conspicuously round.**

- The bark is rough and dark brown to black.

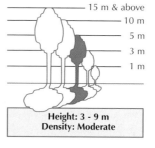

15 m & above
10 m
5 m
3 m
1 m

Height: 3 - 9 m
Density: Moderate

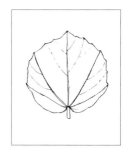

WILD PEAR (COMMON WILD PEAR)

Dombeya rotundifolia

Links with animals

Many butterflies are attracted to the flowers, and the caterpillars of three species of butterfly eat the leaves.

Human uses

The wood is used for mine props and yokes. The bark fibre is used to make rope. The tree is widely used for medicinal purposes: the inner bark to treat heart weakness and nausea in pregnant women; infusions of the bark or wood as enemas and for intestinal ulceration; the flowers for a love potion.

Gardening

This tree is very attractive in spring. It can be grown easily from seed, and grows fast and well in good soil with adequate moisture. It is resistant to light frost and drought. It is suitable as a bonsai tree.

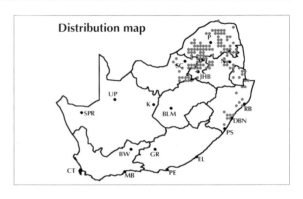

Distribution map

Pale pinky-brown heartwood; creamy-brown sapwood; holds nails well; varnishes to a good finish.

This is a single-stemmed tree with a straight trunk and a densely branched moderate, irregular canopy. Large branches are normally visible in the canopy.

Leaves   Simple leaves are alternate on older twigs and spiral on young twigs. The margins of the round leaves are irregularly and roundly toothed. The leaves are rigid and covered by coarse hairs, giving the leaf a sandpapery feel. The upper-surface is dark green with a paler under-surface. Three to five thick veins originate at the base and protrude from the leaf-surface. (Leaf: 30 x 150 mm)

Flowers
In early spring, before the leaves appear, conspicuous white to light pink, star-shaped flowers grow in abundance in sprays at the end of twigs. Flowers turn brownish when old. This is one of the first trees to flower in spring and is very striking from July to October. (Individual: 15 - 20 mm; spray: 70 x 60 mm)

Fruit   The seeds grow in small capsules that are surrounded by the brownish, dry flower petals. Seeds are covered by silky hairs and are dark when mature (October to December). (6 mm)

Bark   The bark is smooth in young branches and trees, but is very rough and dark, and deeply fissured into irregular, long blocks in older trunks.

Seasonal changes
Semi-deciduous. This tree is easiest to identify in early spring when it is conspicuously covered with white flowers. It is difficult to identify when no leaves or flowers are present.

	Oct	Nov	Dec	Jan	Feb	Mar	Apr	May	Jun	Jul	Aug	Sep
Leaf												
Flower												
Fruit/Pod												

You find trees

COAST – DUNE AND SAND FORESTS

These two Habitats are among the easiest places to start
tree spotting because the trees growing here have to be
specialists. They have to cope with sandy soil and salty
sea winds. Check the Maps, pages 406 - 409, as well as
the Destination and Habitats Grids, on pages 386 - 388,
and you should have no trouble working out if you are in
either of these very specialised areas. Then you should
first look for the trees listed here.

Black Monkey Orange	p. 146
Coast Silver Oak	p. 150
Coastal Red Milkwood	p. 154

Monkey Oranges are easy to find by Habitat and by fruit.
The adventure lies in distinguishing between Green and
Black Monkey Oranges.

BLACK MONKEY ORANGE
Strychnos madagascariensis

**WILD ELDER FAMILY
LOGANIACEAE**

SA Tree Number 626

AFRIKAANS Swartklapper, Botterklapper **N. SOTHO** Morapa **TSONGA** Nkwakwa
TSWANA Mogorwagorwana **VENDA** Mukwakwa **ZULU** umGluguza, umKwakwa

The term **madagascariensis** means from Madagascar.

Where you'll find this tree easily

The Black Monkey Orange grows singly among other
species of trees, and often as a loner.

🌱 It is easiest to find in the Sand Forest of the Coast (C).

🌱 It is also common in the Woodland and Thornveld of
the Bushveld-Savannah (B) and occurs in most of the
forests of the Coast (C).

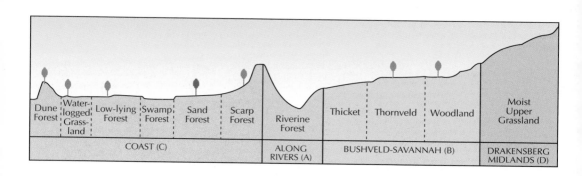

Striking features

- This is a single- or multi-stemmed tree with a spreading
irregular, angular canopy.

- The leaves are hairy, dark green and leathery, with
three to five distinct veins radiating from the base.

- **The leaves are clustered on the ends of short, thick
twigs.**

- **The conspicuous, very hard, orange-like fruit is green
for most of the year, but turns yellow-orange when
ripe.**

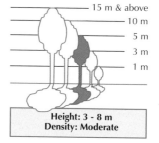

Height: 3 - 8 m
Density: Moderate

146

147

BLACK MONKEY ORANGE
Strychnos madagascariensis

Links with animals

The leaves are eaten by Duiker, Giraffe, Kudu, Impala, Steenbok, Nyala and Elephant. The fruit is eaten by Baboons, Monkeys, Bushpig, Nyala and Eland. Dung Beetles help with seed dispersal as the seeds mimic one of the compounds in dung. The Dung Beetle rolls away the seeds in the dung ball which is then buried.

Human uses

The flesh around the seeds is edible after it has been sun-dried and pounded. The dried shells are the traditional sounding boxes of the musical instrument known as the mbila or marimba. They are also made into flutes.

Gardening

This is a very interesting addition to the landscape garden. It can be grown easily from seed and will grow fairly fast when cultivated. It is sensitive to frost and prefers well-drained soils.

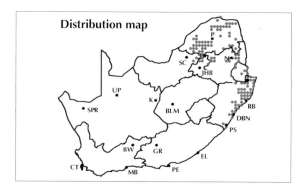

Distribution map

Finely textured wood; strong, resistant, durable; difficult to plane and saw; not suitable for bending; polishes well.

Look-alike tree

The Green Monkey Orange (*Strychnos spinosa*) is also common in the Sand Forest, and is a huge, striking tree in other Coastal forests. It has slender, paired, straight or slightly curved, woody spines at the base of the leaves. The leaves are opposite and not clustered. They are softer and greener than those of the Black Monkey Orange. The fruit turns yellowish-brown when ripe.

GROWTH DETAILS

This is a very variable tree. It may have a single-grooved and dented stem, or it may be multi-stemmed, branching low down. The leaves are crowded towards the ends of new branches and twigs, and form a moderate, irregular, angular, canopy. The side branches tend to come off at right angles.

Leaves   The leaves are simple and opposite or are clustered at the tips of thick, knobbly twigs. Broadly elliptic leaves are velvety, shiny, blue-green above and paler below. The margins are smooth with a round tip and a wedge-shaped base. Leaves have 3 - 5 veins radiating from the base with two secondary veins that run parallel to the margin. (Leaf: 20 - 90 x 10 - 60 mm)

Fruit   The big, round, fleshy, orange-like fruit is characteristic. It has a hard, woody shell. The fruit may take a long time to ripen to yellow-orange, and fruit may still be present into the next flowering season. Large seeds are tightly packed inside the shell, and each seed is covered by yellow pulp (March to August). (70 - 120 mm)

Bark   The bark is light grey and smooth and does not have spines, but has knobbly side shoots of 10 - 30 mm. The bark of young trees and branches is light grey and smooth, becoming rougher with age. The pale grey twigs can be smooth or hairy.

Flowers   Small, inconspicuous, greenish-yellow, trumpet-shaped flowers grow in small clusters at the base of the leaves on the old wood. Flowers tend to appear only after good rains (November to December). (8 - 10 mm diameter)

Seasonal changes
Semi-deciduous. This tree will be easy to find as long as some fruit is present.

	Oct	Nov	Dec	Jan	Feb	Mar	Apr	May	Jun	Jul	Aug	Sep
Leaf												
Flower												
Fruit/Pod												

149

COAST SILVER OAK

Brachylaena discolor

DAISY FAMILY
ASTERACEAE

SA Tree Number 724

AFRIKAANS Kusvaalbos, Kreukelboom **N. SOTHO** Mphahla **XHOSA** umPhahla **ZULU** iPhahla

The term **discolor** refers to the two-coloured leaves.

Where you'll find this tree easily

The Coast Silver Oak grows in groups.

🌿 It is very common and easy to find in the Dune Forest of the Coast (C), where it grows in groups.

🌿 It can also be found in the Low-lying, Sand and Scarp forests of the Coast (C), Along Rivers (A), and in the Woodland of the Bushveld-Savannah (B).

A	B
C	D

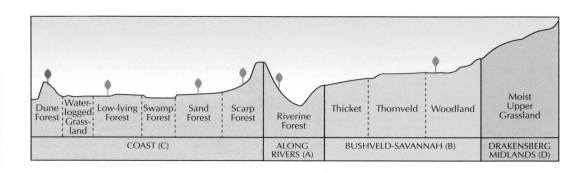

Striking features

- This is a single- or multi-stemmed tree that branches low down to form an irregular to V-shaped canopy.

- The trunk divides into several large branches that tend to grow upwards and then horizontally to form bows.

- **The tree has a characteristic silvery-blue appearance from a distance, that stands out amongst other vegetation.**

- **The leaves are dark green and shiny on the upper-surface, and are covered by thick, white, felt-like hairs below, looking distinctly bi-coloured.**

- The bark is pale brown to grey and has shallow, lengthways grooves.

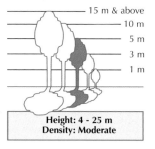

Height: 4 - 25 m
Density: Moderate

151

COAST SILVER OAK

Brachylaena discolor

Links with animals

The leaves are very bitter and unpalatable and are only occasionally browsed by Nyala, Bushbuck, Red and Blue Duiker. When in flower, the entire tree is covered in flowers that produce large amounts of nectar and attract many birds and insects.

Human uses

The wood is durable in water and buoyant. It is used for boat-building and as shafts of fishing spears and the floats of fishing nets. Long, straight branches are used to construct the roofs of huts. The ashes of the tree were used by early settlers to provide the alkali needed in soap making. The leaves were used medicinally by Europeans and Africans as a diabetes remedy and for kidney conditions. The roots were used as an enema, and to stop haemorrhage of the stomach. An infusion of the leaves was used as a tonic, to treat intestinal parasites and for chest pains. The roots and stems were used by Zulu diviners to communicate with the ancestors.

Gardening

The Coast Silver Oak makes a good hedge-plant and the root system is not invasive. It grows easily from seed and is drought- and frost-resistant. It will grow well in deep shade and full sun. It grows best in sandy to loamy soils, and is a good container plant.

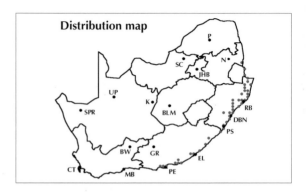

Distribution map

Yellow-brown heartwood; yellow sapwood; straight grain; turns well.

GROWTH DETAILS

This is a single- or multi-stemmed tree that branches low down into several large branches that tend to grow upwards and then horizontally. The branches develop slender branchlets that form drooping bows. The leaves grow towards the ends of the thin twigs leaving the inner branches uncovered. The moderate, irregular, V-shaped canopy is distinctly blue-silver-grey.

Leaves   The simple, alternate leaves are spirally arranged towards the ends of the branchlets and twigs. The margin is distinctly toothed in young leaves, but is irregularly toothed in older leaves. The upper-surface is shiny, dark green and the under-surface is densely covered by short, white to silver-grey hairs. The leathery leaves are elliptic with rounded tip and narrow base. Leaves have an intensely bitter taste. (Leaf: 25 - 120 x 13 - 60 mm, but new leaves may be up to 180 mm long)

Flowers   The white, thistle-like flowers grow in sprays at the end of the branchlets. Similar male and female flowers grow on separate trees (July to September). (Individual: 8 - 12 x 5 mm)

Fruit   The seeds are in a small nutlet with a brown capsule that is tipped with yellowish, paintbrush-like hairs (November to January). (12 mm)

Bark   The bark is pale brown to grey and is fissured lengthways. The branches and branchlets are light brown and also have shallow, lengthways grooves.

Seasonal changes
Usually deciduous, but may be evergreen, under higher rainfall conditions.

	Oct	Nov	Dec	Jan	Feb	Mar	Apr	May	Jun	Jul	Aug	Sep
Leaf												
Flower												
Fruit/Pod												

153

COASTAL RED MILKWOOD

Mimusops caffra

SAPOTACEAE
MILKWOOD FAMILY

SA Tree Number 583

AFRIKAANS Kusrooimelkhout   **XHOSA** umNtunzi, umThunzi   **ZULU** umKhakhayi, umThunzi

The term **caffra** refers to the Hebrew "Kafri", meaning person living on the land.

Where you'll find this tree easily

The Coastal Red Milkwood grows in large uniform groups or singly.

🌴 It is easiest to find in large groups in the Dune Forest of the Coast (C).

🌴 It can also be found in the Low-lying Forest of the Coast (C), where it grows singly as a much larger tree.

A	B
C	D

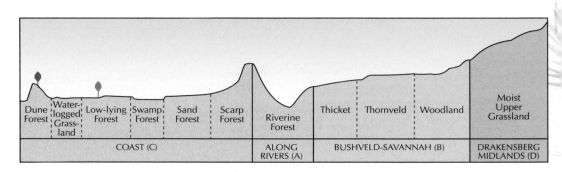

Dune Forest	Water-logged Grass-land	Low-lying Forest	Swamp Forest	Sand Forest	Scarp Forest	Riverine Forest	Thicket	Thornveld	Woodland	Moist Upper Grassland
COAST (C)						ALONG RIVERS (A)	BUSHVELD-SAVANNAH (B)			DRAKENSBERG MIDLANDS (D)

Striking features

• This tree often grows in large uniform groups, creating extensive areas of forest on the sand dunes.

• **The canopies are shaped by the wind and salt spray, giving the impression of a mowed lawn when looked at from the beach.**

• This is a single- or multi-stemmed tree that branches low down and spreads to form a moderate to dense, rounded canopy.

• **Simple leaves are spirally arranged, forming distinct rosettes towards the end of the branches.**

• The leaves are dark blue-green above and greyish below. They are leathery and have a rounded tip.

• All parts contain a milky latex.

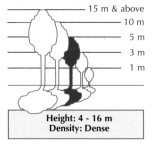

15 m & above
10 m
5 m
3 m
1 m

Height: 4 - 16 m
Density: Dense

Largest tree currently registered

Diameter: 0,82 m
Girth: 2,57 m
Height: 18 m

I.F. Garland & Sons
'Twin Streams',
Mlalazi,
Dist. Mtunzini

COASTAL RED MILKWOOD

Mimusops caffra

Links with animals

The fruit forms an important food source for Monkeys along the coast, and fallen fruit is eaten by Bushpigs. The leaves are eaten by the caterpillars of the Chief False Acraea butterfly (*Pseudacraea lucretia*). Cape Parrots, Blackbellied Glossy Starlings and Yellowstreaked Bulbuls eat the fruit.

Human uses

The fruit is tasty. The wood is used to build boats, while branches make the framework of large conical fish traps and fish kraals. Bark infusions were taken as emetics. In Zululand it is considered a royal timber tree of excellent quality.

Gardening

This is a decorative tree for gardens along the coast. It is slow-growing from seed and not frost- or drought-resistant.

Look-alike tree
This tree can be confused with the Red Milkwood (*Mimusops obovata*), which has a straight, tall stem and thin, leathery, shiny leaves that have a bluntly pointed tip.

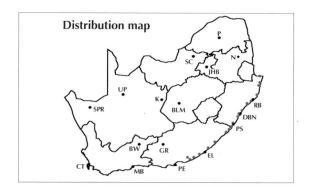

Distribution map

Pinkish-red; close grain; heavy; strong and elastic.

GROWTH DETAILS

The name "Red Milkwood" is based on the colour of the wood and the fact that all parts contain a milky latex. It is a single-stemmed tree that branches low down and spreads to form a moderate to dense, rounded canopy.

Leaves   Simple leaves are spiral, with a leaf-stem of 6 - 15 mm. They tend to be crowded towards the tips of the branches, forming rosettes. The leaves are thick and leathery, with thickened margins. The broadly elliptic leaves have a tapering base and a distinctly rounded tip. Leaves are dark blue-green above and paler, with whitish hairs below. (Leaf: 25 - 80 x 15 - 40 mm)

Flowers   Creamy-white, hairy flower-tufts on slender stalks develop from the clusters of rusty-brown buds in leaf rosettes (June to October). (10 mm diameter)

Fruit   The bunches of oval, berry-like, succulent fruit are orange-red when ripe. The fruit has a hair-like tip (June to January). (15 - 20 x 10 - 15 mm)

Bark   The bark is rough, dark grey and fissured, becoming blocky in older trees. Young growth is covered in velvety, reddish hairs.

Seasonal changes
Evergreen. Can be identified throughout the year.

	Oct	Nov	Dec	Jan	Feb	Mar	Apr	May	Jun	Jul	Aug	Sep
Leaf												
Flower												
Fruit/Pod												

You find trees

COAST – SWAMP, MANGROVE AND WATERLOGGED GRASSLAND

KwaZulu-Natal has greater tree diversity than any other province. This makes tree spotting exciting, but difficult. However in these three Habitats you will find trees that are specialists, able to cope, and thrive, with their feet in water or soggy soil. There are only a few to choose from, and as long as you have checked your Ecozone on the Maps, pages 406 - 409, as well as the Destination and Habitats Grids, pages 386 - 388, you should be looking for the right trees, in the right places.

SWAMP AND MANGROVE FORESTS

Black Mangrove	p. 160
White Mangrove	p. 164
Powder-puff Tree	p. 168

WATERLOGGED GRASSLAND

Water Berry	p. 172
Wild Medlar	p. 176

Charter's Creek, part of the Greater St. Lucia Park, is not only a fisherman's paradise. It has a wide range of Habitats, and therefore diversity of trees. This Wild Medlar in Waterlogged Grassland is on the edge of a magnificent forest.

BLACK MANGROVE

Bruguiera gymnorrhiza

MANGROVE FAMILY **RHIZOPHORACEAE**	**SA Tree Number 527**

AFRIKAANS Swartwortelboom **XHOSA** isiKhangathi **ZULU** isiHlobane

The term **gymnorrhiza** is based on the Greek word meaning "naked root".

Where you'll find this tree easily

The Black Mangrove is the most common mangrove in South Africa and can be found in most of the Mangrove Forests. It probably lives longer than any other mangrove.

🌱 It is found in well-developed Mangrove Forests of the Coast (C), often deeper into the muddy flats.

A	B
C	D

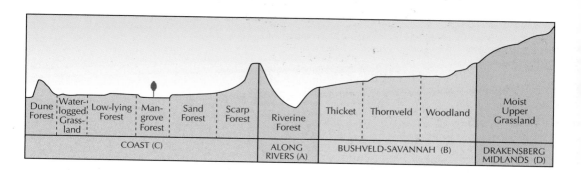

Dune Forest	Water-logged Grass-land	Low-lying Forest	Man-grove Forest	Sand Forest	Scarp Forest	Riverine Forest	Thicket	Thornveld	Woodland	Moist Upper Grassland
COAST (C)						ALONG RIVERS (A)	BUSHVELD-SAVANNAH (B)			DRAKENSBERG MIDLANDS (D)

Striking features

- It is a small, sturdy tree with a straight trunk and often a buttressed stem-base and knee-like root.
- **The bark on the trunk is dark, red-brown and rough.**
- The leaves grow at the tips of sturdy twigs and branchlets.
- **The leaves are firm, leathery, glossy and lime-green in colour.**
- Growing seeds can be seen in the vicinity, or hanging from the trees.
- **The rubbery flowers, often with long cigar-shaped fruit hanging from them, are characteristic.**

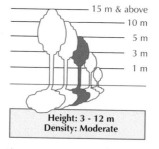

15 m & above
10 m
5 m
3 m
1 m

Height: 3 - 12 m
Density: Moderate

160

161

BLACK MANGROVE

Bruguiera gymnorrhiza

Links with animals

Flowers are visited by ants, moths and wasps, and are eaten by Vervet Monkeys and Bats. The Wattle-eyed Flycatcher is often seen foraging on these in *Bruguiera* groves, while Sunbirds eat the nectar. The leaves are eaten by large Mangrove Crabs.

Human uses

The wood is hard and red and used as posts and for building huts. This tree is used to make fish-trap baskets and fish kraals. The bark is rich in tannin and is used for tanning, yielding a reddish-yellow leather. Bits of bark are added to the water in which fish nets are boiled to preserve them.

Gardening

It is occasionally grown to stabilise soil along shores. It tolerates complete shade in which no other species can survive.

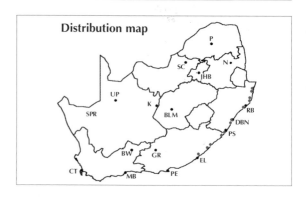

Distribution map

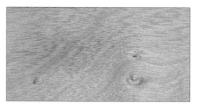

Look-alike trees

The White Mangrove (*Avicennia marina*), page 164, has a pale grey bark, and duller grey-green leaves.

The Red Mangrove (*Rhizophora mucronata*), page 23, is only found in large mature Mangrove Forests and is more widespread world-wide. It is a smaller tree, with dark bark, sharp pointed leaves, four-petalled and star-shaped flowers, with large cigar-shaped fruit and stilt roots that stand high up above the soil or water surface forming a branched pedicle.

162

It is a small, sturdy tree with a straight trunk and often buttressed stem-base and knee-like roots. The branchlets are spirally arranged around the straight branches and stems and the leaves come off the ends of the branchlets and twigs to form a moderate canopy of bright green leaves.

Leaves   Simple, opposite leaves are crowded towards the ends of the branchlets and twigs, forming rosettes. The hairless leaves are elliptic, tapering towards the tips and base. They have a smooth margin. They are almost lime-green in colour with a slightly paler under-surface with a raised central vein.
(Leaf: 76 - 230 x 25 - 70 mm)

Flowers   Single flowers grow on long stalks in the angles formed by the leaves. They are creamy to white with many hard, thick, rubbery petals. The body (calyx) of the flower is red on the outside and green inside (July to April). (25 - 40 mm diameter)

Fruit   The seed develops inside the fruit which grows inside the flower. The developing fruit looks like a cigar hanging down from the remains of the flower. The flower is still attached to the seedling when it drops (September to April). (Fruit: 25 mm; growing seed: 250 mm)

Bark and roots   The bark is dark to red-brown and is coarse and knobbly on older trees. It has horizontal bands formed by grooves. The branches are dark grey to yellow and have a smooth bark.

Seasonal changes
Evergreen. This tree can be identified throughout the year by its leaves.

	Oct	Nov	Dec	Jan	Feb	Mar	Apr	May	Jun	Jul	Aug	Sep
Leaf												
Flower												
Fruit/Pod												

163

WHITE MANGROVE
Avicennia marina

VERBENA FAMILY
VERBENACEAE

SA Tree Number 669

AFRIKAANS Witseebasboom **XHOSA** isiKhungathi **ZULU** isiKhungathi

The word **marina** means "growing near the sea" or "immersed in sea water".

Where you'll find this tree easily

The White Mangrove is found growing in large, uniform groups in the Mangrove Forests. Unlike other mangroves it is a sun lover, often fringing the other mangroves.

🌱 It is found in the Mangrove Forests of the Coast (C).

A	B
C	D

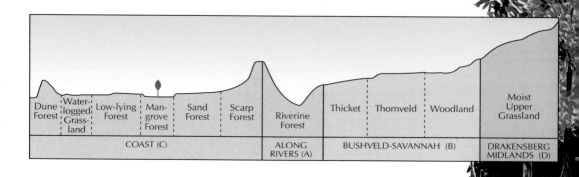

Dune Forest	Water-logged Grass-land	Low-lying Forest	Man-grove Forest	Sand Forest	Scarp Forest	Riverine Forest	Thicket	Thornveld	Woodland	Moist Upper Grassland
COAST (C)						ALONG RIVERS (A)	BUSHVELD-SAVANNAH (B)			DRAKENSBERG MIDLANDS (D)

Striking features

- **The tree has a yellow-green to pink coloured bark with raised dots which flake in small patches to reveal a smoother, brighter-coloured under-bark.**

- This is a single-stemmed tree that branches high up into many small branchlets to form a moderate canopy shaped by the surrounding trees.

- The small, pencil-like roots stick out from the mud around the tree.

- **The leaves are distinctly bicoloured with a shiny, olive-green colour above, and dense grey hairs on the under-surface.**

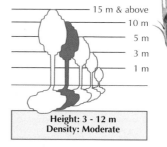

15 m & above
10 m
5 m
3 m
1 m

Height: 3 - 12 m
Density: Moderate

164

Sun-loving White Mangroves are the taller trees, while the Black Mangroves are shorter, often growing deeper in the forest.

165

WHITE MANGROVE

Avicennia marina

Links with animals

Fallen fruit provides food for the tiny, dark Mangrove Crabs that live among the pencil roots. The flowers attract honeybees and ants. The trees provide nesting sites for water birds, such as the Little Egret, Grey Heron, Blackheaded Heron and Golden Weaver. Less common birds associated with this tree are the Wattle-eyed Flycatchers which may be seen feeding on insects. The Mangrove Kingfisher moves between the most northern and southern Mangrove Forests.

Human uses

The wood is grey or yellowish, dotted and fairly dense. It is durable in wet environments and used for ship-building. The frameworks of large fish-traps are made from its branches, and leafy branches are used to close off fish-kraal fences. The bark and roots are used for tanning and brown dye is obtained from the bark. The ash from the wood has been used for washing clothes. The unripe fruit was used to treat sores and to heal the skin lesions of small pox. The wood in the centre yields a resin which was applied to snakebites, and was also used as a contraceptive.

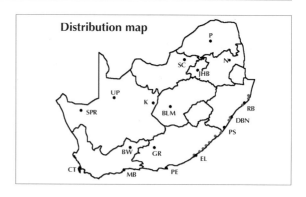

Distribution map

Gardening

This tree has very specialised habitat requirements and cannot be grown in gardens.

Look-alike trees

The Black Mangrove *(Bruguiera gymnorrhiza)*, page 160, is normally found deeper in the Mangrove Forest. It has dark bark, larger, lime-green leaves, many-petalled, rubbery flowers, cigar-shaped fruit and knobbly, knee-like roots.

The Red Mangrove *(Rhizophora mucronata)*, page 23, is only found in large, mature Mangrove Forests and is more widespread world-wide.

It is a smaller tree, with dark bark, sharp pointed leaves, four-petalled flower-stars with large, cigar-shaped fruit and stilt roots that stand high up above the surface, forming a branched pedicle.

This is a single-stemmed tree that branches high up into many small branchlets to form a moderate, irregular canopy that is shaped by the surrounding vegetation. It does not have a central tap root, but has horizontal roots that radiate far from the base of the trunk. Small, pencil-like roots develop from these roots and can be seen over large areas where they stand out above the mud, helping the tree to breathe.

Leaves   The simple, opposite leaves are thick and leathery. They are distinctly bicoloured with a shiny, olive-green colour above and dense grey hairs on the under-surface. The elliptic leaves have a smooth margin and a tapering to pointed tip and base. (Leaf: 30 - 100 x 12 - 40 mm)

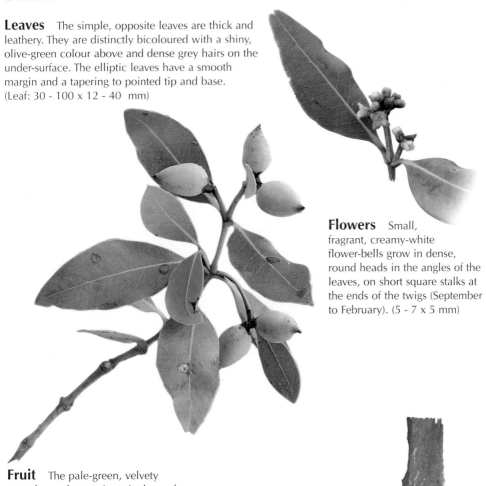

Flowers   Small, fragrant, creamy-white flower-bells grow in dense, round heads in the angles of the leaves, on short square stalks at the ends of the twigs (September to February). (5 - 7 x 5 mm)

Fruit   The pale-green, velvety capsules each contain a single seed and grow in clusters (February to March). (25 mm)

Bark   The bark is yellow-green to pink with raised dots. It may form small flakes in older trees.

Seasonal changes
Evergreen. This tree can be identified throughout the year.

	Oct	Nov	Dec	Jan	Feb	Mar	Apr	May	Jun	Jul	Aug	Sep
Leaf												
Flower												
Fruit/Pod												

167

POWDER-PUFF TREE

Barringtonia racemosa

PARA-NUT FAMILY
LECYTHIDACEAE

SA Tree Number 524

AFRIKAANS Poeierkwasboom   **ZULU** iBoqo

The term **racemosa** means having "racemes", which are the string-like arrangement of stalked flowers.

Where you'll find this tree easily

Powder-puff Trees are often found growing in groups in swamps and marshy areas.

🍃 They are easiest to find on the edge of Swamp and Mangrove forests of the Coast (C).

🍃 They can also be found in the Waterlogged Grassland and the Low-lying Forest of the Coast (C).

A	B
C	D

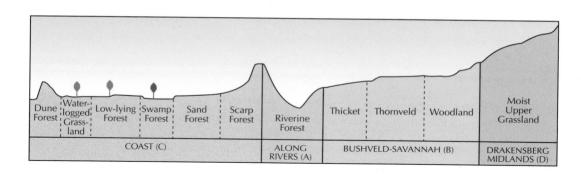

Dune Forest	Water-logged Grass-land	Low-lying Forest	Swamp Forest	Sand Forest	Scarp Forest	Riverine Forest	Thicket	Thornveld	Woodland	Moist Upper Grassland

COAST (C)	ALONG RIVERS (A)	BUSHVELD-SAVANNAH (B)	DRAKENSBERG MIDLANDS (D)

Striking features

- This is a single-stemmed, low-branching tree that branches into only a few large, upright branches.
- The leaves are large and arranged spirally at the ends of thick twigs.
- The short leaf-stem is strikingly purple.
- The bark is grey and has smooth, small dots.
- **The characteristic long strings of powder-puff flowers open late in the evening and are often seen lying on the forest floor or in the water.**
- **The large, guava-sized, poisonous fruit hangs on long strings from the tree from April to October.**

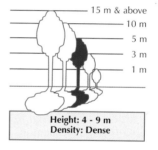

15 m & above
10 m
5 m
3 m
1 m

Height: 4 - 9 m
Density: Dense

169

POWDER-PUFF TREE

Barringtonia racemosa

Links with animals

The caterpillars of the butterfly, the Red-tab Policeman *(Coeliades keithloa)*, feed on the leaves.

Human uses

The wood is light and soft. This tree contains a substance that is poisonous to fish. The bark, seed, fruit, root and wood are widely used to catch fish. Extracts of the plant have proved effective in controlling citrus aphids and the seed may be used as an insecticide. Young leaves, soaked in lime water, are edible as vegetables. The fruit is poisonous and has poisoned wild pigs and humans. The bark of stems and roots are high in tannin and are valuable as tanning material. Root, bark and juice were used to treat fever, and the fruit was used as a remedy for malaria and eye diseases.

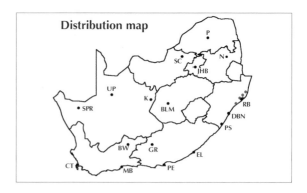

Distribution map

Gardening

This is a very decorative tree, and grows well even if it is not in wet soil. Under the right conditions it grows easily and quickly, and slips planted in wet, black soil take root and grow easily. It cannot tolerate frost at all.

GROWTH DETAILS

This is a single- or multi-stemmed tree with a straight trunk that branches low down into only a few large, upward-growing branches to form a round, dense, canopy.

Leaves   The large, simple, alternate leaves are spirally arranged at the ends of the thick branchlets. They have a smooth or slightly toothed margin. The central vein has a purple tinge at the base of the leaf. The leaf-stem is very short and also has a purple tinge. The side veins are obvious and tend to be alternate. The upper-surface is a dull, dark green with a paler under-surface. There are often scattered, coppery leaves visible in the canopy. (Leaf: 80 - 350 x 40 - 230 mm)

Flowers   The pincushion-flowers grow in a long, hanging spray. Each flower has four, pinky-white petals, with a mass of white stamens. The buds are shiny, deep purplish-red. The flowers open late in the evening or at night and have a very unpleasant smell (November to June). (Spray 120 - 1 000 mm; individual: 35 mm)

Fruit   Several guava-sized, poisonous fruits are attached alternately to long, dangling stalks. While the fruit is still green, it is fleshy, but later it becomes fibrous and hard, and coppery or reddish brown. The ripe fruit is able to float in water. During fruiting season ripe fruit may be seen floating in the surf all around the African coast (July to October). (40 x 30 mm)

Bark   The bark is grey-white, smooth and has small dots. The bark is often covered with lichen that may cause white streaks or blotches.

Seasonal changes
Evergreen. This tree can be recognised throughout the year.

	Oct	Nov	Dec	Jan	Feb	Mar	Apr	May	Jun	Jul	Aug	Sep
Leaf												
Flower												
Fruit/Pod												

171

WATER BERRY

Syzygium cordatum

MYRTLE FAMILY
MYRTACEAE

AFRIKAANS Waterbessie, Waterhout **N. SOTHO** Monhlo, Montlho **SISWATI** umCozi
TSONGA Muthwa, Muhlwa **VENDA** Muṭu **XHOSA** umJome, umSwi **ZULU** umDoni

The term **cordatum** means heart-shaped, referring to the heart-shaped base of the leaves.

Where you'll find this tree easily

The Water Berry is a water-loving, fire-resistant tree and is
found in permanently moist soil and areas of high rainfall.

* It is easiest to find in the Waterlogged Grassland found
  along lagoons and river mouths of the Coast (C).

* In the Bushveld-Savannah (B), it can be found in the
  high rainfall Woodland areas, as well as Along Rivers
  (A) and in most of the forests of the Coast (C).

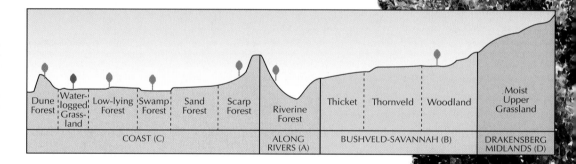

Dune Forest	Water-logged Grass-land	Low-lying Forest	Swamp Forest	Sand Forest	Scarp Forest	Riverine Forest	Thicket	Thornveld	Woodland	Moist Upper Grassland
	COAST (C)					ALONG RIVERS (A)	BUSHVELD-SAVANNAH (B)			DRAKENSBERG MIDLANDS (D)

Striking features

* This is a single-trunked, low-branching tree that
  branches to form a blue-green, dense, semi-circular
  canopy.

* **The stemless leaves are round and are clustered
  towards the ends of thick twigs, forming distinct
  rosettes.**

* The central vein is yellow and conspicuous.

* The characteristic pin-cushion flowers grow at the
  ends of the twigs, in the leaf-rosettes.

* **The succulent berries turn deep purple when ripe
  and are conspicuous from October to May.**

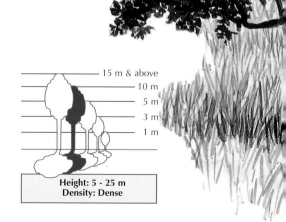

15 m & above
10 m
5 m
3 m
1 m

Height: 5 - 25 m
Density: Dense

WATER BERRY

Syzygium cordatum

Links with animals

Caterpillars of two Charaxes and three Playboy butterflies feed on this tree. The Emperor Moth (*Micragone cana*) also feed on it. Monkeys, Baboons, Bushpigs and Bushbabies eat the fruit, as well as many birds, such as Tambourine Doves, African Green Pigeons, Purplecrested and Knysna Louries. Kudu, Nyala, Bushbuck and Grey Duiker browse the foliage. Ball-like webs are made by the bright ginger Tailor Ant which favours this tree.

Human uses

The succulent berries are edible and are sometimes used to make beer. The wood has a beautiful grain, and is used for furniture and canoes. The powdered bark is sometimes used as a fish poison. An extract of the leaves was used as a purgative, for treatment of diarrhoea, and to treat stomach and respiratory disorders such as tuberculosis, colds and fever. Bark and roots were used for headaches and wounds.

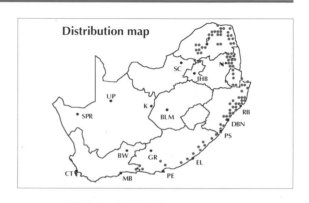

Distribution map

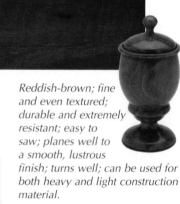

Reddish-brown; fine and even textured; durable and extremely resistant; easy to saw; planes well to a smooth, lustrous finish; turns well; can be used for both heavy and light construction material.

Gardening

This is a very attractive garden tree, but must be planted near water. It has an aggressive root system and grows well in a container. It grows fast from seed but will not withstand severe frost. It can withstand extended periods of waterlogging and can be used to stabilise stream and river banks, or planted as a shade tree in swampy areas.

GROWTH DETAILS

This is a single-trunked, often low-branching tree with branches growing upwards and outwards to form a dense, semi-circular, blue-green canopy. The round leaves are clustered towards the end of the thick twigs, forming distinct rosettes. Young twigs and branchlets are square.

Leaves Simple, opposite leaves are blue-green, leathery and smooth, with a distinct yellow central vein. They are almost round, with a deeply notched base that clamps the twig. The margins are smooth. They grow towards the ends of the branchlets and twigs, with successive pairs at right angles, forming rosettes. New leaves are bright red.
(30 - 100 x 20 - 80 mm)

Fruit The fleshy, berry-like fruit grows in bunches in the leaf-rosettes, resembling posies. The fruit turns deep purple when ripe (June to January).
(13 - 20 x 10 mm)

Flowers The sweet-smelling, pin-cushion-like flowers are creamy-white to pinkish and are rich in nectar. They grow in bunches on the ends of branchlets and twigs in the leaf-rosettes (October to June). (Bunch: 100 mm; individual: 20 x 25 mm)

Bark The bark is dark and coarse and may even be corky in older trees. In young trees the bark is smooth and pale grey, with grey and white blotches.

Seasonal changes
Evergreen. This tree can be identified throughout the year.

	Oct	Nov	Dec	Jan	Feb	Mar	Apr	May	Jun	Jul	Aug	Sep
Leaf												
Flower												
Fruit/Pod												

COAST – WATERLOGGED GRASSLAND
Water Berry

175

WILD MEDLAR
Vangueria infausta

GARDENIA FAMILY
RUBIACEAE

SA Tree Number 702

AFRIKAANS Wildemispel **N. SOTHO** Mmilô **SISWATI** iMandulu **TSONGA** Mpfilwa
TSWANA Monyunwana **VENDA** Muzwilu **XHOSA** umVilo **ZULU** umViyo, umTulwa

The term **infausta** means unlucky and refers to the belief that the wood should not be used as firewood.

Where you'll find this tree easily

The Wild Medlar grows singly.

🌱 It is easiest to find in the Waterlogged Grassland of the Coast (C).

🌱 It can also be found in all the other forests of the Coast (C), Along Rivers (A), on rocky outcrops of the Bushveld-Savannah (B), and in the Drakensberg Midlands (D).

A	B
C	D

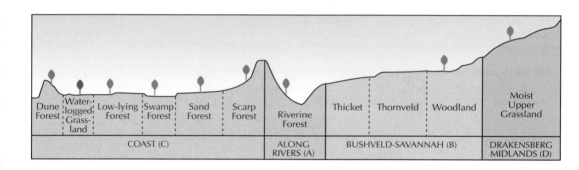

Striking features

- This is a single- or multi-stemmed, low-branching tree with short, stout branches and a moderate, rounded canopy.

- **The large, boat-like, hairy leaves are often partly closed and are bent backwards in a sickle shape.**

- **The plum-like, fleshy fruit is yellow-brown when ripe from November to April.**

- The bark is grey to pale grey and smooth, becoming rough and peeling.

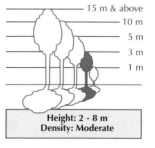

176

177

WILD MEDLAR

Vangueria infausta

Links with animals

The leaves are eaten by antelope. Bushbabies, Monkeys, Baboons, Squirrels and Bushpigs eat the fruit. The flowers are visited by butterflies and flies.

Human uses

The fruit is edible, is high in Vitamin C and can be distilled into brandy. This tree is still used in traditional medicine today: roots and leaves to treat malaria, pneumonia, menstrual problems, infertility in women and for non-traumatic swellings of the limbs. It is also used as a roundworm remedy and a purgative. Sticks placed along the fences are believed to protect the homestead.

Gardening

This is a very attractive tree in the garden. It can be grown from seed and cuttings. It is a slow grower and is frost- and drought-resistant. It is suitable as a bonsai tree.

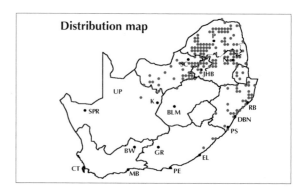

Distribution map

It is believed that it is unlucky to use the wood of this tree as firewood, hence the name "infausta".

GROWTH DETAILS

This can be a low-branching, single- or multi-stemmed tree or shrub. It has short, stout, opposite, upward-growing branches forming a moderate, rounded to V-shaped canopy with a soft appearance. The branchlets are covered by small, raised spots.

Leaves   The large, simple, opposite, broadly elliptic leaves tend to curl backwards along the central vein. They are half-closed in a sickle shape, forming a "boat". Mature leaves are hairy or smooth, but young leaves are velvety and light green. The lateral veins are clearly visible on the under-surface. Leaves have a very short leaf-stalk and smooth margin. In May the leaves change to autumn colours. (Leaf: 50 - 240 x 40 - 200 mm)

Flowers   Inconspicuous, greenish-white, bell-shaped flowers grow in clusters on short side branches from September to November. (2 - 5 mm)

Fruit   The fleshy, plum-like fruit is yellow-brown when ripe from November to April. The remains of the old flower base is still visible at the tip of the fruit. (20 - 40 mm)

Bark   The bark is grey to pale grey and smooth, and may peel in long strips in old trees. The twigs are covered by velvet hairs.

Seasonal changes
Deciduous. This tree is difficult to identify in winter.

	Oct	Nov	Dec	Jan	Feb	Mar	Apr	May	Jun	Jul	Aug	Sep
Leaf												
Flower												
Fruit/Pod												

You find trees

COAST - LOW-LYING AND SCARP FORESTS

KwaZulu-Natal is a tree spotting paradise, but these two zones are not for the faint-hearted, or the real novice. True beginners can enjoy the forests using the Forest Trail, pages 60 - 69. The trees that follow in this section will not be that easy to find unless you already have some tree knowledge from the other sections of this book.

Ngoye Forest, near Empangeni, is famous for birding, and offers the tree spotter days of entertainment.

BROOM CLUSTER FIG

Ficus sur

MULBERRY FAMILY **MORACEAE**	**SA Tree Number 50**

AFRIKAANS Besemtrosvy, Koeman **N. SOTHO** Mogo **TSONGA** Nkuwa **VENDA** Muhuyu-ngala **XHOSA** umKhiwane **ZULU** umKhiwane

The term **sur** is named after an area in Ethiopia.

Where you'll find this tree easily

The Broom Cluster Fig usually grows singly among other species of trees.

🌱 It is easiest to find along rivers in the Low-lying Forest of the Coast (C).

🌱 It can also be found in the Waterlogged Grassland, and most of the other forests of the Coast (C), Along Rivers (A), and on Rocky Outcrops of the Bushveld-Savannah (B).

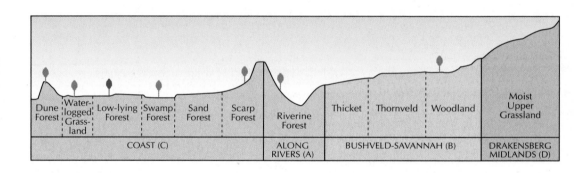

COAST (C)	ALONG RIVERS (A)	BUSHVELD-SAVANNAH (B)	DRAKENSBERG MIDLANDS (D)

Dune Forest · Waterlogged Grassland · Low-lying Forest · Swamp Forest · Sand Forest · Scarp Forest · Riverine Forest · Thicket · Thornveld · Woodland · Moist Upper Grassland

Striking features

- This is a huge, single-stemmed tree that branches low down to form a wide, dense canopy.

- The bark is smooth and grey, and the thick trunk is often conspicuously buttressed.

- **The plum-sized, fleshy figs grow in large, leafless, long-stemmed, broom-like clusters that hang from the trunk and main branches, and turn red when ripe, from June to January.**

- **The simple, large, grey-green to green elliptic leaves have toothed margins, and new leaves can gleam copper-red on twig tips.**

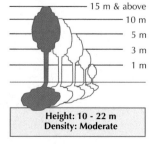

15 m & above
10 m
5 m
3 m
1 m

Height: 10 - 22 m
Density: Moderate

182

Not to scale

Largest tree currently registered

Diameter: 1,25 m
Girth: 3,92 m
Height: 24 m

Buffelskloof Nature Reserve,
Kalmoesfontein,
Dist. Lydenburg

BROOM CLUSTER FIG

Ficus sur

Links with animals

Caterpillars of the Fig Tree Butterfly and the African Map Butterfly feed on the leaves. The fruit is a favourite with Vervet and Samango Monkeys, Baboons and Fruit Bats, and fruit-eating birds such as African Green Pigeons, Brownheaded Parrots, and Knysna, Grey and Purplecrested Louries. Fallen fruit is eaten eagerly by Bushpigs. Leaves are eaten by cattle, Elephant, Kudu, Nyala and Blue Duiker.

Human uses

The ripe figs are edible. Mortars for grinding flour and the major part of drums are made from this wood. Dry pieces of wood were used as the base wood when making fire with sticks by friction. Rope was made from the inner bark. Many medicinal uses are recorded: the milky latex for burns and septic conjunctivitis and sore eyes; bark infusions to stimulate milk production; bark as a powder for rashes; stems and twigs for dysentery, leprosy, epilepsy, rickets, oedema and poisoning. Certain trees have been regarded as sacred shrines and symbolic of Earth and Forest, the two great divinities of productivity.

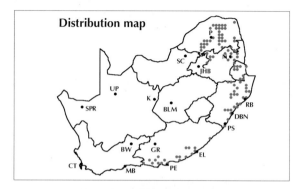

Distribution map

Soft porous wood; yellow-brown heartwood; grey sapwood; not suitable for turning; varnishes and stains well.

Gardening

This is a very attractive garden tree but it has an invasive root system. It is fast-growing and easiest to grow from cuttings. This tree is not resistant to cold and frost. It is a very good tree to attract fruit-eating birds.

Look-alike tree   The Red-leaved Rock Fig *(Ficus ingens)* also has reddish young leaves, but the margins are smooth. The figs are large and fleshy, and grow on short stalks in the leaf angles. They turn red when ripe (June to January).

Other common fig trees

The Natal Fig *(Ficus natalensis)* is a strangler fig, with aerial roots hanging from the branches. The leaves have a rounded tip and the side veins are not very obvious. The fruit is hairless, has long stalks and turns yellow-red when ripe (September to March).

The Common Wild Fig *(Ficus thonningii)* is also a strangler with aerial roots. The leaves are small and dark green, and often have a long stem (up to 45 mm). The net veins are prominent on both surfaces. The small figs (10 mm) have no stalks (August to December).

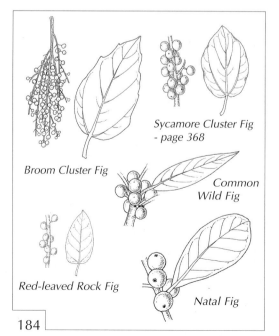

Broom Cluster Fig

Sycamore Cluster Fig
- page 368

Common
Wild Fig

Red-leaved Rock Fig

Natal Fig

GROWTH DETAILS

This is a huge, single-stemmed tree with a thick trunk that is often buttressed, with shallow, spreading roots. The branches grow upwards to form a dense, rounded canopy, with large branches visible.

Leaves   The simple, alternate leaves have a characteristically toothed margin. They are broadly elliptic with a tapering point and rounded base. They are grey-green to green and hairless, and new leaves can gleam copper-red from midwinter. They grow on a long leaf-stem (60 mm) that is furrowed and may be slightly pink. The veins are wide apart, clearly visible and stand out on the under-surface. (Leaf: 80 - 200 x 25 - 90 mm)

Flowers   As in all figs, the flowers are not visible, as they grow inside the fruit.

Fruit   The round, smooth, fleshy, plum-like fruit hangs from large, thick stalks that divide many times to form a broom-like structure. Some figs may hang on main branches on short stalks. The figs may be smooth or slightly hairy and turn deep wine-red when ripe (June to January). (Cluster: 1 m; individual: 20 - 40 mm)

Bark   The bark is smooth and white when young, but becomes darker grey and rougher with age.

Seasonal changes
Evergreen, but the tree may lose its leaves under dry conditions. It is easy to recognise by its leaves and fruit throughout the year.

	Oct	Nov	Dec	Jan	Feb	Mar	Apr	May	Jun	Jul	Aug	Sep
Leaf												
Flower												
Fruit/Pod												

185

COMMON POISON BUSH

Acokanthera oppositifolia

OLEANDER FAMILY
APOCYNACEAE

SA Tree Number 639

AFRIKAANS Boesmansgif, Gewone Gifboom **N. SOTHO** Mothoko-nyepe **SISWATI** inHlungunyembe
VENDA Mutsilili **XHOSA** ubuHlungu behlathi, iNtlugunyembe **ZULU** inHlungunyembe

The term **oppositifolia** refers to the leaves which are opposite one another.

Where you'll find this tree easily

The Common Poison Bush grows singly among other
species of trees.

🌱 It is easiest to find in the Scarp Forest of the Coast (C).

🌱 It can also be found Along Rivers (A), and in the Dune
and Low-lying forests of the Coast (C), on Rocky Outcrops
in the Woodland of the Bushveld-Savannah (B), and in the
Moist Upper Grassland of the Drakensberg Midlands (D).

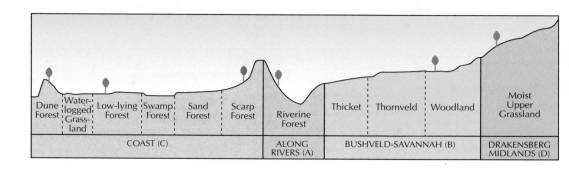

Dune Forest	Water-logged Grass-land	Low-lying Forest	Swamp Forest	Sand Forest	Scarp Forest	Riverine Forest	Thicket	Thornveld	Woodland	Moist Upper Grassland
COAST (C)						ALONG RIVERS (A)	BUSHVELD-SAVANNAH (B)			DRAKENSBERG MIDLANDS (D)

Striking features

- **The canopy is dense, with large, simple, glossy, dark green leaves.**

- It is single- or multi-stemmed and branches low down,
but as it grows among other vegetation, the trunk and
branches are not always easily visible.

- **The simple leaves are thick and leathery and have a
sharp, thorn-like tip.**

- All parts of the tree contain a poisonous, milky latex.

- Conspicuous, sweet-scented bunches of trumpet-
shaped, white flowers appear from June to October.

- The berry-like, fleshy fruit is red to black and grows
among the leaves from September to March.

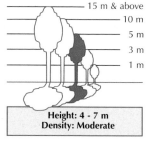

15 m & above
10 m
5 m
3 m
1 m

Height: 4 - 7 m
Density: Moderate

COMMON POISON BUSH

Acokanthera oppositifolia

Links with animals

As this tree is drought-resistant, it still has green leaves when there is little other food. Goats and cattle may then eat the green leaves, with fatal results. Birds may eat the fruit without being poisoned, and the stones that are disgorged grow easily, with seedlings often abundant.

Human uses

The milky latex of the tree is very poisonous and was widely used for poison arrows. It was also used to poison dogs and hyaenas to prevent them from eating livestock. The fruit is also poisonous and causes a burning pain in the stomach, frothing at the mouth and painful vomiting. The fruit is reported to have killed children, cattle and ostriches. Despite being poisonous, the tree was used for medicinal purposes: weak leaf-infusions for abdominal pain; extracts to treat snake- and spider-bites, blood-poisoning and septic spots caused by anthrax; a leaf-paste for swollen and throbbing feet; powder from the root for any sort of pain and immunity to snake-bites; the smoke from burning wood to keep away evil spirits, which were said to choke people in their sleep and cause bad dreams.

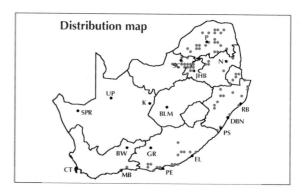

Distribution map

Gardening

This tree grows well from cuttings or from seed and is easily cultivated. It grows fairly fast and is drought- and frost-resistant. It will grow in shade but should not be grown where young children or animals may eat the fruit.

GROWTH DETAILS

This is a multi- or single-stemmed bush or tree that branches low down into only a few main branches. The canopy is dense and dark green, and when the tree grows in the open, the canopy is rounded.

Leaves   The simple, opposite leaves are elliptic, leathery and thick. The leaves are shiny and glossy-green, but paler below and are sometimes tinged with purple. The central vein is raised and the side veins are distinct. The margin is thickened and tapers to form a sharp, thorn-like tip. (Leaf: 50 - 100 x 20 - 50 mm)

Fruit   The small berry-like fruit is fleshy and turns from red to black as it ripens from September to February. (14 - 20 mm)

Bark   The bark is pale and smooth in the forest areas. Elsewhere it is brown and rough, and becomes deeply fissured as the tree grows older. It may be very light in the forest. Young twigs are rich red in summer.

Flowers
The conspicuous white, sweet-scented, flower-trumpets grow in bunches at the ends of the branches. The flowers grow in the angles formed by the leaves (June to October). (Flower-tube: 8 - 11 mm; petal: 3 mm; bunch: 110 mm diameter)

Seasonal changes
Evergreen. This tree can be identified by its leaves throughout the year.

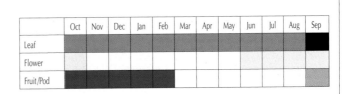

	Oct	Nov	Dec	Jan	Feb	Mar	Apr	May	Jun	Jul	Aug	Sep
Leaf												
Flower												
Fruit/Pod												

189

FLAT-CROWN ALBIZIA
(FLAT-CROWN FALSE-THORN)
Albizia adianthifolia

**THORN-TREE FAMILY
MIMOSACEAE**

SA Tree Number 148

AFRIKAANS Platkroon **VENDA** Muelela, Muvhada-ngoma **XHOSA** umHlandlothi
ZULU uSolo, umHlandlothi

The term **adianthifolia** means "with leaves like a maidenhair fern".

Where you'll find this tree easily

The Flat-crown Albizia grows on the edges of forests.

🌳 It is easiest to find in the Low-lying Forest of the Coast (C).

🌳 It can also be found in the Sand, Dune and Scarp forests of the Coast (C).

A	B
C	D

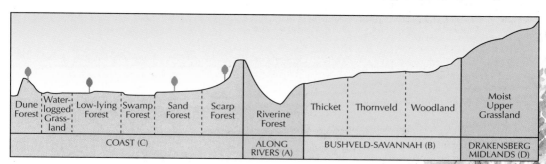

COAST (C)					ALONG RIVERS (A)	BUSHVELD-SAVANNAH (B)			DRAKENSBERG MIDLANDS (D)
Dune Forest	Water-logged Grass-land	Low-lying Forest	Swamp Forest	Sand Forest	Scarp Forest	Riverine Forest	Thicket	Thornveld	Woodland	Moist Upper Grassland

Striking features

- **This is a large, single-stemmed *Albizia* with a huge, flat, medium-umbrella canopy that stands out above the surrounding vegetation.**

- The twice compound leaves are huge, bright green and feathery.

- **The leaflets are distinctly rectangular, with a diagonal central vein and are larger than most *Acacia* leaflets.**

- The conspicuous powder-puff flowers grow above the leaves early in the summer.

- The light brown, papery, bumpy broad bean pods hang from the tree in profusion from September to February.

- In spite of its resemblance to a thorn tree, and being classified as a member of the Thorn-tree family, it has no thorns.

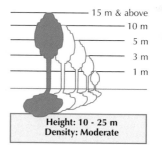

15 m & above
10 m
5 m
3 m
1 m

**Height: 10 - 25 m
Density: Moderate**

191

FLAT-CROWN ALBIZIA
(FLAT-CROWN FALSE-THORN)
Albizia adianthifolia

Links with animals

Elephants eat the leaves and twigs. Many different butterflies are attracted to the tree in bloom, and the Blue-spotted Charaxes *(Charaxes cithaeron)* and the Satyr Charaxes *(Charaxes ethalion)*, common along the Natal coast, breed on this tree. The caterpillars of the Mirza Blue *(Azanus mirza)* feed on the flowers.

Human uses

If this wood is well treated, it can make an attractive-coloured parquet floor. The insoluble sweet-smelling gum, known as "sassa", is used as a cosmetic. A sauce can be made from the seeds. The tree has many traditional medicinal uses: a lotion from the poisonous bark to cure skin ailments, such as scabies and eczema; extracts of the bark to cure internal parasites, snake bites and bronchitis; powdered as a snuff for headaches and sinusitis; a leaf extract to treat eye inflammations, stomach ailments, tooth-ache, dysentery, haemorrhoids and as a purgative. Zulus made a "love-charm" emetic from the bark.

Gardening

This beautifully shaped tree is moderately sensitive to frost. Trees are easily cultivated from seed and grow remarkably fast.

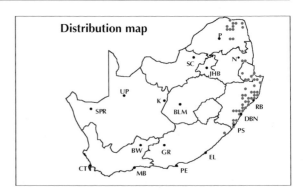

Distribution map

Yellow-brown heartwood, sometimes with a greenish tinge; white sapwood; sawdust has irritant properties; not suitable for turning; stains and varnishes to any required shade.

GROWTH DETAILS

This is a single-stemmed, high-branching tree with a straight trunk. The few large branches grow upwards in a V-shape, and then spread out widely. The branchlets and twigs develop very high up, forming a distinct huge, flat, medium-umbrella canopy. The leaves grow on the ends of branchlets and twigs.

Leaves   The twice compound leaves are alternate. There are 4 - 7 feather pairs, each with 6 - 12 pairs of leaflets. The leaflets are square with a conspicuous central vein running diagonally across them. They are dark green above and paler below. The leaf-stem is covered in light reddish-brown hairs. The feathers close when the leaves are picked and when the sun sets. Young leaves are bright green in spring. (Leaf: 100 - 400 mm; leaflet: 7 - 20 x 4 - 8 mm)

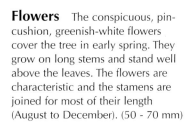

Flowers   The conspicuous, pin-cushion, greenish-white flowers cover the tree in early spring. They grow on long stems and stand well above the leaves. The flowers are characteristic and the stamens are joined for most of their length (August to December). (50 - 70 mm)

Pods   The broad bean pods are pale brown and papery. The pods form bumps over the seeds, and the margins of the pods are thickened (September to February). (125 x 25 mm)

Bark   The bark is smooth and grey to light-brown, and breaks into very fine blocks in older trees. Young twigs are pinkish and hairy.

Seasonal changes
Deciduous. This tree can be identified by its growth form, even when it has no leaves.

	Oct	Nov	Dec	Jan	Feb	Mar	Apr	May	Jun	Jul	Aug	Sep
Leaf												
Flower												
Fruit/Pod												

193

PIGEONWOOD

Trema orientalis

ULMACEAE
ELM FAMILY

SA Tree Number 42

AFRIKAANS Hophout **N. SOTHO** Modutu **SISWATI** umBalalaqane **TSONGA** Mpuka **VENDA** Mukurukuru **XHOSA** umVangazi, uPhakane **ZULU** umSekeseke, umBhangabhanga, umBengebenge, umBengele

The term **orientalis** means of the East.

Where you'll find this tree easily

Pigeonwood is a pioneer tree of the high rainfall forest, and is one of the first trees to regrow where the forest has been disturbed. It normally grows singly among other species of trees.

🌱 It is easiest to find in the margins of the Scarp and Low-lying forests of the Coast (C).

🌱 It can also be found on the margins of the Dune, Swamp and Scarp forests of the Coast (C), Along Rivers (A), and in the Woodland of the Bushveld-Savannah (B).

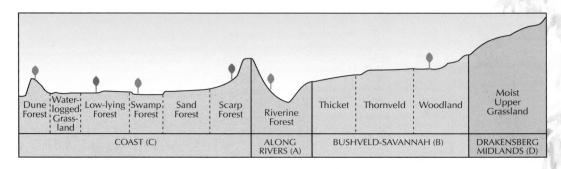

Striking features

- This is a single-stemmed tree that often branches symmetrically upwards to form a moderate, irregular, wide-spreading canopy with drooping branchlets.

- The bark is smooth and grey with conspicuous, small, pale, raised dots.

- **The simple, long, almost triangular leaves are alternate, and the leaf-base is heart-shaped and asymmetrical.**

- **The entire leaf margin is distinctly toothed.**

- Three veins radiate from the base and follow the margin.

- The small, fleshy, berry-like fruit grows in bunches in the angles of the leaves.

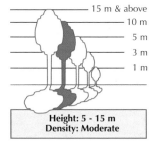

Height: 5 - 15 m
Density: Moderate

194

195

PIGEONWOOD

Trema orientalis

Links with animals

Flowers are pollinated by bees. Fruit is eaten by Bats, and Kudu browse the foliage. Butterflies of at least 13 species breed on the Pigeonwood – one of them is the Bluespotted Charaxes *(Charaxes cithaeron)*. White-eyes, Forest Canaries and Rameron Pigeon relish the fruit.

Human uses

The wood is used for articles such as fruit boxes. Young leaves are eaten as spinach. The bark is used for waterproofing fishing lines. Infusions of fruit and leaves were taken as teas to treat bronchitis, coughs, pneumonia and pleurisy. Leaves were used on sores and wounds. Bark was used to treat hookworm and roundworm infestations, and the wood was used to treat dysentery. Stems and twigs were used for fevers, toothache and venereal diseases. Fruit and seeds were used for tired muscles and aching bones.

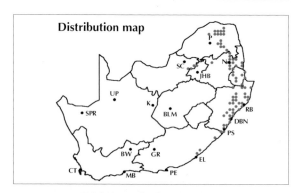

Distribution map

Pinkish-white in colour, mellowing to creamy-yellow; not suitable for turning; non-durable; suitable for decorative veneer.

Gardening

This is an attractive garden tree when planted in good soil. The tree grows very fast and seed germinates easily. It is not frost-resistant.

Look-alike tree
This tree can be easily confused with the White Stinkwood *(Celtis africana)*, page 13, that has very similar leaves, bark and growth form. The leaves of the White Stinkwood are broader, rounder, and only toothed in the upper two-thirds. The main vein is central and the bark is very smooth. The leaf-base is symmetrical.

GROWTH DETAILS

This is a single-stemmed tree with a straight trunk. In forests it is a straight, slender tree with a narrow canopy, but on the forest edge is wide-spreading, with an irregular, rounded canopy and drooping branchlets. Young branchlets and twigs may be slightly zig-zagged. Branches tend to branch out opposite each other.

Leaves Simple, alternate leaves have three distinct veins, radiating from the base. The veins stand out clearly on the under-surface. Leaves are bright green and coarse above, and paler and smoother below. They are almost triangular with a sharply tapering tip. The leaf-base is heart-shaped and asymmetrical, and the entire margin is distinctly toothed. (60 - 200 x 25 - 45 mm)

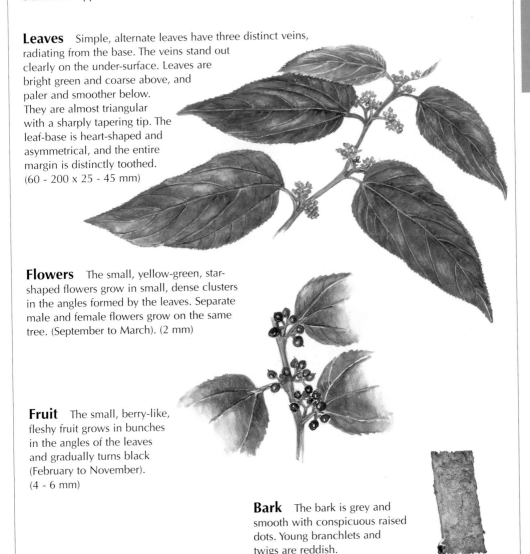

Flowers The small, yellow-green, star-shaped flowers grow in small, dense clusters in the angles formed by the leaves. Separate male and female flowers grow on the same tree. (September to March). (2 mm)

Fruit The small, berry-like, fleshy fruit grows in bunches in the angles of the leaves and gradually turns black (February to November). (4 - 6 mm)

Bark The bark is grey and smooth with conspicuous raised dots. Young branchlets and twigs are reddish.

Seasonal changes Usually deciduous but may be evergreen in conditions of higher rainfall. This tree is difficult to identify when it has no leaves.

	Oct	Nov	Dec	Jan	Feb	Mar	Apr	May	Jun	Jul	Aug	Sep
Leaf												
Flower												
Fruit/Pod												

197

WHITE PEAR

Apodytes dimidiata

WHITE PEAR FAMILY
ICACINACEAE

SA Tree Number 422

AFRIKAANS Witpeer **N. SOTHO** Kgalagangwê **SISWATI** umDzakane **VENDA** Tshiphopha-maḍi **XHOSA** umDakane **ZULU** umDakane

The term **dimidiata** means parted and refers to the two parts of the fruit.

Where you'll find this tree easily

The White Pear usually grows singly among other species of trees.

🌱 It is a forest tree and and is easiest to find in the Low-lying and Scarp forests of the Coast (C).

🌱 It can also be found on Rocky Outcrops in the Woodland of the Bushveld-Savannah (B), Along Rivers (A), and in the Dune Forest of the Coast (C).

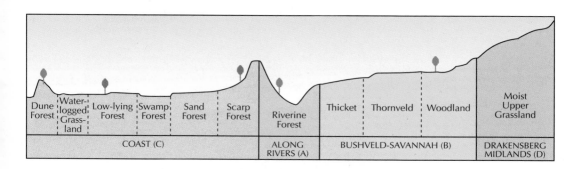

Dune Forest	Water-logged Grass-land	Low-lying Forest	Swamp Forest	Sand Forest	Scarp Forest	Riverine Forest	Thicket	Thornveld	Woodland	Moist Upper Grassland
COAST (C)						ALONG RIVERS (A)	BUSHVELD-SAVANNAH (B)			DRAKENSBERG MIDLANDS (D)

Striking features

- This is a single-stemmed tree with a dense rounded canopy.

- **The bark is pale grey and smooth and has distinct, elevated, horizontal rings around the trunk, and often has white patches of lichen.**

- **The leaves are small and have a striking yellow, central vein that can even be seen on leaves that are high up in the canopy.**

- When a leaf is cracked carefully, and then pulled apart, a thin elastic thread connecting the two halves can be seen against the light.

- The characteristic black and red, succulent berries ripen from December to May.

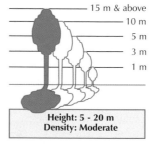

15 m & above
10 m
5 m
3 m
1 m

Height: 5 - 20 m
Density: Moderate

199

WHITE PEAR

Apodytes dimidiata

Links with animals

Both leaves and bark are eaten by the Black Rhino. The fruit is seldom eaten by animals, even Monkeys, but birds such as Redwinged Starlings, Bush and Rameron Pigeons, Blackeyed Bulbuls, Cape White-eyes and Pied Barbets eat it readily. The seeds often become hosts to parasitical insects.

Human uses

The wood is used for furniture, especially benches and tables, agricultural implements, flooring, veneering, panelling, engraving for printing and for rifle stocks. The wood is also used to make baskets for trapping fish and for "fish-kraals". The leaves can be boiled whole and eaten with porridge. The Zulu used an infusion of root, bark and other plants as an enema for intestinal parasites. The leaf was applied to ear inflammations, and an extract of the bark was taken for stomach complaints, and to treat worms in cattle. The bark was also used to ward off evil spirits.

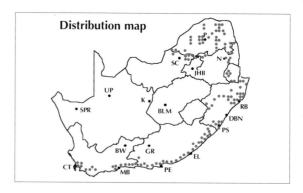

Distribution map

Low-lustre wood; polishes well; dull, pinkish-grey colour; suitable for turning; saws easily.

Gardening

The White Pear can be used as a hedge as it reacts well to pruning. It is also an attractive tree on a wide, open lawn. It has a non-invasive root system, is not resistant to cold, grows slowly and is relatively shade loving. The seeds should be sown in the winter and germination may take up to one year.

Look-alike tree
The Cape Holly *(Ilex mitis)* also has pale bark and shiny leaves, but leaves have a sunken central vein and toothed margin. The Cape Holly is normally only found along the rivers of the Scarp Forests.

This is a single-stemmed, high-branching tree that may have a fluted trunk. The branches grow upwards to form a moderate, rounded canopy.

Leaves   The simple, alternate leaves have a fairly long, often reddish leaf-stem (20 mm). The margin of the hairless, leathery leaf may be wavy. The upper-surface is shiny dark green, with a paler under-surface. The central vein is pale and stands out on the under-surface, but fades towards the tip. (Leaf: 50 - 150 x 20 - 70 mm)

Fruit   The black seed has a fleshy appendage. This appendage is both fatty and succulent, and turns from green to scarlet, eventually ripening to black (December to May). (6 x 3 mm)

Flowers   The small, white, sweet-scented, flower-stars grow in bunches at the ends of the twigs and stand out above the leaves (September to April). (Spray: 80 x 100 mm; individual: 3 - 6 mm)

Bark   The bark is smooth and pale grey and is often marked with small, elevated spots (lenticels). In the forest, the bark may be covered with green or orange lichen. Trees along the coast have distinctive, elevated horizontal bands. Young twigs are purple to red.

Seasonal changes
Evergreen. This tree can be identified by its bark and leaves throughout the year.

	Oct	Nov	Dec	Jan	Feb	Mar	Apr	May	Jun	Jul	Aug	Sep
Leaf												
Flower												
Fruit/Pod												

201

WILD MULBERRY

Trimeria grandifolia

WILD PEACH FAMILY
FLACOURTIACEAE

AFRIKAANS Grootblaarysterhout, Wildemoerbei **SISWATI** isiCandamashane, maHlebe **VENDA** Tshilaphithi
XHOSA iDlebe lendlovu, iGqabela, umNqabane **ZULU** iDlebendlovu

The term **grandifolia** refers to the large leaves.

Where you'll find this tree easily

The Wild Mulberry grows singly. It often leans on other
trees or is closely surrounded by them.

🌿 It is easiest to find in the Low-lying Forest of the
Coast (C).

🌿 It is also found in the Scarp and Swamp forests of the
Coast (C), and Along Rivers (A).

A	B
C	D

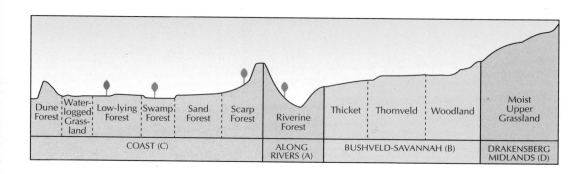

Dune Forest	Water-logged Grass-land	Low-lying Forest	Swamp Forest	Sand Forest	Scarp Forest	Riverine Forest	Thicket	Thornveld	Woodland	Moist Upper Grassland
COAST (C)						ALONG RIVERS (A)	BUSHVELD-SAVANNAH (B)			DRAKENSBERG MIDLANDS (D)

Striking features

- This is a small, single-stemmed tree with a thin,
  smooth, pale yellow-brown trunk and a few branches
  forming a sparse, irregular canopy.

- **The bark often has white or olive-green patches of
  lichen.**

- **The large leaves, with 5 - 9 veins radiating from the
  base, are soft and almost round, like those of a
  mulberry leaf.**

- Large branches are visible in the canopy.

- The small, fleshy, berry-like fruit generally resembles a
  mulberry and turns yellow to bright coral-red (February
  to April).

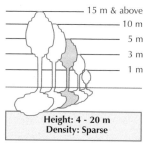

15 m & above
10 m
5 m
3 m
1 m

Height: 4 - 20 m
Density: Sparse

203

WILD MULBERRY

Trimeria grandifolia

Links with animals

Caterpillars of the Common Orange Butterfly, the African Leopard *(Phalantha phalantha aethiopica)*, eat this species.

Human uses

The heartwood is red, hard and tough and little used, except in making yoke-keys. An infusion of the leaf was taken for abdominal problems.

Gardening

This is a good garden tree in frost-free areas.

Look-alike tree   The Forest Raisin *(Grewia lasiocarpa)* also has round leaves but they have a rough upper-surface, and a duller under-surface covered with reddish hairs. It has only three veins from the base, and the leaf-stem is covered with short, russet hairs.

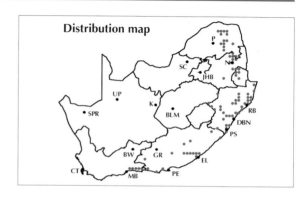

Distribution map

GROWTH DETAILS

This is a small, single-stemmed tree with a slender, straight stem that branches into a few large branches which are visible in the sparse, rounded canopy.

Leaves   The simple, alternate leaves are almost round and have 5 - 9 distinct veins radiating from the base. The margin is strongly toothed and may be so deeply indented that it appears to be lobed. The leaves are dark, shiny green above and paler below. Leaves are hairy when young, but become smooth with age. The stems are sturdy and hairy. (50 - 200 mm)

Fruit   The small, fleshy, berry-like fruit is packed in dense spikes generally resembling a mulberry, although it is not related to the mulberry. It turns yellow to the bright coral-red when ripe (February to April). (5 x 3 mm)

Flowers   Small, inconspicuous and similar male and female flowers grow separately. The male flowers are in branched sprays (70 mm), and female flowers in spikes in the angle of the leaves (30 mm) (August to February).

Bark   The bark is pale yellow-brown and smooth, and is often marked with white or olive-green lichen. In older trees it is grey to grey-brown and flakes off in large scabs. New twigs are reddish, with pale, raised dots.

Seasonal changes
Deciduous. This tree is difficult to identify without leaves.

	Oct	Nov	Dec	Jan	Feb	Mar	Apr	May	Jun	Jul	Aug	Sep
Leaf	■	■	■	■	■	■	■	■			■	■
Flower												
Fruit/Pod					■	■	■					

205

CAPE BEECH

Rapanea melanophloeos

CAPE MYRTLE FAMILY
MYRSINACEAE

SA Tree Number 578

AFRIKAANS Boekenhout **N. SOTHO** Mogônô **SISWATI** iGcolo, uDzilidzili **VENDA** Tshikonwa
XHOSA isiQwane sehlathi **ZULU** uMaphipha, iKhubalwane

The term **melanophloeos** refers to the dark bark.

Where you'll find this tree easily

The Cape Beech is a forest tree, growing in loose groups,
often as saplings in the under-storey, but also as a tall tree.

🌱 It most easily found in the Scarp Forest of the Coast (C).

🌱 It can also be found in the Dune, Swamp and Low-lying
forests of the Coast (C), Along Rivers (A), and in the
Woodland of the Bushveld-Savannah (B).

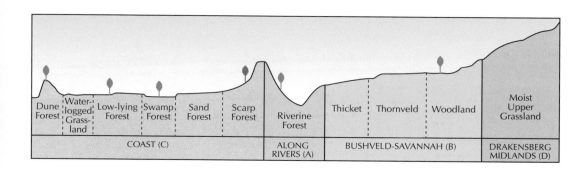

Striking features

• This is a single-stemmed tree that branches low down
to form a moderate, narrow, V-shaped canopy.

• **The stems of the younger trees and branches are pale
grey and covered with small knobs resembling ostrich
skin.**

• **The simple leaves are crowded towards the ends of
the branchlets and twigs, and are dark green above
and distinctly paler below.**

• The leaf-stems are dark purple, and young leaves and
twigs are purplish-red.

• The fruit and flowers grow in rows on twigs below the
leaves, leaving permanent scars when they drop.

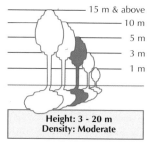

Height: 3 - 20 m
Density: Moderate

207

CAPE BEECH

Rapanea melanophloeos

Links with animals

Bees and flies are attracted to the flowers, which in turn attract insect-eating birds. The berries are eaten by Bushpigs, Baboons and Samango and Vervet Monkeys, and by fruit-eating birds such as Crested Guineafowl, African Green Pigeons, Rameron Pigeons, Knysna and Purplecrested Louries and Barbets.

Human uses

The Cape Beech is not a relative of the beeches of Europe despite the fact that they have similar wood. It is popular for furniture, especially dining-room tables and chairs, since the reticulated effect gives the wood a beautiful texture. The bark was used by herbalists to strengthen the heart, as an expectorant, to treat sore throats and control fevers, for acidity and to treat stomach and muscular pain. The leaves were used as astringent to stop bleeding. The bark was used in a sprinkling charm against lightning and to counteract evil.

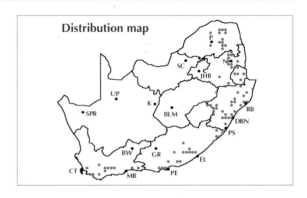

Distribution map

Rare wood; almost white when freshly sawn; darkens on exposure; turns well; stains, polishes and varnishes well.

Gardening

This is an attractive tree for coastal gardens as it is tolerant of sea winds. It is easily cultivated, fairly fast-growing and can withstand moderate drought and a fair degree of frost.

GROWTH DETAILS

This is a single-stemmed tree that branches low down to form a moderate, narrow, V-shaped canopy in the forest. On the forest edge it is a much-branched, wide-spreading tree with a rounded canopy. In the Riverine Forest it is often only a bush. The roots send up numerous suckers. Small trees are normally found among the larger ones.

Leaves   The simple, broadly elliptic, alternate leaves are thick and leathery and are crowded towards the ends of the branchlets and twigs. They are smooth, dark green above and paler below. Light-coloured gland-dots are visible when the leaf is held against the light. The margin is thickened and the leaf-stem is dark purple. The central vein is sunken on the upper-surface and stands out on the under-surface. Young leaves and twigs are purplish red. (50 - 150 x 20 - 40 mm)

Flowers   The greenish-white, star-shaped flowers are crowded on twigs, mostly below the leaves. Similar male and female flowers grow on separate trees (May to July). (5 mm)

Fruit   The small, berry-like, fleshy fruit has a hair-like tip. It is packed on twigs mostly below the leaves and turns purple when ripe (August to November). (5 - 8 mm)

Bark   The bark is dark, rough and corky, and fissured lengthways in old trees. Younger trees and branches have a pale grey bark that is covered in knobs and resembles ostrich skin.

Seasonal changes
Evergreen. This tree can be identified throughout the year.

	Oct	Nov	Dec	Jan	Feb	Mar	Apr	May	Jun	Jul	Aug	Sep
Leaf												
Flower												
Fruit/Pod												

209

CORAL TREE (COMMON CORAL TREE)

Erythrina lysistemon

PEA FAMILY
FABACEAE

SA Tree Number 245

AFRIKAANS Gewone Koraalboom **N. SOTHO** Mokhupye, Mmalê, Mokhungwane **SISWATI** umSisi **TSONGA** Nsisimbane, Muvale **TSWANA** Mophêthê **VENDA** Muvhale **XHOSA** umSintsi **ZULU** umSinsi

The term **lysistemon** refers to the stamen that stands separate in the tube-like flower.

Where you'll find this tree easily

The Coral Tree is found growing among other species of trees.

🌱 It is easiest to find in the Low-lying Forest of the Coast (C).

🌱 It can also be found in the Dune, Swamp and Scarp forests of the Coast (C), in the Thornveld and Woodland of the Bushveld-Savannah (B), Along Rivers (A), and in the Moist Upper Grassland of the Drakensberg Midlands (D).

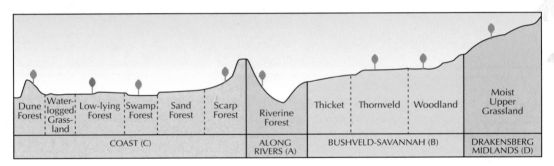

Striking features

- This is a single-trunked tree that forms a moderate, rounded canopy, with large branches visible among the leaves.

- The bark is light grey-brown and smooth in between shallow lengthways grooves and dark, slightly hooked thorns on the trunk and branches.

- **The compound leaves have three heart-shaped leaflets, the terminal one being distinctly larger, with a longer leaflet-stem.**

- **The red flowers are aloe-like and conspicuous in early spring on the leafless tree.**

- The bumpy bean pods burst open on the tree to reveal the characteristic black and red seeds (September to February).

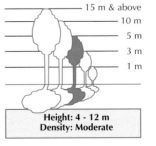

15 m & above
10 m
5 m
3 m
1 m

Height: 4 - 12 m
Density: Moderate

211

CORAL TREE (COMMON CORAL TREE)

Erythrina lysistemon

Links with animals

The leaves and bark are eaten by Black Rhino, Elephant, Baboons, Kudu, Nyala and Klipspringer. Unripe seeds and nectar are a favourite of the Brownheaded Parrot. Many insects are attracted to the tree when it flowers, and Vervet Monkeys regard flower-buds as a delicacy. Nectar in flowers attracts many sunbirds such as the Greater Doublecollared, Collared, Olive, Scarletchested and Grey Sunbirds.

Human uses

Canoes and troughs are made from hollowed trunks, and wood is used as floats for fishing nets. It has many medicinal uses: a poultice of the bark is used for swellings, sores, wounds, abscesses and arthritis; an infusion of bark is used for toothache and an infusion of leaves for ear drops to relieve earache; crushed leaves clear the maggots from infested wounds and counteract inflammation. A branch from this tree growing near a man's hut was often planted on his grave, and the seeds are often still used as lucky charms.

Gardening

This is a very attractive, fast-growing garden tree. It is easily cultivated from seed and may flower within a year. It is fairly drought-resistant and will stand several degrees of frost.

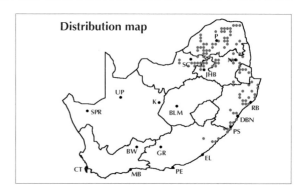

Distribution map

White heartwood and sapwood; straight grain; poor nail-holding properties; saws cleanly; not suitable for turning.

Look-alike trees

The Coast Coral Tree *(Erythrina caffra)* is very similar. It also grows in the Coastal Forest but is taller when mature (10 - 18 m) and has broader leaflets and leaf-stems without thorns. The orange-red flower-spikes are more rounded, with the petal curving backwards at the tip to expose the stamens.

The Dwarf Coral Tree *(Erythrina humeana)*, page 22, is a small, straggly shrub (4 m). It has dark green, thin, leathery leaflets and long, narrow flower-heads.

The Broad-leaved Coral Tree *(Erythrina latissima)* has similar flowers, but the leaves are large (200 - 600 mm), rounded and very hairy, and the bark is coarse and rough.

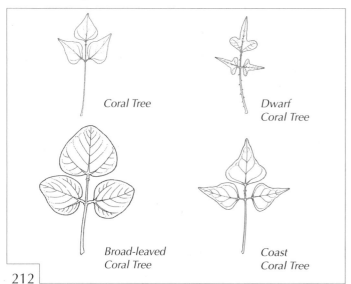

Coral Tree

Dwarf Coral Tree

Broad-leaved Coral Tree

Coast Coral Tree

GROWTH DETAILS

This is a single-trunked tree that forms a moderate, rounded canopy, with large branches visible among the leaves.

Leaves The three-leaved compound leaves are alternate and are crowded towards the ends of the branchlets and twigs. The heart-shaped, dark green leaflets have smooth margins, and the central vein is prominent on both surfaces. New leaves are a bright, light green. The end leaflet is larger with a longer leaf-stem than the side leaflets. The leaf-stems are long (160 mm) and may have scattered thorns. (Leaf: 60 - 220 mm; end leaflet: 110 - 125 mm; side leaflets: 80 - 110 mm)

Thorns Slightly hooked thorns are dark brown, with a broad base and a very sharp point, resembling those of a rose. Thorns are sparsely scattered on the main trunk and branches, but are much closer together on the smaller branchlets and twigs. (3 - 7 mm)

Flowers Conspicuous, erect, red flower-spikes appear before the leaves in early spring. The tightly packed, tubular flowers consist of a large, tube-like petal enclosing the stamens and smaller petals so that they are not visible (June to October). (Spray: 90 mm; individual: 40 - 60 mm)

Bark The bark is pale grey-brown, fairly smooth and often grooved lengthways, with scattered brown, hooked thorns on the trunk.

Fruit Tightly constricted, bumpy bean pods hang in clusters. When ripe, they burst open to expose shiny, scarlet and black, bead-like seeds that resemble lucky beans. Fruit stays on the tree for long periods (September to February). (90 - 200 x 11 - 15 mm)

Seasonal changes

Deciduous. Leaves turn yellow in autumn. The trees can often still be identified by their bark, thorns and pods even when no leaves are present.

	Oct	Nov	Dec	Jan	Feb	Mar	Apr	May	Jun	Jul	Aug	Sep
Leaf												
Flower												
Fruit/Pod												

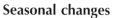

213

MITZEERI

Bridelia micrantha

EUPHORBIA FAMILY
EUPHORBIACEAE

AFRIKAANS Mitserie, Bruinstinkhout **N. SOTHO** Motsêrê **TSONGA** Ndzerhe **VENDA** Munzere
XHOSA umHlahla-makhwaba **ZULU** umHlalamagwababa, umHlalamkhwaba, umHlalamahubulu,
umHlalamangcwibi

The term **micrantha** refers to the small flowers.

Where you'll find this tree easily

The Mitzeeri normally grows singly among other species
of trees.

🌶 It is easiest to find in the Low-lying and Swamp forests
of the Coast (C).

🌶 It can also be found in the Scarp Forest of the Coast
(C), in the Woodland of the Bushveld-Savannah (B) and
Along Rivers (A).

A	B
C	D

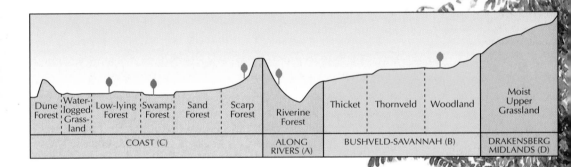

Striking features

- This is a single-stemmed tree with a dense, semi-
  circular canopy with branchlets that stand out
  loosely from the canopy outline.

- **Flower- and leaf-scars form knobbly protrusions on
  exposed twigs that are clearly visible in the canopy.**

- The large, simple, glossy leaves are alternate.

- **The herringbone veins come off the central vein
  alternately and stop at the leaf margin.**

- The bark on the trunk is dark and rough, while the
  smaller branches have contrasting, smooth, grey to
  yellowish bark.

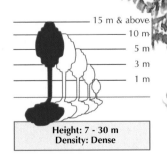

Height: 7 - 30 m
Density: Dense

215

MITZEERI

Bridelia micrantha

Links with animals

The bark and leaves are eaten by Black Rhino. The leaves are eaten by Nyala, Bushbuck and Grey Duiker. Caterpillars of the Giant Charaxes and the Merant's Charax butterflies feed on the leaves. The fruit is popular with fruit-eating birds such as Green Pigeons, Cape Glossy Starlings, Pied, Blackcollared and Crested Barbets, Doves, Louries and Bulbuls.

Human uses

The wood is used for parquet flooring, furniture, fence poles and panelling. The fruit is edible. Branchlets are used to make the frameworks of fish traps. Root extracts were used for infant coughs, aching joints, as a purgative or to treat gastric ulcers. Powdered roots were rubbed into the scalp for headaches and fevers. The leaves were used to terminate pregnancies. Bark extracts were taken for stomach ache, tapeworm, diarrhoea, and to cause vomiting. These extracts were also administered as tonics to children and were applied to burns.

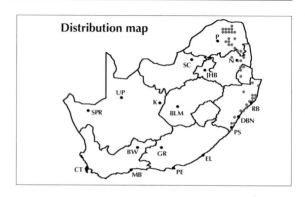

Distribution map

Light sapwood; reddish-brown heartwood; fine texture; durable; saws and planes well.

Gardening

The Mitzeeri has an invasive root system that affects buildings and paved areas. It can grow in soil that is temporarily waterlogged because the roots are extensive and bind soil effectively. It can be grown from seed easily, but the seed must be fresh when planted. The Mitzeeri attracts birds to the garden.

Look-alike tree   The Tassel Berry (*Antidesma venosum*), page 124, has a very similar growth form to the smaller Mitzeeri trees. The leaf of the Tassel Berry is darker green and appears velvety, the veins curl along the margin, and the flowers and fruit hang in long, thin bunches from the branchlets.

GROWTH DETAILS

This is a single-stemmed tree with a straight trunk that develops into large branches high up, but smaller branches may form lower down. The canopy is dense and rounded.

Leaves   The simple, alternate leaves are elliptic, with a tapering tip and base. The upper-surface is bright green and smooth with a paler under-surface. The light-coloured veins form a herringbone pattern with veins that come off alternately. The leaf is attached to the twig by a short, hairy leaf-stem. The leaves turn bright red and gold in autumn and winter. (Leaf: 60 - 180 x 25 - 100 mm)

Flowers   The inconspicuous, small, yellow-green, flower-stars grow in the angle formed by the leaves. Male and female flowers grow on separate trees (August to October). (5 mm)

Fruit   The small, oval, berry-like, fleshy fruit grows in the angles formed by the leaves and turns black as it ripens, from January to April. The trees do not bear fruit every year. (8 - 10 x 4 - 7 mm)

Bark   The bark of the trunk and main branches is grey-brown, dark and rough, almost forming blocks. In contrast, the young branches and branchlets have a smooth, yellowish to grey-brown bark that is covered with knobs. The grey twigs have knobbly protrusions, caused by old flowers and leaves, that are clearly visible on the exposed twigs in the canopy.

Seasonal changes

Deciduous to semi-deciduous. The Mitzeeri changes to beautiful autumn colours before the leaves drop. The tree is usually bare for only a few weeks in late winter or early spring, and can then still be identified by the knobbly twigs.

	Oct	Nov	Dec	Jan	Feb	Mar	Apr	May	Jun	Jul	Aug	Sep
Leaf												
Flower												
Fruit/Pod												

217

SMALL KNOBWOOD

Zanthoxylum capense

**CITRUS/BUCHU FAMILY
RUTACEAE**

SA Tree Number 253

AFRIKAANS Kleinperdepram, Wildekardamon **N. SOTHO** Monokwane, Senekomaropa
SISWATI umNungwane **TSONGA** Manhungwana **TSWANA** Monokomabêlê **VENDA** Murandela,
Munungu **XHOSA** umNungumabele, umLungumabele **ZULU** umNungumabele, umNungwane omncane

The term **capense** means of the Cape.

Where you'll find this tree easily

The Small Knobwood grows singly.

🌿 It is easiest to find in the Low-lying and Scarp forests
along the Coast (C).

🌿 It can also be found in the Dune and Swamp forests
of the Coast (C), on rocky hillsides of the Woodland
of the Bushveld-Savannah (B), and Along Rivers (A).

A	B
C	D

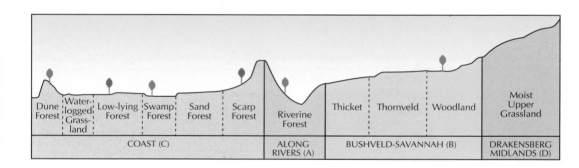

| COAST (C) | ALONG RIVERS (A) | BUSHVELD-SAVANNAH (B) | DRAKENSBERG MIDLANDS (D) |

Dune Forest | Water-logged Grass-land | Low-lying Forest | Swamp Forest | Sand Forest | Scarp Forest | Riverine Forest | Thicket | Thornveld | Woodland | Moist Upper Grassland

Striking features

- This is a single-stemmed, low-branching tree which
  branches upwards to form a moderate, V-shaped
  canopy.

- **Prominent, knob-like swellings, ending in a rose-like
  thorn, cover the main stems and branches of mature
  trees.**

- **The shiny, compound leaves are spirally arranged
  towards the ends of twigs and branchlets.**

- The leaflets have a strong citrus smell when crushed.

- There are small, hooked thorns on the under-surface of
  the leaf-stem.

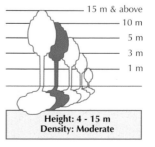

15 m & above
10 m
5 m
3 m
1 m

**Height: 4 - 15 m
Density: Moderate**

218

219

SMALL KNOBWOOD

Zanthoxylum capense

Links with animals

Some mammals browse the leaves. The flowers attract beetles. Birds such as Mousebirds and Barbets eat the fruit.

Human uses

The wood can be used to make pick handles, knobkieries, planks and yokes. The seeds are used to make perfume. A wide range of medicinal uses is recorded. The tree is still used in traditional medicine today: the bark and root to treat violent chronic coughs, pleurisy, tuberculosis and paralysis; powdered bark was rubbed into incisions along the sides of the body to treat paralysis; an infusion of the leaf was drunk for colic and gastro-intestinal disorders; the leaf was used to cure sores, and crushed leaves to cure colds, and for snakebite and toothache; the plant itself was used to disinfect anthrax-infected meat.

Gardening

This is an attractive garden tree, but it is difficult to grow from seed. It is frost- and drought-resistant.

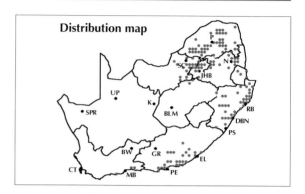

Distribution map

Logs lemon-yellow when freshly cut; darker heartwood; wavy grain; turns well.

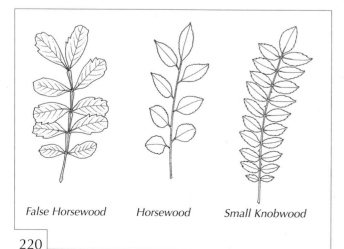

False Horsewood   *Horsewood*   *Small Knobwood*

Look-alike trees   The Horsewood *(Clausena anisata)* has very similar leaves, but the tree is always slender and straggly. The leaflets of the Horsewood are alternate (not opposite), the central vein is off-centre, and crushed leaves have a pungent aniseed smell.

The False Horsewood *(Hippobromus pauciflorus)* is also a straggling tree of the forest and is often multi-stemmed. It has alternate leaflets with the top of the leaflet deeply toothed. Crushed leaves have a resinous smell, and the leaf-stem is winged on alternate sides.

The Forest Knobwood *(Zanthoxylum davyi)* has a trunk covered in spine-tipped knobs that point upwards. It has longer leaflets that are dull on the under-surface and have 16 - 20 side veins.

GROWTH DETAILS

This is a single-stemmed tree with a straight trunk that branches upwards to form a V-shaped canopy. A few large branches are visible in the canopy, acutely branching into thin, delicate branchlets and twigs.

Leaves Compound leaves are spirally arranged towards the ends of twigs and branchlets, and their leaf-stems may have small, hooked thorns on the under-surface. There are 3 - 10 pairs of leaflets with a single leaflet at the tip that may be absent or very small. Elliptic leaflets have sharply toothed margins, may be opposite or alternate, and do not have leaf-stems. Leaflets have 8 pairs of side veins, and are shiny above and duller below. The leaves have a strong citrus smell when crushed. The scent comes from oil glands that are visible when the leaf is held against the light. (Leaf: 40 - 200 mm; leaflet: 1 - 4 x 1 - 2 mm)

Fruit Small, round, fleshy, berry-like fruit grows in clusters, and the skin is covered by tiny glands. The berries turn red to red-brown when ripe and split open on the tree to reveal a single, black seed with an oily appendage (November to June). (50 - 130 x 13 mm)

Flowers Inconspicuous, greenish-white, sweet-scented flowers grow in sprays at the end of the twigs. Similar male and female flowers are on separate trees (October to February). (20 - 60 mm)

Bark The bark is grey and smooth with hooked, rose-like thorns on prominent, knob-like swellings on the main stems and branches of mature trees.

Seasonal changes
Deciduous. Mature trees can be identified by their typical bark throughout the year.

	Oct	Nov	Dec	Jan	Feb	Mar	Apr	May	Jun	Jul	Aug	Sep
Leaf	■	■	■	■							■	■
Flower	■	■	■	■	■							
Fruit/Pod		■	■	■	■	■	■	■	■			

221

THORNY ELM
Chaetachme aristata

ELM FAMILY ULMACEAE	S A Tree Number 43

AFRIKAANS Doringolm **SISWATI** umBangabangwe **TSONGA** Pumbulu **VENDA** Mula-nguluvhe, Muṱhavhalunzhi **XHOSA** umKhovothi **ZULU** umBhangbangwe, umKhovothi

The term **aristata** means bristle-like.

Where you'll find this tree easily

The Thorny Elm grows singly. This is one of the first trees to re-establish itself after a forest has been cleared. It is the predominant tree in Durban parks.

🌱 It is easiest to find in the Low-lying Forest of the Coast (C).

🌱 It can also be found in the Swamp, Scarp and Dune forests of the Coast (C) and Along Rivers (A).

A	B
C	D

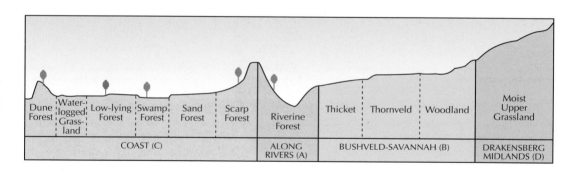

Dune Forest	Water-logged Grass-land	Low-lying Forest	Swamp Forest	Sand Forest	Scarp Forest	Riverine Forest	Thicket	Thornveld	Woodland	Moist Upper Grassland
COAST (C)						ALONG RIVERS (A)	BUSHVELD-SAVANNAH (B)			DRAKENSBERG MIDLANDS (D)

Striking features

- **This is a conspicuously multi-stemmed tree with young branches covered in thorns often growing low down.**

- The canopy is moderate and is dark green, formed by leaves that look small for the size of the tree.

- The smooth, pale grey to green, new branches constrast strongly with the darker, older branches, and are covered in spines.

- **The leaf edge is toothed in young leaves and leaves crack audibly as if varnished when folded in half.**

- The upper-surface of the leaf is smooth, shiny and dark green, with a lighter under-surface that is very rough and feels like sandpaper.

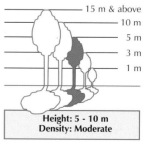

15 m & above
10 m
5 m
3 m
1 m

Height: 5 - 10 m
Density: Moderate

young   *mature*

Largest tree currently registered

Diameter:	3,80 m
Girth:	11,93 m
Height:	11 m

Dr L. Kritzinger
Weltevreden,
Dist. Waterberg

THORNY ELM

Chaetachme aristata

Links with animals

Leaves are readily eaten by Nyala and Bushbuck, and larger trees usually show a distinctive browse line. Black Rhino eat the bark and leaves. The caterpillars of the Blue Spotted Charaxes butterfly *(Charaxes cithaeron)* feed on this tree. Bats eat the fruit, while Purplecrested Louries and Thickbilled Weavers seem to be the only birds that are fond of the fruit.

Human uses

The wood is yellow, heavy, hard, strong and tough but is little used except as fighting sticks. The bark was used in the treatment of haemorrhoids.

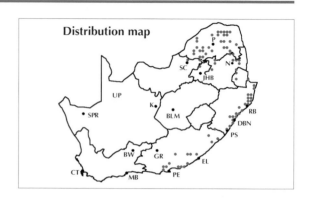

Distribution map

Durable; heavy, yellow wood; turns well.

Gardening

Due to its spines and irregular growth form, this is not a popular garden tree.

Look-alike tree

This tree can be confused with the Green Thorn in the Sand Forest. The Green Thorn *(Balanitis maughamii)* has zig-zag twigs and compound leaves with two leaflets, and the spines are usually forked. The fruit is often found under the tree and is large and plum-like. See **Sappi Tree Spotting Lowveld**.

GROWTH DETAILS

This is a multi-stemmed tree with young branches covered in thorns often coming from low down. The canopy is moderate and dark green, formed by leaves that look small for the size of the tree.

Leaves   Simple, alternate leaves have a smooth margin, although young leaves are strongly toothed. The central vein is conspicuous on both sides, but the side veins are only visible on the under-surface. The leaves are elliptic with a broadly tapering to rounded tip with a hair-like point and rounded base; they crack as if varnished when folded. The upper-surface of the leaf is smooth, shiny and dark green, with a lighter under-surface that is very rough and feels like sandpaper.
(Leaf: 20 - 150 mm)

Flowers   The greenish, star-shaped flowers are inconspicuous. Male and female flowers grow on separate trees, male flowers in clusters, and female flowers individually.
(October to December). (5 mm)

Fruit   The berry-like, fleshy fruit is pinkish-yellow when ripe from March to June. (15 mm)

Thorns   The long spines arise on either side of the leaf and may be paired or single. The name "umBambangwe" means "it catches the leopard" which is very descriptive of the long spines. (30 - 150 mm)

Bark   The bark is light brown-grey and fissured lengthways, sometimes forming rectangular blocks. New branchlets are contrastingly whitish-grey to green and are covered in sturdy thorns.

Seasonal changes
Deciduous but may be evergreen. This tree is easy to identify throughout the year by its thorny branches.

	Oct	Nov	Dec	Jan	Feb	Mar	Apr	May	Jun	Jul	Aug	Sep
Leaf												
Flower												
Fruit/Pod												

225

THORNY ROPE (HLUHLUWE CREEPER)

Dalbergia armata

PEA FAMILY
FABACEAE

SA Tree Number 231

AFRIKAANS Doringtou, Bobbejaantou **ENGLISH** Hluhluwe Creeper **N. SOTHO** Sehlokootswa
SISWATI umGcophe **XHOSA** umZungulu **ZULU** umHluhluwe

The term **armata** refers to the spines on the trunk.

Where you'll find this tree easily

The Thorny Rope is a climber.

🌱 It is most easily found in the Scarp and Low-lying
forests of the Coast (C) where the thorny trunk crosses
pathways.

🌱 It is also common in the Dune and Swamp forests of
the Coast (C), and Along Rivers (A).

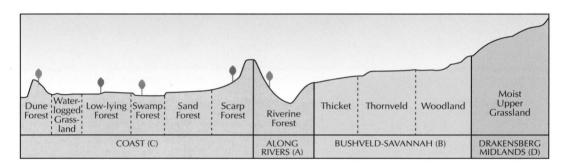

| | | COAST (C) | | | | | ALONG RIVERS (A) | BUSHVELD-SAVANNAH (B) | | | DRAKENSBERG MIDLANDS (D) |

Dune Forest | Water-logged Grass-land | Low-lying Forest | Swamp Forest | Sand Forest | Scarp Forest | Riverine Forest | Thicket | Thornveld | Woodland | Moist Upper Grassland

Striking features

- This is a multi-stemmed climber that resembles a thick,
  thorny rope and leans on the surrounding vegetation.

- **The trunk is smooth, dark and covered in huge
  conspicuous spines that are often clumped on
  swellings.**

- The compound leaves have very small leaflets and
  are very delicate and often only visible high up in
  the canopy.

- The white, pea-like flowers cover this creeper from
  October to November.

- The twigs form tight curls around the surrounding
  vegetation for support.

- **The flat, yellow-brown, winged pods hang in bunches
  and are visible among the leaves from March to May.**

227

THORNY ROPE (HLUHLUWE CREEPER)

Dalbergia armata

The Zulu name "umHluhluwe" gives the name to the whole area and in particular to the Hluhluwe Game Reserve.

Links with animals

Bark and leaves are eaten by Black Rhino. Leaves are browsed by Bushbuck. The caterpillars of the Common Sailor Butterfly *(Neptis laeta)* feed on this tree.

Human uses

The slender branches were used to make a muzzle to fix around the noses of calves to keep them from stealing milk from the cows. The tree was used as a love charm.

Gardening

Due to its very spiny trunk this is not a good garden plant. It is however suitable to grow as a bonsai.

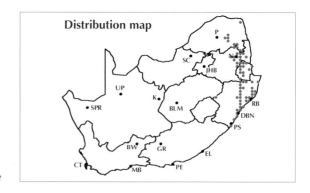

Distribution map

Bark   The bark is dark grey to black and smooth. The young stems and twigs are smooth and form tight curls where they attach to the surrounding vegetation.

Spines   Dark, stout spines are long and sharp, growing singly or in clumps of up to six on swellings on all sides of the main trunk. (50 - 100 mm)

GROWTH DETAILS

This is a multi-stemmed climber with a thick, spiny stem and huge spines. The leaves grow high up on slender twigs to form a delicate lace-like canopy in the open areas.

Leaves Compound leaves are alternate and grow on delicate twigs at the top of the canopy where they can reach the sun. The small leaflets are elliptic with a rounded tip and base and are dark green above and paler below. Young leaves are bright green and are covered by velvety hairs, becoming smooth as they mature. Leaflets close in overcast weather. There are 10 - 20 pairs of leaflets with a single leaflet at the tip. (Leaf: 15 - 80 mm; leaflet: 6 - 9 x 3 - 6 mm)

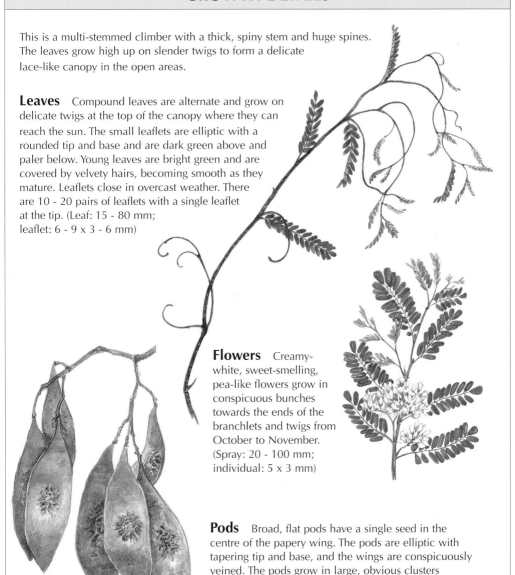

Flowers Creamy-white, sweet-smelling, pea-like flowers grow in conspicuous bunches towards the ends of the branchlets and twigs from October to November. (Spray: 20 - 100 mm; individual: 5 x 3 mm)

Pods Broad, flat pods have a single seed in the centre of the papery wing. The pods are elliptic with tapering tip and base, and the wings are conspicuously veined. The pods grow in large, obvious clusters towards the ends of the branchlets and ripen from March to May. (50 x 20 mm)

Seasonal changes

Deciduous. This climber can be identified easily throughout the year by its obvious spines.

	Oct	Nov	Dec	Jan	Feb	Mar	Apr	May	Jun	Jul	Aug	Sep
Leaf												
Flower												
Fruit/Pod												

229

FOREST KARREE (RED CURRANT)

Rhus chirindensis

MANGO FAMILY
ANACARDIACEAE

SA Tree Number 380

AFRIKAANS Bostaaibos **N. SOTHO** Motha-thaa **VENDA** Muvhadela-phanga
XHOSA iNtlokolotshane enkulu, umHlakothi **ZULU** inHlokoshiyane enkulu, umHlakothi, umHlabamvubu

The term **chirindensis** refers to the Chirinda Forest in Zimbabwe.

Where you'll find this tree easily

The Forest Karree grows singly among other trees.

† It is easiest to find in the Scarp Forest of the Coast (C) where it is a very large tree.

† It can also be found in the Low-lying, Dune and Swamp forests of the Coast (C), Along Rivers (A), and on rocky outcrops in higher rainfall areas of the Bushveld-Savannah (B).

A	B
C	D

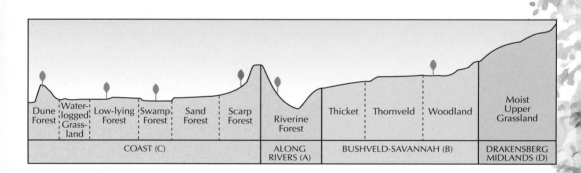

Dune Forest	Water-logged Grass-land	Low-lying Forest	Swamp Forest	Sand Forest	Scarp Forest	Riverine Forest	Thicket	Thornveld	Woodland	Moist Upper Grassland
COAST (C)						ALONG RIVERS (A)	BUSHVELD-SAVANNAH (B)			DRAKENSBERG MIDLANDS (D)

Striking features

- This is a large, often crooked-trunked, low-branching tree with an irregular, spreading canopy.

- **The drooping, compound leaves have three leaflets and a long, reddish leaf-stem.**

- **The elliptic leaflets have a wavy margin and a prominent central vein.**

- The bark is dark and cracked lengthways revealing deep red under-bark.

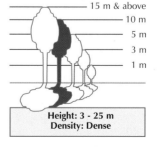

15 m & above
10 m
5 m
3 m
1 m

Height: 3 - 25 m
Density: Dense

230

Largest tree currently registered

Diameter: 0,67 m
Girth: 2,10 m
Height: 20 m

State Forest Hangklip,
Dist. Soutpansberg

FOREST KARREE (RED CURRANT)

Rhus chirindensis

Links with animals

Leaves and bark are eaten by Black Rhino, and the leaves are eaten by Kudu, Nyala, Bushbuck and Red Duiker. The fruit attracts Vervet and Samango Monkeys, African Green Pigeons, Knysna and Purplecrested Louries, Blackeyed Bulbuls, Pied and Crested Barbets, Cape White-eyes and Cape Parrots.

Human uses

The ripe fruit is edible and has a sweet-sour taste. Zulu herbalists used the sap as medicine for treating heart complaints; the bark to strengthen the body, stimulate circulation and for rheumatism; bark extracts for mental disturbances.

Gardening

This is a very attractive garden tree and does not have an aggressive root system. It grows easily and fast from cuttings and is frost- and drought-resistant. It prefers well-drained soil.

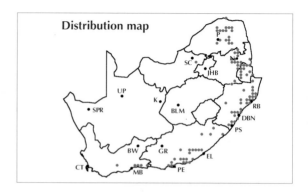

Distribution map

Red heartwood; yellow sapwood; heavy; can be polished to an attractive sheen.

232

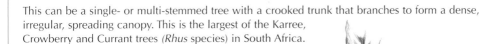

This can be a single- or multi-stemmed tree with a crooked trunk that branches to form a dense, irregular, spreading canopy. This is the largest of the Karree, Crowberry and Currant trees *(Rhus* species) in South Africa.

Leaves   The three-leaflet compound leaves have broadly elliptic leaflets on short stems that are attached at a single point to the long, often reddish leaf-stem (70 mm). Leaflets are smooth and glossy dark green above and slightly paler below. Young leaflets are reddish. Prominent central and side veins are often pinkish. The tips of the sharply tapering leaflets are hair-like and the margins are wavy. (Leaf: 130 - 200 x 100 - 130 mm; central leaflet: 60 - 130 x 25 - 40 mm)

Fruit   The small, round bunches of grape-like fruit can weigh down the branches. The fleshy fruit ripens to red-brown or pink (December to March). (4 - 7 mm)

Flowers   Small, yellow-green, star-shaped flowers grow in long, delicate sprays at the ends of the branchlets and twigs (August to January). (Spray: 160 - 200 mm; individual 3 mm)

Bark   In mature trees the bark is dark and cracked lengthways revealing deeper red under-bark. It is light brown to grey and smooth when young. The stems of young plants and new shoots may be spiny.

COAST – LOW-LYING / SCARP
Distinctive leaves – Forest Karree

Seasonal changes
Usually deciduous, but may be evergreen in the forest. This tree can be found as long as some leaves are present.

	Oct	Nov	Dec	Jan	Feb	Mar	Apr	May	Jun	Jul	Aug	Sep
Leaf												
Flower												
Fruit/Pod												

RED BEECH

Protorhus longifolia

MANGO FAMILY ANACARDIACEAE	SA Tree Number 364

AFRIKAANS Rooiboekenhout, Rooimelkhout **SISWATI** umHlangothi, imFuce **XHOSA** umHluthi, umKomiso **ZULU** umHlangothi, umHluthi

The term **longifolia** means long leaves.

Where you'll find this tree easily

The Red Beech grows singly among other species of trees, but where one is found, others will be found in the vicinity.

🌱 It is easiest to find in the Scarp Forest of the Coast (C).

🌱 It may also be found in the Low-lying and Dune forests of the Coast (C), on Rocky Outcrops of the Bushveld-Savannah (B), and along major Rivers (A).

A	B
C	D

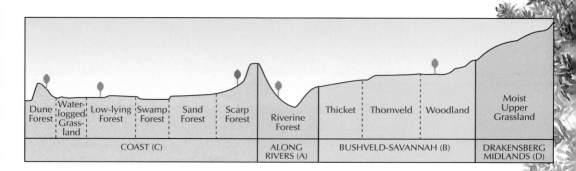

Striking features

- This is a single-trunked tree that may branch low down to form a dense, round canopy.

- **The simple leaves are long and elliptic and have striking, herringbone side veins.**

- **The leaves spiral towards the ends of thick twigs and branchlets in the outer canopy.**

- **Occasional red leaves among the foliage, especially at the top of the canopy, are characteristic.**

- All parts of the tree have a milky latex.

- The kidney-shaped, purple, berry-like, fleshy fruit grows above the leaves in bunches at the ends of branchlets and twigs (September to December).

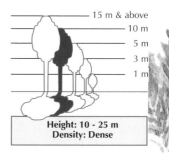

Height: 10 - 25 m
Density: Dense

234

235

RED BEECH

Protorhus longifolia

Links with animals

The bark and leaves are eaten by Black Rhino. The ripe fruit is eaten by Vervet and Samango Monkeys, Bushpigs and Red Duiker, as well as fruit-eating birds such as Plumcoloured Starlings, Parrots, Louries, Mousebirds, Barbets and Bulbuls.

Human uses

The wood is used for rafters, beams, planks and furniture. Women used the strong-smelling fruit as perfume. The bark was used for tanning, giving a distinct colour to tanned skins. The gum which exudes from the injured bark was used to stick blades into assegai handles. The powdered bark is very poisonous, causing paralysis, but was injected to cure paralysis believed to be caused by witchcraft. Bark extracts were taken to relieve heartburn and bleeding from the stomach. Parts of the plant were used by herbalists as medicine to strengthen the heart.

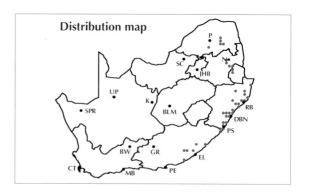

Distribution map

Fine-grained; purplish or grey, tinged with red; dark heartwood.

Gardening

This can be a very attractive garden tree and will provide dense shade. The root system is not aggressive. It can be grown from fresh seed and grows moderately fast. The tree can tolerate very mild frost and is drought-resistant.

Look-alike trees   Resin Trees

(*Ozoroa* species), page 21, have the same herringbone vein pattern on the leaves and a very similar growth form. The leaves of these trees are normally shorter and do not produce a white latex when broken. There are no reddish leaves visible in the canopy.

GROWTH DETAILS

This is a single-stemmed tree with a thick, straight trunk that branches low down or has a long, straight trunk in dense forests. It forms a dense, round canopy. The branches of young trees hang down to the ground. All parts have milky latex.

Flowers   The greenish-pink to white, star-shaped flowers are small and grow in dense sprays at the ends of the branchlets and twigs. Similar male and female flowers grow on separate trees (July to September). (Spray: 100 - 150 mm; individual: 4 - 6 mm)

Leaves   The simple, long, elliptic leaves have long leaf-stems (25 mm). They spiral towards the ends of thick twigs and branchlets in the outer canopy. They are dark green above and paler below, and have slightly wavy, thickened margins. The central and side veins stand out clearly on the under-surface. The side veins have a striking herringbone pattern that runs to the edge of the leaf. Occasional red leaves are always visible in the top of the canopy. (Leaf: 50 - 160 x 20 - 40 mm)

Fruit   The berry-like, fleshy fruit is slightly kidney-shaped, and grows in bunches at the ends of the branchlets and twigs. It turns purple when ripe (September to December). (10 - 13 mm)

Bark   The thin bark is grey to brown and produces a white latex when injured. It can become rough and fissured in older trees but is smooth in younger trees. The light brown branchlets have prominent, knobbly leaf-scars.

Seasonal changes
Evergreen. This tree can be identified by its foliage throughout the year.

	Oct	Nov	Dec	Jan	Feb	Mar	Apr	May	Jun	Jul	Aug	Sep
Leaf												
Flower												
Fruit/Pod												

SNEEZEWOOD

Ptaeroxylon obliquum

**SNEEZEWOOD FAMILY
PTAEROXYLACEAE**

AFRIKAANS Nieshout **SISWATI** umThathi **TSONGA** Ndzari **TSWANA** Thate **VENDA** Munari-mulari **XHOSA** umThathi **ZULU** umThathe, uBhaqa

The term **obliquum** refers to the asymmetrical leaflets.

Where you'll find this tree easily

The Sneezewood is a widely distributed tree that prefers well-drained soils, and grows singly among other species of trees.

🍃 It is easiest to find in the Sand Forest of the Coast (C).

🍃 It can also be found in the Low-lying and Scarp forests of the Coast (C), in Thornveld and Rocky Outcrops in the Bushveld-Savannah (B), and Along Rivers (A).

A	B
C	D

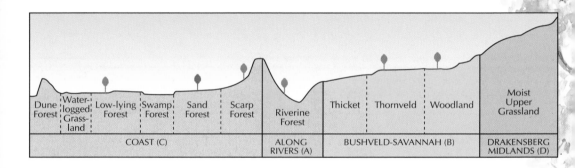

Dune Forest	Water-logged Grass-land	Low-lying Forest	Swamp Forest	Sand Forest	Scarp Forest	Riverine Forest	Thicket	Thornveld	Woodland	Moist Upper Grassland
	COAST (C)					ALONG RIVERS (A)	BUSHVELD-SAVANNAH (B)			DRAKENSBERG MIDLANDS (D)

Striking features

- This is a single-trunked tree that branches low down to form a narrow, moderate, V-shaped canopy.
- The bark is pale grey and rough.
- **The feathery canopy is grey-green and lighter than those of the surrounding trees.**
- The compound leaves grow towards the ends of the branchlets, and large branches are visible in the canopy.
- **The leaflets are sickle-shaped, with an off-centre central vein.**
- Leaflets decrease in size from the tip to the base of the leaf.

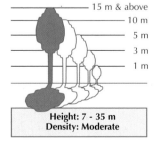

15 m & above
10 m
5 m
3 m
1 m

**Height: 7 - 35 m
Density: Moderate**

Largest tree currently registered

Diameter: 1,29 m
Girth: 4,05 m
Height: 45 m

The Downs,
Lekgalameetse Nature
Reserve

SNEEZEWOOD

Ptaeroxylon obliquum

Links with animals

Leaves and young shoots are eaten by Impala, Giraffe and Kudu.

Human uses

The wood is very durable and valuable for use as fence posts. Extracts of the wood were used in cattle dips and to treat anthrax in cattle, as well as for the treatment of rheumatism and heart diseases. Pieces of wood, or the sawdust, were kept between clothes to repel insects. Burnt wood was used to discover an evildoer.

Gardening

This tree grows fast, and seedlings must be watered regularly. It can withstand moderate frost and is very drought-resistant.

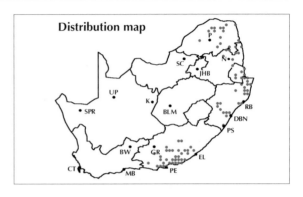

Distribution map

Reddish-brown heartwood; white sapwood; pungent essential oil in wood causes irritation to humans.

GROWTH DETAILS

This is a single or multi-stemmed tree with a straight trunk that branches low down to form a narrow, V-shaped canopy. In the forest it is high branching with a more rounded canopy.

Leaves   The compound leaves are opposite with a pair of leaflets at the tip. They grow towards the ends of the branchlets and twigs. There are 3 - 8 pairs of leaflets that are almost opposite and have very short or no leaf-stems. Leaflets decrease in size from the tip to the base of the leaf. The leaflets are asymmetrical and sickle-shaped, with the smaller part hanging below the central vein. The tip is rounded and the margin smooth. The leaflets are grey-green to bright green, shiny above and slightly paler below. Young leaf-stems are hairy. (Leaf: 80 - 250 mm; leaflet: 25 - 55 x 6 - 15 mm)

Flowers   The sweet-scented, yellow, star-shaped flowers grow in abundance in branched bunches in the angles formed by the leaves. The male and female flowers grow on separate trees (October to November). (Spray: 30 - 50 mm; individual: 5 - 7 mm)

Fruit   The papery, distinctly veined, red-brown, capsuled fruit grows in bunches. Ripe fruit splits into two, releasing winged seeds from December to January. (20 - 15 mm)

Bark   The bark is pale grey, rough and may be fibrous. There are knobs of leaf-scars on the twigs and branchlets.

Seasonal changes

Deciduous, but may be evergreen in the forest, where it can be found throughout the year.

	Oct	Nov	Dec	Jan	Feb	Mar	Apr	May	Jun	Jul	Aug	Sep
Leaf												
Flower												
Fruit/Pod												

WHITE IRONWOOD
Vepris lanceolata

CITRUS / BUCHU FAMILY
RUTACEAE

SA Tree Number 261

AFRIKAANS Witysterhout **TSONGA** Muruvula **VENDA** Muhondwa **XHOSA** umZane **ZULU** umOzane

The term **lanceolata** refers to the shape of the leaves.

Where you'll find this tree easily

The White Ironwood occurs singly among other species of trees, in a wide variety of habitats.

🌱 It is easiest to find in the Scarp and Low-lying forests of the Coast (C) and Along Rivers (A).

🌱 In the Dune Forest (C) and the Woodland of the Bushveld-Savannah (B), it is a much smaller tree.

A	B
C	D

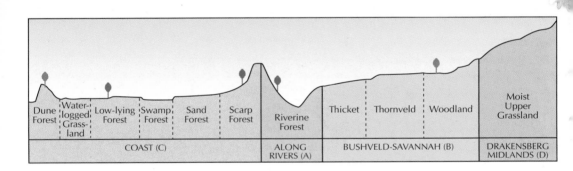

Dune Forest | Water-logged Grass-land | Low-lying Forest | Swamp Forest | Sand Forest | Scarp Forest | Riverine Forest | Thicket | Thornveld | Woodland | Moist Upper Grassland

COAST (C) — ALONG RIVERS (A) — BUSHVELD-SAVANNAH (B) — DRAKENSBERG MIDLANDS (D)

Striking features

- This is a large, single-trunked tree that branches high up.
- **The compound leaves have three dark green, rigid, glossy leaflets with distinctly wavy margins.**
- The leaflets have no leaflet stems.
- **Leaves have a faint lemon smell when crushed.**
- The bark is smooth and whitish-grey to pink.

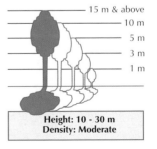

15 m & above
10 m
5 m
3 m
1 m

Height: 10 - 30 m
Density: Moderate

242

243

WHITE IRONWOOD

Vepris lanceolata

Links with animals

The caterpillars of three species of Swallowtail Butterfly feed on this tree, the best known of which is the Citrus Swallowtail *(Papilio demodocus)*. Porcupines eat the bark and in some areas destroy the tree over a period of years by ringbarking it. The dry fruit is eaten by birds such as the Redwing Starlings, all the Lourie species, Rameron and Delagorgue's Pigeons, Redeyed Doves, Crested Barbets and Blackeyed Bulbuls.

Human uses

The wood is used for tent hoops, hammer and pick handles, spokes and beams, implement handles and furniture. The powdered roots were used as a remedy for influenza and colic. The fruit was used as a spice and for treatment of gonorrhoea and bronchitis. It was also used to throw out the devil by casting it on to a fire, and making the possessed person breathe the smoke.

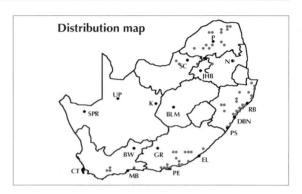

Distribution map

White wood; strong; elastic; close grain.

Gardening

This is a good garden subject, does not have an aggressive root system and can be pruned to any shape. It is a good tree to attract birds and a very successful container- and house-plant, flowering and bearing fruit without problems. The tree grows fast, and young plants transplant well. It tolerates some frost and is quite drought-resistant.

GROWTH DETAILS

This is a single-stemmed tree, buttressed in older trees, that branches high up to form a moderate canopy. Large branches only divide into smaller ones, high up in the canopy. Branches and branchlets form a "wavy" pattern.

Leaves   The compound, alternate leaves have a long, rigid leaf-stem (150 mm). The three leaflets (occasionally four) have no leaflet-stems and emerge from a single, central indentation at the top of the leaf-stem. The leaflets are dark glossy-green with a wavy margin and are seen to be gland-dotted when held against the sun. The central vein stands out on both surfaces. Leaves have a lemon smell when crushed.
(Leaf: 140 x 200 mm; leaflet: 50 - 120 x 15 - 40 mm)

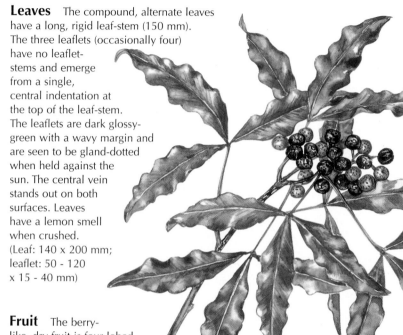

Fruit   The berry-like, dry fruit is four lobed and grows in bunches at the ends of twigs and branchlets. It is leathery and black when ripe (February to April). (5 mm)

Flowers   The inconspicuous, small, star-shaped flowers grow in sprays at the ends of the twigs (December to January).
(Spray 100 - 150 mm; individual: 5 mm)

Bark   The bark is smooth and whitish-grey to pink.

Seasonal changes
Evergreen. This tree can be identified by its leaves throughout the year.

	Oct	Nov	Dec	Jan	Feb	Mar	Apr	May	Jun	Jul	Aug	Sep
Leaf												
Flower												
Fruit/Pod												

245

WILD PLUM

Harpephyllum caffrum

MANGO FAMILY **ANACARDIACEAE**	**SA Tree Number 361**

AFRIKAANS Wildepruim, Suurpruim **N. SOTHO** Mothêkêlê **SISWATI** umGwenye **XHOSA** umGwenye
ZULU umGwenye

The term **caffrum** refers to the Hebrew "Kafri", meaning person living on the land.

Where you'll find this tree easily

The Wild Plum grows singly and is a huge, distinctive tree.

� It is easiest to find in the Low-lying Forest of the Coast (C).

🌱 It is also found in most of the other dense Coastal
forests (C), as well as Along Rivers (A).

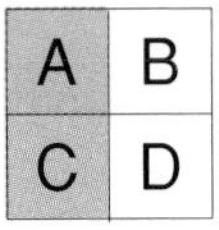

A	B
C	D

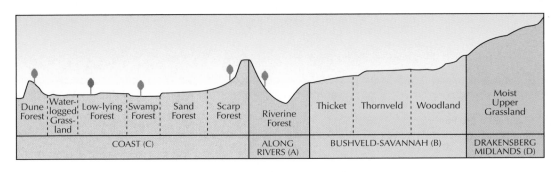

Striking features

- This is a very large, single-stemmed tree that branches
  high up to form a round, dense canopy.

- **The sickle-shaped leaflets have an off-centre central
  vein.**

- **The leaves are crowded towards the ends of thick
  branchlets, creating very visible whirlpools of leaves, all
  over the tree.**

- **The brown bark has shallow, darker brown, lengthways fissures.**

- Some red leaves are usually visible on the tree all year
  round.

- The plum-like, fleshy, red fruit on the forest floor is
  conspicuous (March to October).

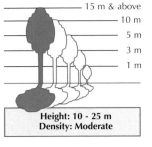

Height: 10 - 25 m
Density: Moderate

246

Largest tree currently registered

Diameter: 1,22 m

Girth: 3,83 m

Height: 28 m

Buffelskloof Nature
Reserve Trust,
Kalmoesfontein,
Dist. Lydenburg

WILD PLUM

Harpephyllum caffrum

Links with animals

Many insects are associated with the tree, such as the Common Hairtail butterfly *(Anthene definita)* and the Eggar Moth *(Lasiocampa kollikerii)* whose caterpillars feed on the leaves. Baboons, Monkeys, Bushbabies, Bushpigs and Bushbuck love the fruit, as do fruit-eating birds such as Knysna Louries, Cape Parrots, Green Pigeons, Mousebirds, Barbets, Bulbuls and Starlings.

Human uses

The wood is used for tables and chairs, planking, beams and rafters. The fruit is edible with a sour pulp and makes a good jelly. Xhosas sow their sorghum when the fruit matures. A bark extract was used as an emetic and blood purifier, and to treat skin problems such as acne and eczema. Powdered, burnt bark was applied to broken skin to treat sprains and fractures.

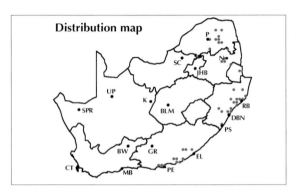

Distribution map

Finely textured hardwood; pinkish-red in colour; suitable for decorative veneers; difficult to nail; polishes well.

Gardening

This is a beautiful garden tree and the root system is not invasive. It grows easily and fast from seed or cuttings in areas without severe frost. It is easy to train and grow as a bonsai, forming an attractive, thick trunk.

Look-alike tree

The Cape Ash *(Ekebergia capensis)*, page 274, has very similar-looking leaves, but they are less sickle-shaped and shinier, tend to droop more and do not form whorls. The bark is darker and smoother with no distinct lengthways markings. The round, berry-like fruit grows in bunches.

GROWTH DETAILS

This is a very large, high-branching, single-stemmed tree with a straight trunk. The branches are often opposite each other. The leaves are clustered towards the ends of thick twigs, forming conspicuous whorls.

Leaves
The compound leaves cluster in a spiral towards the ends of thick, unbranched twigs. There are 4 - 10 pairs of opposite, sickle-shaped, stalkless leaflets with a single leaflet at the tip. The central vein of the leaflets is off-centre. Leaflets are leathery, shiny dark-green above and paler below, and often with a wavy margin. Leaves live for about two years and then turn red before falling. There are usually some red leaves present on the tree all year round. (Leaf: 150 - 400 mm; leaflet: 50 - 100 x 15 - 30 mm)

Fruit
The plum-like, fleshy fruit is smooth and oblong and hangs in bunches from the centre of the whirlpool. It ripens to an apple-red colour, from March to October. (25 - 35 x 13 - 25 mm)

Flowers
The small, white, star-shaped flowers grow in long sprays in the centre of leaf whirlpools. Similar male and female flowers grow on separate trees (November to March). (5 mm)

Bark
The bark is light brown and smooth in young trees, becoming darker and rougher, breaking up into regular, shallow, lengthways fissures in older trees.

Seasonal changes
Evergreen. This tree can be easily recognised throughout the year by its striking features.

	Oct	Nov	Dec	Jan	Feb	Mar	Apr	May	Jun	Jul	Aug	Sep
Leaf												
Flower												
Fruit/Pod												

249

You find trees

BUSHVELD-SAVANNAH – THICKETS

Thickets are areas where one species of tree dominates an area and grows in massed clumps that are not very tall. The trees that follow in this section are very easy to identify, as long as they are in groups. Once you have learned to recognise the main features when they are crowded together, you will develop enough of a Search Image to be able to find them when they are growing alone.

Magic Guarri, growing in thickets, is often found in areas where soil has been disturbed.

CAMPHOR BUSH

Tarchonanthus camphoratus

DAISY FAMILY
ASTERACEAE

SA Tree Number 733

AFRIKAANS Wildekanferbos, Saliehout **N. SOTHO** Sefahlane **S. SOTHO** Mofahlana **TSWANA** Mofatlha **VENDA** Moologa **XHOSA** isiDuli, umGqeba **ZULU** iGqeba elimhlophe

The term **camphoratus** refers to the camphor-like smell of the crushed leaves.

Where you'll find this tree easily

The Camphor Bush grows as a small tree in large uniform groups. Where it grows singly among other trees, it is often a large tree.

🌿 It is easiest to find in the Thickets of the Bushveld-Savannah (B).

🌿 It can also be found in the Low-lying and Sand forests of the Coast (C), and in the Woodland of the Bushveld-Savannah (B).

A	B
C	D

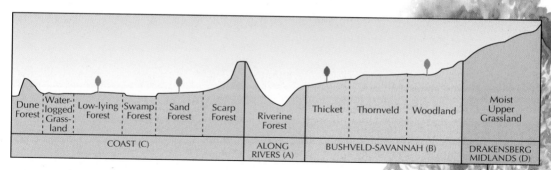

Dune Forest	Water-logged Grass-land	Low-lying Forest	Swamp Forest	Sand Forest	Scarp Forest	Riverine Forest	Thicket	Thornveld	Woodland	Moist Upper Grassland
COAST (C)						ALONG RIVERS (A)	BUSHVELD-SAVANNAH (B)			DRAKENSBERG MIDLANDS (D)

Striking features

• Growing in groups as a small tree, it is multi-stemmed and branches low down to form a moderate, irregular, V-shaped canopy.

• **The leaves are dull, grey-green above and pale grey underneath, often giving the canopy a pale appearance.**

• The bark on the main stem is light grey-brown and fissured lengthways, and on young branchlets and twigs is pale grey and forms distinct ridges.

• The fruit grows as a branched spray of tiny fruit covered by cottonwool-like hairs. (March to November).

• **Most parts of the tree have a strong camphor smell when crushed.**

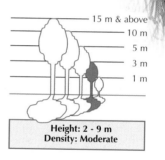

15 m & above
10 m
5 m
3 m
1 m

Height: 2 - 9 m
Density: Moderate

CAMPHOR BUSH

Tarchonanthus camphoratus

Links with animals

Although the foliage is unpalatable, it may be useful during drought as a fodder plant. Giraffe, Black Wildebeest, Grey Duiker, Eland, Kudu, Sable, Nyala, Impala and Springbok utilise the tree.

Human uses

The wood is heavy and was used for musical instruments and cabinet work. San hunter-gatherers made their bows from it. The leaf was used for massaging the body and as a perfume. Dried leaves were smoked like tobacco, with a slight narcotic effect. The woolly flower-heads were sometimes used to stuff cushions, but are strong-smelling. Smoke from burning green branches was inhaled for headache, blocked sinuses and rheumatism. A poultice of the leaves treats asthma, whooping cough, tooth-ache, internal haemorrhage, abdominal pain, bronchitis, inflammation and venereal diseases.

Gardening

This tree germinates easily and transplants well but has an aggressive root system. It is a favourite species for bonsai. It is one of the few trees that can tolerate sea-breezes, severe frost and drought.

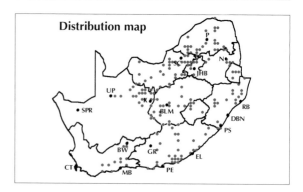

Distribution map

Grey-brown or yellow sapwood; whitish heartwood; close grain; durable; polishes to an attractive finish.

GROWTH DETAILS

This can be a single- or multi-stemmed tree. It is low-branching, with branches growing upwards to form a moderate, irregular, V-shaped canopy. Leaves grow on twigs that stand upright on the canopy outline. The main branches are bare. In forests the single trunk is often crooked and branches high up, creating a dense, rounded canopy. The trees are smaller in drier areas where they tend to grow in large groups (Bushveld-Savannah) and taller in areas of high rainfall where they occur singly. Most parts of the tree have a strong camphor smell when crushed.

Fruit   The tiny fruit is covered by cottonwool-like hairs. The fruit grows together as a branched spray of small, white balls. This makes a striking display of white from March to November. (50 - 130 x 13 mm)

Leaves   The simple, alternate leaves are very variable in size. The upper-surface is dull grey-green, the under-surface is pale grey and velvety. Young leaves are covered in velvety hairs and may have toothed margins. The mature leaves have smooth margins. The central vein and net veining stand out on the under-surface. (Leaf: 20 - 150 x 10 - 70 mm)

Flowers   The small, creamy flowers grow in groups of three, in branched sprays towards the end of the branchlets and twigs, standing out above the leaves (March to November). (Spray: 90 x 50 mm; individual: 8 - 12 mm)

Bark   The bark is pale brown and fissured lengthways. Young branches and twigs are pale grey and form distinct ribs.

Seasonal changes   Semi-deciduous, but in the winter the leaves can look wilted and pale. This tree can be identified throughout the year.

	Oct	Nov	Dec	Jan	Feb	Mar	Apr	May	Jun	Jul	Aug	Sep
Leaf												
Flower												
Fruit/Pod												

MAGIC GUARRI
Euclea divinorum

EBONY FAMILY	
EBENACEAE	**SA Tree Number 595**

AFRIKAANS Towerghwarrie, Hemelsghwarrie **N. SOTHO** Mohlakola **TSONGA** Nhlangula
TSWANA Motlhakola **VENDA** Muṱangule **ZULU** umHlangula

The term **divinorum** refers to the use of tree parts by diviners.

Where you'll find this tree easily

The Magic Guarri is mostly found growing in large, uniform groups.

🌳 It is easiest to find in the Thickets of the Bushveld-Savannah (B).

🌳 It can also be found among the smaller trees growing on old Termite Mounds in the Bushveld-Savannah (B), and in the Low-lying and Sand forests of the Coast (C).

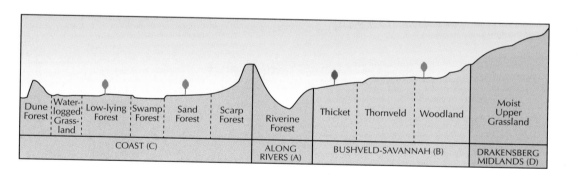

COAST (C)	ALONG RIVERS (A)	BUSHVELD-SAVANNAH (B)	DRAKENSBERG MIDLANDS (D)
Dune Forest / Water-logged Grass-land / Low-lying Forest / Swamp Forest / Sand Forest / Scarp Forest	Riverine Forest	Thicket / Thornveld / Woodland	Moist Upper Grassland

Striking features

• **It is a small, multi-stemmed tree with a dense, rounded canopy of olive-green leaves.**

• **The margins of the simple, elliptic leaves are distinctly wavy.**

• The bark of the stem is dark grey and broken into blocks, but is smooth and distinctly pale grey on branchlets and twigs.

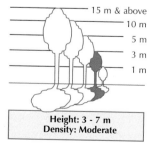

15 m & above
10 m
5 m
3 m
1 m

Height: 3 - 7 m
Density: Moderate

257

MAGIC GUARRI

Euclea divinorum

Links with animals

The fleshy fruit is eaten by birds such as Hornbills. The leaves are unpalatable and only eaten by browsers when food is scarce.

Human uses

The wood is pale brown to red-brown, heavy, hard and tough, with a fine grain. Leafy branches are broken off and used to beat out veld fires. It was used medicinally: the fruit as a purgative; the roots to cure toothache and headache, and bark and root to kill intestinal worms and as a purgative and tonic. The berries were used to make a purple ink and brewed for beer, and the roots as a brown dye to colour baskets. The frayed ends of the twigs were used as toothbrushes. A brew made from the leaves was given to help diviners judge a guilty person – hence the name *divinorum*.

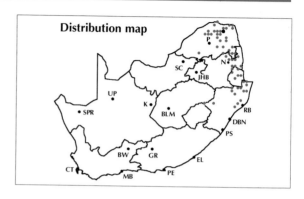

Distribution map

Gardening

This is an attractive garden plant and can be used very effectively as a hedge. It can be grown from seed and is fairly frost-resistant, but grows slowly.

Bush Guarri

Small-leaved Guarri

Magic Guarri

Natal Guarri

Look-alike trees   The Small-leaved Guarri *(Euclea undulata)* is a shrub that grows with the Bush Guarri and the Magic Guarri in the Woodland of the Bushveld-Savannah. It has smaller, darker green leaves (20 - 30 x 5 - 15 mm), with a very wavy margin, which are tightly packed around the tips of the branches and twigs. The leaves and young twigs are often covered with minute, rusty-brown glands which spread the surface with a granular, dust-coloured film. The Natal Guarri *(Euclea natalensis)* has dark green, alternate leaves that are often larger and broader (80 - 120 x 8 - 40 mm) than those of the Bush Guarri and have a longer leaf-stem (10 mm). The veins are prominent on the upper-surface and leaves are covered by velvety, rusty hairs. The margin is wavy and slightly thickened. The Bush Guarri *(Euclea schimperi)*, page 270, has distinct blue-green leaves that are arranged spirally at the ends of the twigs, looking like stars. It is a single-stemmed tree with a pale grey bark that branches high up.

This is a multi-stemmed, small tree or shrub that branches low down to form a dense, rounded canopy.

Leaves The simple, narrow elliptic leaves are opposite and have a short leaf-stem (4 - 6 mm). The leathery leaves are olive-green above and paler below. The central vein stands out on the under-surface. The margin is usually very wavy, but may be virtually flat.

Flowers Inconspicuous, creamy, bell-shaped flowers grow in dense clusters in the angles formed by the leaves. They have a sweet, citrus scent. The male and female flowers grow on separate trees (August to December). (3 - 5 mm)

Fruit The small, berry-like fruit is fleshy and grows on short stalks among the leaves. It ripens to purplish black from October to March. (5 - 7 mm)

Bark The stem is covered by smooth, light grey bark in young trees. It becomes darker grey, coarser and broken into blocks in older trees. The twigs and branchlets have smooth, pale grey bark.

Seasonal changes
Evergreen. This tree can be recognised easily throughout the year.

	Oct	Nov	Dec	Jan	Feb	Mar	Apr	May	Jun	Jul	Aug	Sep
Leaf												
Flower												
Fruit/Pod												

259

RED THORN ACACIA

Acacia gerrardii

THORN-TREE FAMILY
MIMOSACEAE

SA Tree Number 167

AFRIKAANS Rooidoring, Rooibas **N. SOTHO** Mooka **SISWATI** siNga **TSONGA** Bota **TSWANA** Moki **VENDA** Muunga **ZULU** umPhuze

The term **gerrardii** is in honour of the English botanist, WT Gerrard, who collected the first specimen in Natal.

Where you'll find this tree easily

The Red Thorn Acacia grows singly or in small groups.

- It is easiest to find where it grows in uniform groups in the Thickets of the Bushveld-Savannah (B).
- It can also be found in the Thornveld and Woodland of the Bushveld-Savannah (B), and in the Sand Forest of the Coast (C).

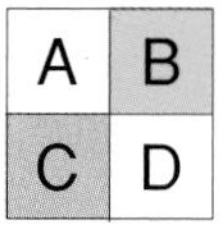

A
B
C
D

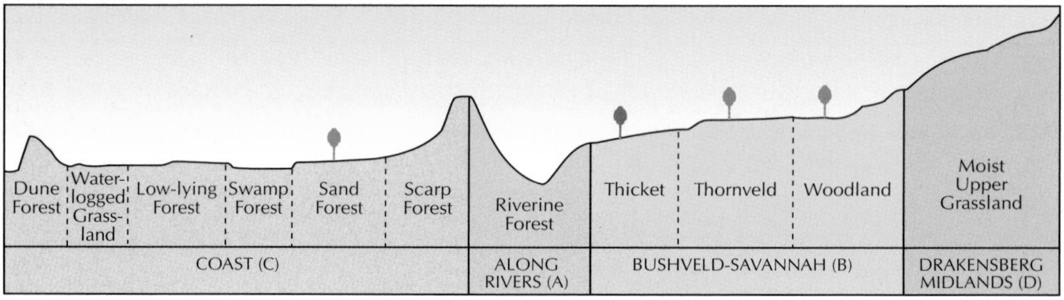

Dune Forest
Water-logged Grass-land
Low-lying Forest
Swamp Forest
Sand Forest
Scarp Forest
Riverine Forest
Thicket
Thornveld
Woodland
Moist Upper Grassland
COAST (C)
ALONG RIVERS (A)
BUSHVELD-SAVANNAH (B)
DRAKENSBERG MIDLANDS (D)

Striking features

- In the Thickets this single-stemmed thorn tree divides into only a few upward-growing branches to form a sparse, spindly, V-shaped canopy.
- The bark is reddish-grey and there are paired, straight, shortish, very stout, white thorns on the branches, branchlets and twigs.
- **The leaves are long and droopy, with very short leaf-stems, and appear to be attached directly to branches. They create the image of continuous green sleeves that cover the length of most branchlets.**
- **The sickle-shaped pods ripen to red or grey-brown from December to May.**

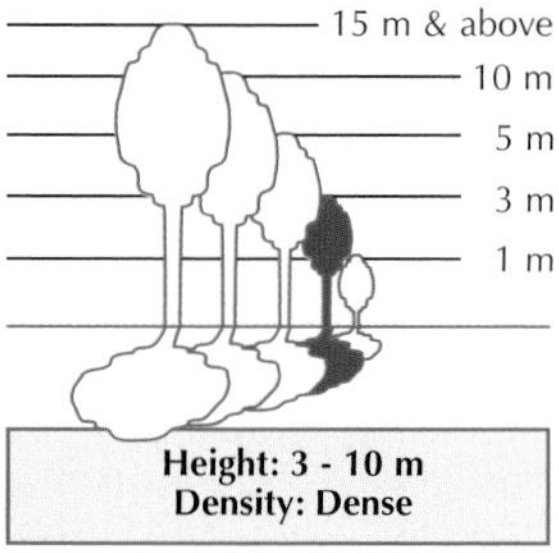

15 m & above
10 m
5 m
3 m
1 m
Height: 3 - 10 m
Density: Dense

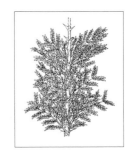

RED THORN ACACIA

Acacia gerrardii

Links with animals

Pods and young shoots are eaten by Baboons. The bark and leaves are eaten by Black Rhino, Giraffe, Duiker, Kudu, Steenbok, cattle and goats. Insects are attracted to the flowers.

Human uses

The wood is very pale with a brown tint. Depending on where the tree grows, the wood may be soft, or tough and strong. It is often damaged by wood borers and is of little value. The inner bark is used to make twine. The bark contains tannin and was used to make an infusion for coughs and sore throats. The Zulus had a belief that they would be in favour with their companions if they used a brew of this bark as an emetic and enema.

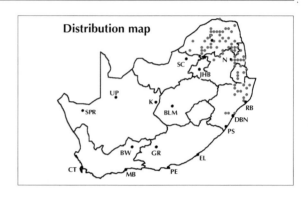

Distribution map

Gardening

This can be an attractive addition to the indigenous garden. The seed germinates very easily and will grow in most gardens, but is slow growing. The tree will withstand some frost and is drought-resistant.

Look-alike trees The Black Monkey Thorn Acacia (*Acacia burkei*), page 312, is a large tree with a strikingly dark green, dense, thick-umbrella canopy, yellowish under-bark and hooked thorns.

The Scented Thorn Acacia (*Acacia nilotica*), page 316, has a less dense, bottle-green, moderate-umbrella canopy, with longer thorns, shorter, stiffer leaves and characteristic necklace-like pods.

The Umbrella Thorn Acacia (*Acacia tortilis*), page 320, has a flat, grey-green, fine feathery, thin-umbrella canopy, straight and hooked thorns and tightly coiled pods. In the Thickets the Red Thorn Acacia looks similar to the Sickle Bush (*Dichrostachys cinerea*), page 264. It is a more branched, intertwined tree with single, straight, pale brown spines and tightly coiled pods in dense clusters.

GROWTH DETAILS

In the Thickets this is a single-stemmed tree that has only a few upward-growing branches to create a sparse, spindly, V-shaped canopy. In the Thornveld lone trees branch high up and spread horizontally to form a dense, thick-umbrella canopy. In both growth forms, the leaves are attached closely to branches, forming soft, feathery sleeves.

Leaves The long, twice compound, dark green leaves have very short leaf-stems. The leaves are droopy with 5 - 10 pairs of feathers and 15 - 20 pairs of leaflets. The young leaves, twigs and pods are covered with thick grey hairs. (Leaf: 80 - 100 mm; leaflet: 3 - 8 x 1 - 2 mm)

Pods The sickle-shaped, flat pods are velvety and grow in bunches. The pods ripen to red or grey-brown from December to May and burst open while still on the tree. (80 - 160 x 8 - 16 mm)

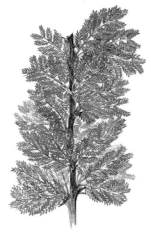

Flowers The conspicuous, round, creamy-white, sweet-scented flowers are crowded near the thorns among the leaves. The flower-stalks are long (30 mm) and are covered with hairs (October to February). (10 - 20 mm)

Bark The bark of the trunk is dark grey to reddish with lengthways fissures, often revealing red under-bark. In young trees, and trees that grow in thickets, the bark is smooth, more reddish and is often wrinkled like an elephant's trunk, showing a rusty under-layer. The common name "red thorn" refers to the colour of the bark.

Thorns
The paired thorns are normally shortish, straight or slightly curved, and very stout. The base of the thorn is often swollen and is covered by soft hairs, especially in young thorns. (25 - 100 mm)

Seasonal changes
Deciduous. The form of the tree and the reddish bark should help with identification in winter.

	Oct	Nov	Dec	Jan	Feb	Mar	Apr	May	Jun	Jul	Aug	Sep
Leaf	▓	▓	▓	▓	▓	▓	▓	▓				▓
Flower		▓	▓	▓	▓							
Fruit/Pod			▓	▓	▓	▓	▓	▓				

SICKLE BUSH

Dichrostachys cinerea

THORN-TREE FAMILY
MIMOSACEAE

SA Tree Number 190

AFRIKAANS Sekelbos, Soetpeul **N. SOTHO** Morêtšê **SISWATI** umSilazembe **TSONGA** Ndzenga
TSWANA Mosêlêsêlê **VENDA** Murenzhe **ZULU** uGagane, umThezane

The term **cinerea** refers to the ashy colour of the bark.

Where you'll find this tree easily

The Sickle Bush prefers loamy soils and is often found close to rivers and on the flats. It normally grows in uniform groups.

🌱 It is easiest to find in the Thickets of the Bushveld-Savannah (B).

🌱 It can also be found in the Sand and Low-lying forests of the Coast (C), in the Bushveld-Savannah (B), and the Drakensberg Midlands (D).

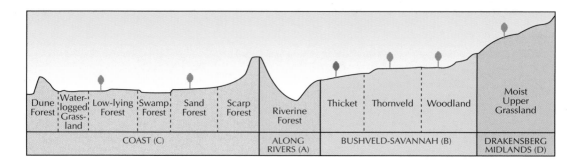

Striking features

- **This multi-stemmed small tree is low-branching and has a heavily intertwined or matted canopy, with long, fine feathery leaves.**

- The branches and twigs have long, straight, pale brown spines.

- The mauve-pink and yellow flower-spikes resemble Chinese lanterns.

- **Groups of tightly coiled pods growing in dense clusters are distinctive.**

- The delicate twice compound leaves stand out against the pale bark.

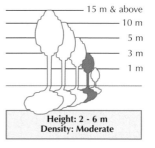

15 m & above
10 m
5 m
3 m
1 m

Height: 2 - 6 m
Density: Moderate

Largest tree currently registered

Diameter: 0,67 m

Girth: 2,10 m

Height: 6 m

JJH Engelbrecht
Maroelasfontein,
Dist. Waterberg

SICKLE BUSH

Dichrostachys cinerea

Links with animals

Pods are very nutritious and eaten by a wide variety of animals such as Rhino, Monkey, Giraffe, Bushpig, Impala, Nyala, Kudu and even Buffalo. Caterpillars of the Satyr Charaxes butterfly *(Charaxes ethalion ethalion)* feed on the Sickle Bush.

Human uses

The tree is used widely medicinally: pods to treat sores and scabies; leaves as a local anaesthetic; chewed leaves are placed on scorpion stings and snake bites to draw the poison; leaf extracts as a remedy for earache, sore throat, and headache; leaf and root extracts to relieve toothache, sore eyes and stomach troubles; powdered bark placed locally to draw skin abscesses and to treat indigestion, chest complaints, gonorrhoea, leprosy, syphilis, colic and diarrhoea.

Gardening

Although it grows slowly unless well watered, the Sickle Bush can be an attractive tree or hedge, and is used by insects and thus birds. It can be grown easily from seed or root cuttings. It is not frost-resistant, but very drought-resistant. It is a good plant to grow as a bonsai.

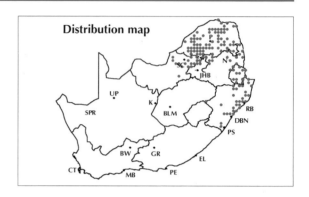

Distribution map

Hard, dark, durable wood; borer- and termite-proof; suitable for turning; produces a good quality charcoal.

Look-alike tree In the Thornveld of the Bushveld-Savannah, the tree that can be confused with the Sickle Bush is the spindly form of the Red Thorn Acacia *(Acacia gerrardii)*, page 260. The Red Thorn Acacia has paired white thorns, not spines, reddish bark, leaves with very short leaf-stems forming sleeves around the branchlets, creamy-white, ball-flowers, and sickle-shaped pods.

GROWTH DETAILS

This is a multi-stemmed, low-branching, small tree. The stems and branches divide profusely to form a densely intertwined, matted canopy of branchlets and twigs, with fine, feathery foliage.

Leaves   The long, twice compound, olive-green leaves are opposite. The leaflets are elliptic with a smooth margin and very small and delicate. There are 8 - 12 pairs of feathers and 15 - 30 pairs of leaflets. (Leaf: 30 - 200 mm; leaflet: 3 x 0,5 mm)

Flowers
The flower-spikes are like Chinese lanterns. They grow on long stems towards the ends of the branchlets and twigs. The fluffy, mauve-pink filaments at the base of the flowers are sterile. The yellow tip consists of minute, fertile flowers closely packed together (October to January). (40 - 60 mm)

Pods   The closely packed, fertilised flowers mature to form many tightly coiled pods, growing bunched together from each flower tip. The pods ripen to dark brown and do not split on the tree. Pods may remain on the tree even after the leaves have dropped (May to September). (Cluster: 70 mm diameter)

Spines   The long, straight, light grey spines are modified side branchlets and sometimes have leaves growing from them. They are so tough that they can puncture tractor tyres. (20 - 40 mm)

Bark   The bark is light brown to grey, with shallow lengthways grooves.

Seasonal changes
Deciduous. This tree can be identified in winter by its growth form, spines and pods.

	Oct	Nov	Dec	Jan	Feb	Mar	Apr	May	Jun	Jul	Aug	Sep
Leaf	▓	▓	▓	▓	▓	▓						▓
Flower	▓	▓	▓	▓								
Fruit/Pod							▓	▓	▓	▓	▓	▓

You find trees

BUSHVELD-SAVANNAH – WOODLAND

The Bushveld-Savannah Ecozone offers wonderful opportunities for tree spotting, but the Woodland is not the place to start. Literally hundreds of different species of trees crowd together here, in different stages of growth. Woodland is a Habitat of excitement and challenge to the more experienced tree spotters, who have worked their way through the easier sections of the book first.

The game reserves of Natal offer unique opportunities to enjoy the wild. Hluhluwe Nature Reserve is a paradise of animals, birds and trees.

BUSH GUARRI

Euclea schimperi (Euclea racemosa)

EBONY FAMILY	
EBENACEAE	SA Tree Number 600

AFRIKAANS Bosghwarrie **N. SOTHO** Mohlakola **TSONGA** Nhlangula **ZULU** iChithamuzi, iDungamuzi

The term **schimperi** is in honour of the German botanist W Schimper.

Where you'll find this tree easily

The Bush Guarri grows singly among other species of trees.

🌱 It is easiest to find in the Woodland of the Bushveld-Savannah (B).

🌱 It can also be found in the Sand, Dune and Low-lying forests of the Coast (C).

A	B
C	D

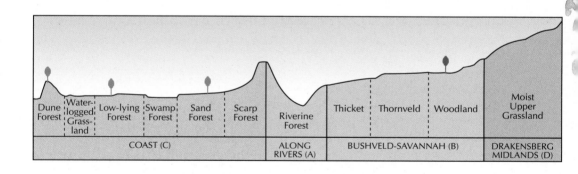

Striking features

- This is a single- or multi-stemmed small tree with smooth, light grey bark.

- It spreads high up to form a dense, round canopy.

- **The blue-green leaves are tightly clustered in spirals towards the ends of twigs.**

- **These clusters of leaves are star-like and form a strong contrast to the pale bark.**

- The margin of the leaf is smooth.

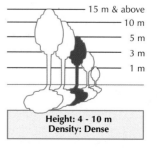

Height: 4 - 10 m
Density: Dense

270

BUSH GUARRI
Euclea schimperi (Euclea racemosa)

Links with animals

Black Rhino eat the bark. The leaves are unpalatable and only eaten by browsers when food is scarce. The flowers attract insects. The fruit is eaten by birds. *Euclea* species are preferred nesting sites for the Greater Doublecollared Sunbird.

Human uses

The fleshy fruit is edible and the wood is hard and heavy. The roots are used as a dark brown dye for woven baskets. It was used to make wooden screws and wagon wheels. Small branches make superb beaters to put out veld fires. Medicinally the major uses were: bark infusions to relieve painful menstruation and to treat splenic pain and swelling; the powdered leaf for snakebite. This tree was never used for firewood as this was believed to lead to domestic quarrels.

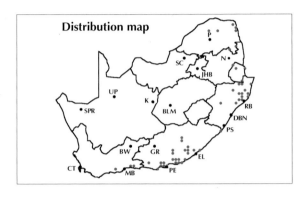

Distribution map

Gardening

This tree can be a very attractive addition to the garden. It can be grown from seed easily but grows slowly at first. It is fairly drought-resistant but not frost-resistant.

Look-alike trees   The Small-leaved Guarri *(Euclea undulata)* is mostly a shrub of the Woodland areas. It has small (20 - 30 x 5 - 15 mm), dark green leaves, with a very wavy margin. They are tightly packed around the tips of the branches and twigs. The leaves and young twigs have minute, rusty-brown glands which cover the surface with a granular, dust-coloured film. See **Sappi Tree Spotting Highveld**.

The Natal Guarri *(Euclea natalensis)* has dark green, alternate leaves that are often larger and broader (80 - 120 x 8 - 40 mm) than those of the Bush Guarri and have a longer leaf-stem (10 mm). The veins are prominent on the upper-surface and leaves are covered by velvety, rusty hairs. The margin is wavy and slightly thickened.

The Magic Guarri *(Euclea divinorum)*, page 256, often grows in pure stands with no other species amongst them. It has darker, coarser bark. The leaves are larger, opposite, olive-grey-green and have a very wavy margin and a short leaf-stem (4 - 6 mm).

GROWTH DETAILS

This tree is very variable depending on the habitat where it is found. It can be single- or multi-stemmed, and branches to form a rounded, dense canopy of blue-green leaves. The leaves grow towards the ends of the branchlets and twigs, leaving the larger branches bare.

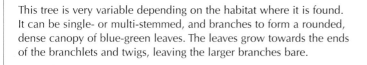

Leaves   Simple, alternate to sub-opposite leaves grow in spirals towards the ends of the branchlets and twigs. The leaves are hairless, blue-green above and paler below. The central vein is obvious on the upper-surface and there is virtually no leaf-stem. (Leaf: 30 - 110 x 7 - 40 mm)

Fruit   The round, berry-like fruit is thinly fleshed and grows in bunches on long stalks, among the leaves. They ripen to deep red or purple (March to December). (6 - 11 mm)

Flowers   The inconspicuous, small, white, bell-shaped flowers grow in unbranched sprays in the angles formed by the leaves. They are sweetly scented and the male and female flowers are on separate trees (November to April). (Spray: 40 - 50 mm; individual: 7 mm)

Bark   The bark is smooth and light grey becoming rougher and darker in older trees.

Seasonal changes
Evergreen. This tree is easy to identify throughout the year by its blue-green leaves.

	Oct	Nov	Dec	Jan	Feb	Mar	Apr	May	Jun	Jul	Aug	Sep
Leaf												
Flower												
Fruit/Pod												

CAPE ASH
Ekebergia capensis

MAHOGANY FAMILY **MELIACEAE**	**SA Tree Number 298**

AFRIKAANS Essenhout **SISWATI** iNyamati **TSONGA** Nyamarhu **VENDA** Muḓouma, Muṱovuma
XHOSA umGwenyezinja, umGwenye wezinya **ZULU** umGwenya wezinja

The term **capensis** means "of the Cape".

Where you'll find this tree easily

The Cape Ash normally grows singly among other species
of trees.

🌱 It is easiest to find in the Woodland of the Bushveld-
Savannah (B).

🌱 It can also be found in most of the forests of the Coast
(C), and Along Rivers (A).

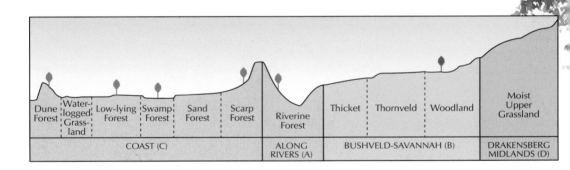

Dune Forest	Water-logged Grass-land	Low-lying Forest	Swamp Forest	Sand Forest	Scarp Forest	Riverine Forest	Thicket	Thornveld	Woodland	Moist Upper Grassland
COAST (C)						ALONG RIVERS (A)	BUSHVELD-SAVANNAH (B)			DRAKENSBERG MIDLANDS (D)

Striking features

- This is a tall, single-trunked tree that divides fairly high
  up, with the leaves crowded towards the ends of the
  branchlets, to form a dense, semi-circular canopy.
- The shiny, compound leaves have a single leaflet at the
  tip and are bi-coloured with a pale under-surface.
- **The central vein of the pointed leaflets is often off-
  centre.**
- The bark is dark and broken into irregular blocks.
- There are white spots on the branchlets and twigs.
- **The berry-like, fleshy fruit grows in bunches and turns
  red when ripe, from November to April.**

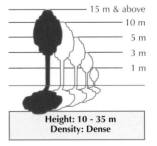

Height: 10 - 35 m
Density: Dense

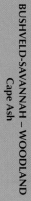

Largest tree currently registered

Diameter: 1,66 m

Girth: 5,21 m

Height: 35 m

Lekgalameetse Nature Reserve

275

CAPE ASH

Ekebergia capensis

Links with animals

The fleshy fruit is eaten off the tree by Baboons, Monkeys and Bushpigs; Bushbuck and Nyala eat the fallen fruit. Most fruit-eating birds are attracted to the fruit, including the Knysna and Purplecrested Louries, Barbets, Hornbills, Bulbuls and Mouse-birds. The leaves are eaten by amaCimbimbi caterpillars, the larva of the Common Emperor Moth and the White-barred Charaxes in the rain forests in Pondoland.

Human uses

The bark is used to treat vomiting and diarrhoea, roots and leaf extracts to treat skin ailments, and leaves as a purgative. The bark was traditionally used to protect chiefs against witchcraft and was also taken in love charm emetics.

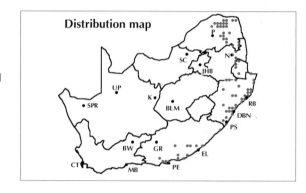

Distribution map

Rare wood; pale, straw-coloured heartwood; yellow sapwood; straight grain; fine, even texture; planes easily and gives a good finish.

Gardening

This is an attractive shade tree and should be planted near or at water points. It is fast-growing from seed but is susceptible to frost.

Look-alike tree

Because the central veins of the leaflets of the Wild Plum *(Harpephyllum caffrum)*, page 246, are also off-centre, it can be confused with the Cape Ash. The Wild Plum has a distinct whirlpool leaf arrangement, characteristic, lengthways marked bark and plum-like fruit.

276

This is a single-trunked tree that divides fairly high up to form a densely branched, semi-circular canopy. The leaves are crowded towards the ends of thin branchlets and twigs. The trunk is often fluted in trees that grow in forests.

Leaves

The compound leaves are large and droop down. They are spirally arranged towards the ends of the young branchlets and twigs, but in older growth are opposite. The leaf-stem is often winged. There are 3 - 5 pairs of opposite, or nearly opposite leaflets, with a single leaflet at the tip. Leaflets are variable in form and may be narrow or broadly elliptic with a sharp tip. They are distinctly bi-coloured with a much paler under-surface. The central vein is often off-centre, and the margins are wavy. (Leaf: 200 - 500 mm; leaflet: 110 - 150 x 35 - 50 mm)

Flowers

The small, sweetly scented, greenish-white, star-shaped flowers are not very conspicuous and grow in sprays in the angles of the leaves. Very few flowers are produced in dry years. The male and female flowers grow on separate trees (October to December). (Spray: 150 - 200 mm; individual: 75 mm)

Fruit

The fleshy, berry-like fruit is produced in profusion in good rainy years, and hangs in bunches. Green fruit turns red when ripe and is very conspicuous from November to April. (15 - 20 mm)

Bark

The bark is dark grey to grey-brown, and rough and flaking in old trees, but is smooth in younger trees and branches. Branchlets are marked by old circular leaf-scars and by raised grey dots.

Seasonal changes

Deciduous. It can be identified throughout the year in areas where the leaves have not dropped. Leaves change to yellow and red in autumn where trees are deciduous.

	Oct	Nov	Dec	Jan	Feb	Mar	Apr	May	Jun	Jul	Aug	Sep
Leaf												
Flower												
Fruit/Pod												

BUSHVELD-SAVANNAH – WOODLAND
Cape Ash

277

NATAL MAHOGANY

Trichilia emetica

**MAHOGANY FAMILY
MELIACEAE**

SA Tree Number 301

AFRIKAANS Rooiessenhout, Basteressenhout   **N. SOTHO** Mmaba   **SISWATI** umKhuhlu   **TSONGA** Nkuhlu
TSWANA Mosikiri   **VENDA** Muḓouma, Muṱshikili   **ZULU** umKhuhlu, uMathunzini

The term **emetica** refers to the bark being used to induce vomiting.

Where you'll find this tree easily

The Natal Mahogany is very widely distributed and grows
singly among other species of trees. Where one is found,
more will be found in the vicinity.

- You will find it most easily in the Woodland of the
  Bushveld-Savannah (B) and in the Low-lying Forest of
  the Coast (C).

- It can also be found in other forests of the Coast (C),
  and Along Rivers (A).

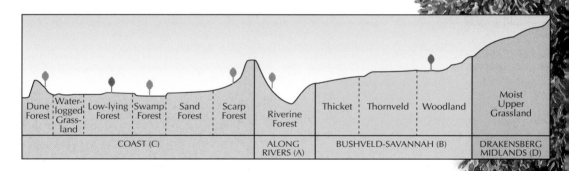

			COAST (C)				ALONG RIVERS (A)	BUSHVELD-SAVANNAH (B)			DRAKENSBERG MIDLANDS (D)
Dune Forest	Water-logged Grass-land	Low-lying Forest	Swamp Forest	Sand Forest	Scarp Forest		Riverine Forest	Thicket	Thornveld	Woodland	Moist Upper Grassland

Striking features

- **This large tree is striking even from afar because of its
  uniform, very dense, deep green, glossy foliage and
  rounded canopy with very few internal branches
  visible.**

- The single trunk branches low down and has a fairly
  smooth bark.

- **The large, compound leaves, with single leaflet at the
  tip, droop down.**

- Leaflets have a very distinctive herringbone vein
  pattern visible on both surfaces.

- When ripe, the fruit bursts open on the tree to show
  striking red and black contents (December to May).

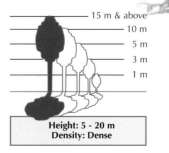

15 m & above
10 m
5 m
3 m
1 m

**Height: 5 - 20 m
Density: Dense**

**Largest tree currently
registered**

Diameter: 1,36 m
Girth: 4,27 m
Height: 14 m

J Nell
Brakspruit,
Dist. Barberton

279

NATAL MAHOGANY

Trichilia emetica

Links with animals

Baboons, Monkeys and Nyala eat the fruit, although the seeds are poisonous to humans. Seeds are also eaten by Crowned, Grey and Trumpeter Hornbills, Blackcollared and White-eared Barbets, Grey and Purple-crested Louries, and Blackbellied Glossy Starlings. Sunbirds feed on the nectar. Fish such as Barbel eat the seeds that fall into the water. Kudu and Giraffe eat the young shoots. The caterpillars of several species of butterfly feed on this tree.

Human uses

The wood is used to make furniture, fish floats, dug-out canoes and musical instruments. Oil extracted from the seeds was used as a body and hair oil for its curative powers, and was said to hasten healing, particularly of fractures. Candles were made from the kernel remains. The bark produces a pinkish dye and was used as a fish poison, and as an emetic to cause vomiting. The root was used as a remedy for fever, to kill intestinal worms and as a purgative. This tree played an important role in the burial rites of the Zulus.

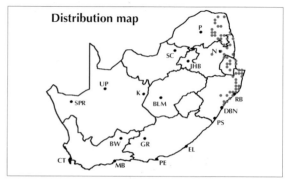

Distribution map

Colour varies from pinkish-brown to brownish-grey to yellow; holds nails well; planes smoothly; not suitable for turning; polishes well; varnishes readily.

Gardening

This dense, evergreen, ornamental tree is an excellent shade tree in the garden, and has a non-aggressive root system. It can be grown easily from seed or cuttings and grows fast when well watered. It is not frost- or drought-resistant, and can be planted in either shade or full sun.

Look-alike tree

The Forest Mahogany (*Trichilia dregeana*), page 28, found in the Dune and Low-lying forests of the Coast (C), is similar. The leaflets are very shiny, have pointed tips, a wavy margin and are much paler on the under- than the upper-surface. The 8 - 12 side veins are further apart.

It has a single, straight trunk that branches to form a very dense, rounded canopy, with very little internal tree structure visible from the outside.

Leaves   The large, alternate, compound leaves are crowded towards the ends of branchlets and twigs. They have 3 - 5 pairs of leaflets, with a single leaflet at the tip. The leaves are dark green above and slightly paler below with brownish hairs, particularly along the 13 - 16 side veins. Leaflets are elliptic with a tapering, rounded tip and base. They are opposite or sub-opposite, with the last pair smaller than the rest. New leaves are shiny, red-brown, and turn very bright lime-green before darkening. (Leaf: 350 - 500 mm; end leaflet: 150 - 160 x 55 mm)

Fruit   The dry, grey-green, capsules grow in bunches. When mature the capsule bursts open to show striking red and black seeds wrapped in bright red pulp. (December to March). (10 - 25 mm diameter)

Flowers   Small, green, sweet-smelling, trumpet-shaped flowers appear in dense sprays at the ends of the branches (August to November). (15 - 18 mm)

Bark   The bark is dark brown and fairly smooth, especially in smaller branches, becoming slightly grooved in older trees.

Seasonal changes
Evergreen. This tree can be found throughout the year.

	Oct	Nov	Dec	Jan	Feb	Mar	Apr	May	Jun	Jul	Aug	Sep
Leaf	█	█	█	█	█	█	█	█	█	█	█	█
Flower												
Fruit/Pod		█	█	█	█	█						

RED IVORY

Berchemia zeyheri

DOGWOOD FAMILY
RHAMNACEAE

SA Tree Number 450

AFRIKAANS Rooi-ivoor, Rooihout **N. SOTHO** Monee **SISWATI** umNeyi **TSONGA** Xiniyani
TSWANA Moye **VENDA** Muṇiane, Muṇia-ṇiane, Muhukhuma **XHOSA** umNini **ZULU** umNini, umNcaka

The term **zeyheri** is named after KLP Zeyher, a famous German botanist.

Where you'll find this tree easily

The Red Ivory normally grows singly in dense groups of other trees.

🍃 It is easiest to find on hillsides in the Woodland of the Bushveld-Savannah (B).

🍃 It can also be found in the Sand and Low-lying forests of the Coast (C), Along Rivers (A), and in the Moist Upper Grassland of the Drakensberg Midlands (D).

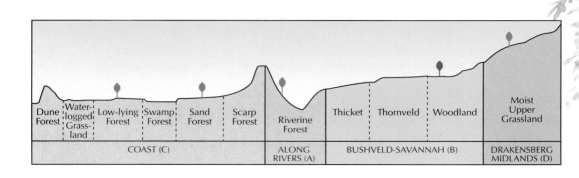

Striking features

• It is a single-stemmed tree that branches fairly high up to form a dense, irregular canopy, shaped by the surrounding vegetation, or a rounded canopy when growing singly.

• **The roundish leaves are shiny, dark green and stand out among the surrounding vegetation.**

• **The side veins are arranged in a herringbone pattern which curl in slightly at the margin and are very distinct on the under-surface.**

• The leaf-stems are often reddish.

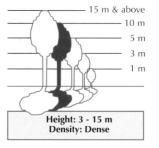

Height: 3 - 15 m
Density: Dense

283

RED IVORY

Berchemia zeyheri

Links with animals

Vervet Monkeys, Baboons, Bushbabies and goats as well as many fruit-eating birds such as Doves, Mousebirds, Blackeyed Bulbuls, Crested, Pied and Blackcollared Barbets, Red-winged Starlings, Grey and Purplecrested Louries, Rameron and Green Pigeons eat the succulent fruit. Meyer's Parrots eat the fruit, probably for the seeds. Leaves are browsed by Giraffe, Blue Wildebeest, Eland, Kudu, Nyala, Bushbuck and Impala. Porcupines eat the bark.

Human uses

The wood is much sought after for carving, mainly ornamental work, wooden bowls and walking sticks which are sold as curios. It is a good furniture wood. The fleshy fruit is edible. The bark is used as a dye for fibre and woven material, giving it a purplish colour. The powdered root was smoked as a headache cure. An extract of the inner bark was used to relieve back pain, for enemas and to cure dysentery. In parts of Zululand it was considered as a royal tree, the chief alone carrying knobkieries made from it.

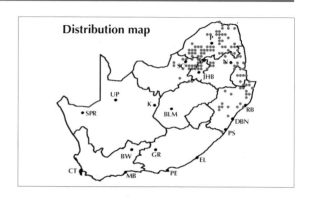

Distribution map

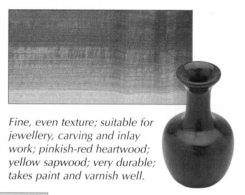

Fine, even texture; suitable for jewellery, carving and inlay work; pinkish-red heartwood; yellow sapwood; very durable; takes paint and varnish well.

Gardening

This is an attractive tree, with its non-invasive root system and is one of the best trees to plant in the garden to attract birds. It is an ideal container-plant requiring little pruning to maintain its neat shape. The tree is drought-resistant and can take a little frost. Seedlings take slowly but grow fast once they are established.

Look-alike tree
The Brown Ivory *(Berchemia discolor)* looks very similar, but the leaves are larger and dark green above and below, have a more tapering tip and do not have a red leaf-stem.

284

GROWTH DETAILS

This is a single-stemmed tree with a straight trunk and spreading branches forming a dense, irregular canopy when growing among other trees, but rounded when growing singly. In Hluhluwe many branches have small, dark swellings (galls), that look as though they are part of the tree, but in fact are caused by insects.

Leaves
The simple, opposite to sub-opposite leaves have short, reddish leaf-stems. The broadly elliptic leaf has a rounded base and tip, and a smooth margin. The upper-surface is shiny blue-green, with the under-surface paler. The leaves have distinct herringbone veins that curl in slightly at the margin. Leaves turn golden-yellow in autumn and new young leaves are bright green. (Leaf: 25 - 60 x 15 - 35 mm)

Flowers
Inconspicuous, greenish-white, star-like flowers grow in small clusters on long stems in the angles formed by the leaves (September to February). (10 - 13 mm)

Fruit
The oval, berry-like fruit is fleshy and grows on long stalks. It is yellow-orange to deep red when ripe (January to April). (6 - 13 x 5 mm)

Bark
The bark is grey-brown, smooth in younger trees and branches, but coarse and splitting into neat rows of irregular blocks in older trees.

Seasonal changes
Deciduous, but may be evergreen under very favourable circumstances. This tree will be difficult to identify in winter.

	Oct	Nov	Dec	Jan	Feb	Mar	Apr	May	Jun	Jul	Aug	Sep
Leaf												
Flower												
Fruit/Pod												

285

WILD OLIVE

Olea europaea

OLIVE FAMILY
OLEACEAE

AFRIKAANS Olienhout, Swartolienhout **N. SOTHO** Mohlware **SISWATI** umNquma **S. SOTHO** Mohloaare **TSWANA** Motlhware **VENDA** Muṱwari **XHOSA** umNquma **ZULU** umNqumo

The term **europaea** refers to its close relationship with the European Olive.

Where you'll find this tree easily

The Wild Olive normally grows singly and occurs in a wide variety of habitats ranging from kloofs and river banks, to grasslands and rocky outcrops.

🌱 It is easiest to find in the densely wooded areas of the Woodland of the Bushveld-Savannah (B).

🌱 It can also be found Along Rivers (A) and in the Low-lying and Scarp forests of the Coast (C).

A	B
C	D

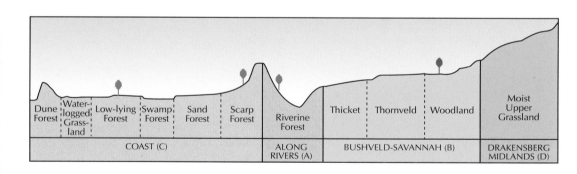

Dune Forest	Water-logged Grass-land	Low-lying Forest	Swamp Forest	Sand Forest	Scarp Forest	Riverine Forest	Thicket	Thornveld	Woodland	Moist Upper Grassland
COAST (C)						ALONG RIVERS (A)	BUSHVELD-SAVANNAH (B)			DRAKENSBERG MIDLANDS (D)

Striking features

- This is a single-trunked tree with a dense, bi-coloured canopy, with a regular, round outline.
- The trunk is often fluted and usually gnarled.
- **The simple, narrowly elliptic, leathery, rigid leaves are shiny dark-green above, and paler below.**
- The side veins and the leaves are opaque when the leaf is held against the light.

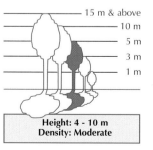

15 m & above
10 m
5 m
3 m
1 m

Height: 4 - 10 m
Density: Moderate

Largest tree currently registered
Diameter: 1,59 m
Girth: 4,99 m
Height: 14 m

Ds AMJD Alberts
Schaaphok,
Dist. Potgietersrus

WILD OLIVE

Olea europaea

Links with animals

Although the foliage is tough and unpalatable, it may be useful as a fodder plant during drought . The fruit is eaten by birds such as Redwinged and Pied Starlings and Rameron Pigeons.

Human uses

The juice of the fruit can be made into ink, and the leaves into palatable tea. The wood makes beautiful furniture and is good for fencing posts. The tree is still used in traditional medicine today: an infusion of the bark to relieve colic; infusion of the leaves as an eye lotion and gargle; the leaf and bark for intermittent fever.

Gardening

This is an attractive tree, and is easy to cultivate. It is drought- and frost-resistant, but it grows slowly. The commercial olive tree can be successfully grafted onto this tree as they are very closely related. It is excellent as a bonsai tree.

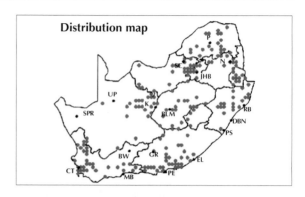

Distribution map

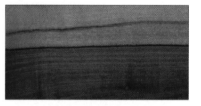

Attractive yellow-brown heartwood; yellow sapwood; wavy grain; very durable; too hard to nail; turns well; oily surface but polishes well.

Look-alike trees

This tree can easily be confused with the Bush Guarri *(Euclea crispa)*, page 270. The Bush Guarri has a less regular outline, formed by clumped, upright leaves. The leaf margin is wavy and the side veins are transparent when held against the light. Fruit and flowers grow among the leaves.

The False Olive Sage *(Buddleja saligna)*, has pale, peeling, lengthways fissured bark. The canopy is irregular and tangled, with leaves only on the outside of the canopy. The leaf-bearing twigs are square and the flower-heads are large, white and conspicuous. See **Sappi Tree Spotting Highveld**.

GROWTH DETAILS

This is a single-trunked tree with a crooked, often fluted, gnarled trunk that branches low down to form a dense, round, bi-coloured canopy with a smooth outline. More exposed trees are smaller, while those in very windy areas may be weather-beaten and more irregular. Young stems are square with four ridges.

Leaves Simple, narrowly elliptic leaves are opposite. They are leathery, rigid, shiny and dark green above, becoming greyer with maturity. The leaves are distinctly bi-coloured, the under-surface is much paler and covered with silvery or brownish scales. The tips end in a sharp point that may turn slightly downwards. The base is tapering and the margin is thickened. The side veins and the leaf are opaque when the leaf is held against the sun. (Leaf: 20 - 100 x 7 - 16 mm)

Fruit The berry-like, fleshy fruit turns purplish-black when ripe from March to July. (8 x 10 mm)

Flowers Inconspicuous, small, cream-green flowers are faintly scented, and grow in short, branched sprays in the angles of the leaves (October to February). (6 - 10 mm)

Bark The bark is smooth and grey-brown in younger branchlets and twigs, turning darker and rougher with age, flaking in irregular strips and blocks. Twigs are covered with small, raised dots, from old leaf-stems.

Seasonal changes
Evergreen. This tree can be found throughout the year.

	Oct	Nov	Dec	Jan	Feb	Mar	Apr	May	Jun	Jul	Aug	Sep
Leaf												
Flower												
Fruit/Pod												

You find trees

BUSHVELD-SAVANNAH – THORNVELD

Southern Africa is well known for its thornveld country. Some of the most beautiful of these areas, with their scattered trees, can be found in KwaZulu-Natal. This is a superb area for tree spotting as the trees often stand well apart, and the variety is exciting and challenging, without being overwhelming. Check the Maps, pages 406 - 409, as well as Destinations and Habitats Grids, pages 386 - 388 to be sure you are in the right areas. Then check the trees listed in this section and build up Search Images of those you are most likely to find in your area.

The sun rising over the Thornveld of Umfolozi promises an ideal day – bird, game and tree spotting.

BUFFALO-THORN

Ziziphus mucronata

DOGWOOD FAMILY/BLINKBLAAR FAMILY
RHAMNACEAE

SA Tree Number 447

AFRIKAANS Blinkblaar-wag-'n-bietjie, Haak-en-steek-wag-'n-bietjie **N. SOTHO** Mokgalwa
SISWATI umLalhabantu **TSONGA** Mphasamhala **TSWANA** Mokgalo **VENDA** Mukhalu, Mutshetshete
XHOSA umPhafa **ZULU** umPhafa, isiLahlankosi, isiLahla, umHlahlankosi

The term **mucronata** refers to the pointed leaves on the tree.

Where you'll find this tree easily

This tree occurs in a wide variety of habitats.

🌿 It is easiest to find in the Thornveld of the Bushveld-Savannah (B), where it is often a large tree.

🌿 It also grows in the Drakensberg Midlands (D), Along Rivers (A), in the Woodland of the Bushveld-Savannah (B), and in most of the forests of the Coast (C).

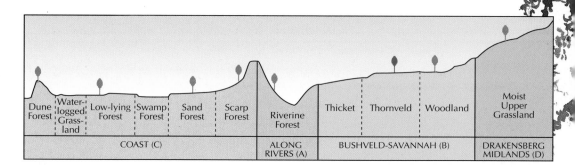

Striking features

- This is a single-trunked tree with a moderate, spreading canopy.

- Branchlets divide into fine twigs that are slightly zig-zagged.

- Leaves tend to grow on the same flat plane, facing the light.

- **The leaves are distinctly shiny and have three veins radiating from the base.**

- **Pairs of reddish-brown thorns, one hooked and one straight, grow at the base of the leaves, in the angles of the twigs.**

- The large, round, red-brown berries are dry and conspicuous, and stay on the tree for long periods.

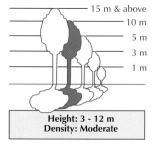

15 m & above
10 m
5 m
3 m
1 m

Height: 3 - 12 m
Density: Moderate

Largest tree currently registered

Diameter: 1,37 m
Girth: 4,30 m
Height: 12 m

CG & MM Cunningham
Meseg Cemetary, Enzelsberg,
Dist. Marico

BUFFALO-THORN

Ziziphus mucronata

Links with animals

The leaves are eaten by Giraffe, antelope, cattle and goats, and the fruit by many animals such as small antelope, Baboons, Monkeys and Warthog, as well as Green Pigeons. The caterpillars of many butterflies feed on this tree.

Human uses

The fruit is edible, and is used to make porridge and meal. The seeds can be roasted as a coffee substitute. The wood is yellow and warps easily. It is used for fencing posts, dishes and spoons. This was an important medicinal plant, and is still used in traditional medicine today: it was used for stomach ailments, skin ulcers and chest problems; a paste of the leaves was used to treat boils and glandular swellings. It was the burial tree of the Zulu and the Sotho. Trees were planted to surround the body, and branches were used to attract the ancestral spirits from one dwelling place to the next.

Gardening

This is a very pretty tree but it tends to drop thorny branches. The tree grows fast from seed and is fairly drought- and frost-resistant. It is suitable as a bonsai tree.

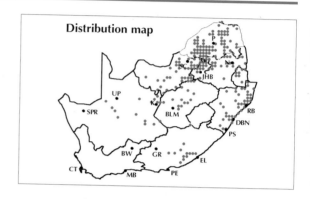

Distribution map

Yellow-brown heartwood, sometimes with reddish-brown, dark streaks; yellow sapwood; hard, durable; suitable for turning.

GROWTH DETAILS

This is a single-trunked tree with a short, often crooked trunk that branches fairly low down to form a shiny, moderate, spreading canopy. It can grow very tall in the forest. Long, slender branchlets and twigs are red-brown. Twigs and leaves create a flat plane with leaves facing the light. Twigs are slightly zig-zag.

Flowers Inconspicuous, small, star-like, yellow-green flowers grow in clusters at the base of the leaves. They produce copious nectar (October to January). (6 mm)

Leaves Simple, alternate, elliptic leaves are slightly folded and grow on the angles of the twigs. They are distinctly shiny with slightly toothed edges and have three veins radiating from the base. Young leaves may be hairy and are bright, spring-green. In protected areas the leaf-stem is long and prominent. (30 - 120 x 20 - 70 mm)

Fruit The hard, round, berry-like fruit is shiny and red-brown when ripe. The fruit is often still visible on the leafless trees in winter (Ripens February to June). (15 - 25 mm)

Thorns Pairs of reddish-brown thorns, one straight and one hooked, grow at the base of the leaves, in the angles of the twigs. Mature trees may have virtually no thorns. Trees in drier areas, younger trees and younger branchlets and twigs tend to be more thorny. (Straight: 10 - 20 mm; curved: 5 - 7 mm)

Bark The bark is light grey-brown and smooth when young, becoming grooved with age. In forests the bark is distinctive, flaking in rectangular blocks that run lengthways down the trunk.

Seasonal changes

Semi-deciduous. The presence of fruit makes it possible to identify this tree in winter.

	Oct	Nov	Dec	Jan	Feb	Mar	Apr	May	Jun	Jul	Aug	Sep
Leaf												
Flower												
Fruit/Pod												

KNOB THORN ACACIA
Acacia nigrescens

THORN-TREE FAMILY MIMOSACEAE	SA Tree Number 178

AFRIKAANS Knoppiesdoring, Perdepram **N. SOTHO** Moritidi **SISWATI** umKhaya **TSONGA** Nkaya **TSWANA** Mokala, Mokoba **VENDA** Munanga **ZULU** umKhaya

The term **nigrescens** means black and probably refers to the pods.

Where you'll find this tree easily

Knob Thorn Acacia do not grow in dense groups, but many trees will be found near one another in suitable Habitats.

🌱 This tree is easiest to find in the Thornveld of the Bushveld-Savannah (B), where it stands out among the other species of trees.

🌱 It can also be found in the Woodland of the Bushveld-Savannah (B), Along Rivers (A) and in the Sand Forest of the Coast (C).

A	B
C	D

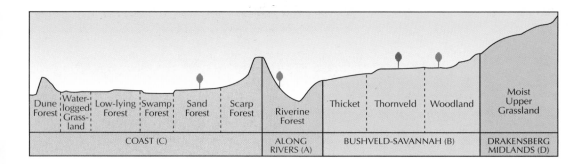

Dune Forest	Water-logged Grass-land	Low-lying Forest	Swamp Forest	Sand Forest	Scarp Forest	Riverine Forest	Thicket	Thornveld	Woodland	Moist Upper Grassland
COAST (C)						ALONG RIVERS (A)	BUSHVELD-SAVANNAH (B)			DRAKENSBERG MIDLANDS (D)

Striking features

- This is an upright thorn tree, with a straight, single trunk that branches high up to form a moderate, irregular canopy.

- **There are woody knobs on the trunks and on the large branches of many of the trees.**

- **The leaflets are large for an *Acacia*, and paired. Each pair resembles a butterfly leaf.**

- In early spring, before the new leaves appear, the tree is covered with creamy-white flower-spikes.

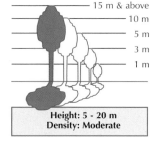

15 m & above
10 m
5 m
3 m
1 m

Height: 5 - 20 m
Density: Moderate

Largest tree currently registered

Diameter: 0,97 m
Girth: 3,05 m
Height: 13 m

Nwanedi Resort
Northern Province

KNOB THORN ACACIA

Acacia nigrescens

Links with animals

This tree is vulnerable to insects. When the bark has been removed from the trees, is often attacked, and may even be killed, by wood-borers. The flowers are eaten by Baboons, Monkeys and Giraffe. However, in the process many of the flowers are pollinated by Giraffe! Leaves and shoots form an important food source for Elephant, Kudu, Giraffe, cattle and goats. The pods supply an important protein for Giraffe in winter. Holes in the trunk and branches provide nesting sites for birds.

Human uses

The wood is used for fence posts and also for knobkieries (fighting sticks). The knobs on the bark play no part in this. Poles were planted in the ground to stop lightning striking the village. The bark was used for tanning leather.

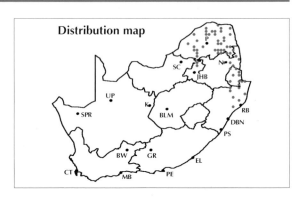

Distribution map

Yellow-brown heartwood; yellow sap-wood; irregular grain; difficult to saw; planes well to a smooth finish; turns readily; does not hold nails well; varnishes satisfactorily.

Gardening

This tree grows well in most gardens. It likes warm conditions, is susceptible to frost but is fairly drought-resistant. The tree is a disadvantage in home gardens as it tends to drop thorny twigs. It germinates very easily but grows very slowly.

GROWTH DETAILS

This tree has a single, straight trunk that branches to form a moderate, irregular canopy.

Leaves   The twice compound, opposite leaves have pale green leaflets that are almost round and have a smooth margin. There are 1 - 3 feather pairs, each feather consisting of 1 - 2 pairs of leaflets, each pair resembling a butterfly leaf. (Leaf: 35 x 80 mm; leaflet: 10 - 30 x 8 - 25 mm)

Flowers   From late June to early July the tree has a plum-coloured sheen from the developing flower-buds. They open to form a spectacular creamy-white display covering the leafless trees in spring (July to September). The sweet-scented flower-spikes grow in clusters of 2 - 3 at the leaf-buds. Flowers are most abundant after good, late summer rains. (80 - 100 mm)

Thorns   Downward-curving, hooked thorns grow on characteristic protruding knobs on the thicker branches and young trunks. Smaller, hooked thorns grow in pairs on branchlets and twigs. (5 - 10 mm)

Pods   The flat bean pods hang down in clusters. They change from pale green to brown as they ripen. Pods never open on the trees but break up on the ground (December to June). (110 - 140 x 70 mm)

Bark   The bark is dark brown, rough and deeply fissured lengthways, revealing a yellowish under-bark. Younger branches and trees have paler bark and have the characteristic knobs with hooked thorns.

Seasonal changes

Deciduous. Leaves turn yellow before they fall in autumn. The knobs are still visible in winter making it easy to find.

	Oct	Nov	Dec	Jan	Feb	Mar	Apr	May	Jun	Jul	Aug	Sep
Leaf												
Flower												
Fruit/Pod												

299

LARGE-LEAVED ALBIZIA
(LARGE-LEAVED FALSE-THORN)
Albizia versicolor

THORN-TREE FAMILY
MIMOSACEAE

SA Tree Number 158

AFRIKAANS Grootblaarvalsdoring, Sandkiaat **N. SOTHO** Mohlalabata **SISWATI** siVangatsane, umVangatana **TSONGA** Mbhesi **TSWANA** Mmola **VENDA** Mutamba-pfunda **ZULU** umVangazi

The term **versicolor** refers to the colour changes of the pods.

Where you'll find this tree easily

The Large-leaved Albizia stands out above the other species of trees.

🌱 It is easiest to find in the Thornveld of the Bushveld-Savannah (B).

🌱 It can also be found in the Low-lying Forest of the Coast (C), Along Rivers (A), and in the Woodland of the Bushveld-Savannah (B).

A	B
C	D

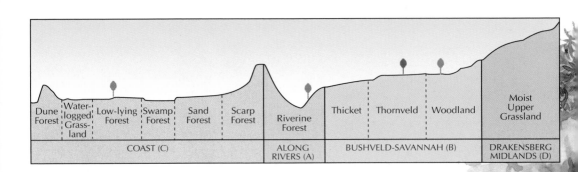

	COAST (C)				ALONG RIVERS (A)	BUSHVELD-SAVANNAH (B)			DRAKENSBERG MIDLANDS (D)
Dune Forest	Water-logged Grass-land	Low-lying Forest	Swamp Forest	Sand Forest	Scarp Forest	Riverine Forest	Thicket	Thornveld	Woodland	Moist Upper Grassland

Striking features

- This is a large, single-trunked tree that separates fairly low down into a few large branches to form a dark green, V-shaped canopy.

- **The twice compound leaves have distinct, large, rounded leaflets that are clearly visible, even from a distance of 30 metres.**

- The large, white, powder-puff flowers appear with the new leaves (August to January).

- **The large, broad pods are present from December to March.**

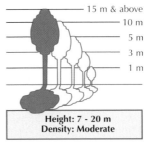

15 m & above
10 m
5 m
3 m
1 m

Height: 7 - 20 m
Density: Moderate

LARGE-LEAVED ALBIZIA
(LARGE-LEAVED FALSE-THORN)

Albizia versicolor

Links with animals

The leaves, pods and young shoots are eaten by
Kudu and Elephant, although the pods have been
reported to have poisoned cattle and sheep. The
flowers are a source of nectar and pollen for bees,
while the seeds are eaten by Brownheaded Parrots.

Human uses

The wood is valued for building beams, doors,
windows and door frames. The wood is also used to
make furniture, cabinets, mortars for stamping corn
and drums. The bark is used for tanning and the
inner bark produces a fairly strong rope. The bark
and roots have a lathering quality and can be used
as a soap. Roots were used as an enema to kill
intestinal worms, as a purgative, and as a headache
remedy if used with the leaves and bark. Extracts of
the bark were used to treat sore eyes and sun rashes.
The gum is reputed to be poisonous.

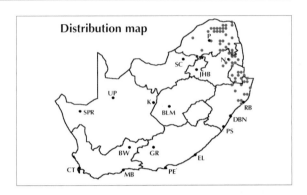
Distribution map

*Dark, almost black
heartwood; fine
grain; durable;
termite-resistant.*

Gardening

This is a beautiful shade tree
for the warmer parts of the
country. It does not have an
invasive root system. Seeds
germinate well and trees
grow relatively fast. It is
drought-resistant but frost-
sensitive.

GROWTH DETAILS

This is a single-trunked tree that branches upwards, fairly low down, to form a wide, V-shaped canopy. The large branches and branchlets are thick, even in the outer canopy, and the leaves grow from thick twigs.

Leaves   The twice compound leaves are alternate, with opposite feathers and leaflets. There are 1 - 3 feather pairs, with 3 - 5 pairs of leaflets. The large, broadly elliptic leaflets have a rounded tip and base. They have a smooth margin, and clearly visible, light-coloured, parallel side and central veins. The leaflets are olive-green above, and slightly paler below, and have a very short leaflet-stem. The under-surface of the leaflet and leaflet-stem are covered in rusty, velvety hairs. The attachment of the leaf to the twig is distinctly thickened. Leaves turn yellow to red in autumn and young leaves are reddish. (Leaf: 100 - 350 mm; leaflet: 25 - 50 x 20 - 35 mm)

Flowers   The large, pin-cushion flowers are conspicuous in summer when they appear with the new leaves. They are lightly scented, white and turn pinkish with age (August to January). (Stamen: 35 mm)

Pods
The flat, broad bean pods have a thickened margin. They turn from green to yellow to red, and then become pale brown when ripe. They do not split open on the tree (December to March). (100 - 200 x 30 - 50 mm)

Bark   The bark is dark grey, rough and corky. In old trees, the bark often breaks up into deeply grooved segments. Young branches are hairy and initially buff-coloured, but they darken with age.

Seasonal changes
Deciduous. This tree may be difficult to find during the winter.

	Oct	Nov	Dec	Jan	Feb	Mar	Apr	May	Jun	Jul	Aug	Sep
Leaf												
Flower												
Fruit/Pod												

MARULA

Sclerocarya birrea

<table>
<tr><td>MANGO FAMILY
ANACARDIACEAE</td><td align="right">SA Tree Number 360</td></tr>
</table>

AFRIKAANS Maroela **N. SOTHO** Morula **SWAZI** UmGana **TSONGA** Nkanyi **TSWANA** Morula
VENDA Mufula **ZULU** umGanu

The term **birrea** is based on the common name of the tree "birr" in Senegal and Gambia.

Where you'll find this tree easily

Marula trees very seldom grow in groups, but once one is found, other trees are usually visible in the vicinity. It grows on most soil types at medium to low altitudes.

🌱 This tree can be found easiest in the Thornveld of the Bushveld-Savannah (B), where it is one of the largest trees.

🌱 It can also be found in the Woodland of Bushveld-Savannah (B), along the banks of larger Rivers (A) and in most of the forests of the Coast (C).

<table>
<tr><td>A</td><td>B</td></tr>
<tr><td>C</td><td>D</td></tr>
</table>

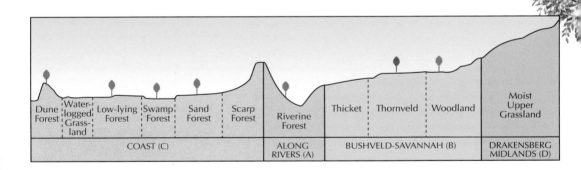

COAST (C)					ALONG RIVERS (A)	BUSHVELD-SAVANNAH (B)			DRAKENSBERG MIDLANDS (D)
Dune Forest	Water-logged Grass-land	Low-lying Forest	Swamp Forest	Sand Forest	Scarp Forest / Riverine Forest	Thicket	Thornveld	Woodland	Moist Upper Grassland

Striking features

- It is a single-trunked tree, dividing high up into a few bare branches and a semi-circular canopy.
- **The bark often peels in conspicuous, characteristic, rounded depressions, revealing a smooth, pink-brown under-bark.**
- In summer blue-green, compound leaves hang, crowded towards the end of thickened twigs; in winter the bare twigs stand out like stubby fingers.
- Unripe green and ripe yellow fruit are often seen on the ground under the female trees (January to March**).**

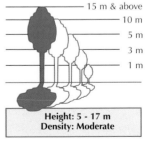

15 m & above
10 m
5 m
3 m
1 m

**Height: 5 - 17 m
Density: Moderate**

Largest tree currently registered

Diameter: 1,33 m
Girth: 4,18 m
Height: 19 m

N.G. Kerk
Kranspoort Mission Station,
Dist. Soutpansberg

MARULA

Sclerocarya birrea

Links with animals

Mosquitoes often breed in the hollows between branches. The caterpillars of eight species of butterfly feed on the foliage. The bark is often infected by insects that cause huge, dark swellings (galls) to form on the main trunk. The fleshy fruit is a favourite of many mammals such as Elephant, Monkeys, Baboons, Kudu, Duiker, Impala and Zebra. The leaves and bark are often eaten by Elephant.

Human uses

The wood is used for furniture, carvings and household articles. The fruit is tasty and rich in Vitamin C. Jelly, jam, beer and Amarula liqueur are made from it. The kernel of the seed is edible, and oil pressed from it can be used as a preservative. An extract of the bark treated dysentery and diarrhoea and prevented malaria, while the inner bark was effective in soothing insect bites and the burns of hairy caterpillars. Newly-born baby girls and their mothers were traditionally washed in water heated on a fire made from the twigs.

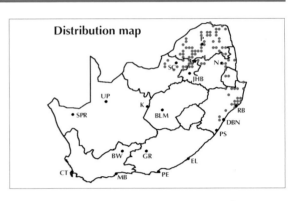

Distribution map

Abundant; soft, perishable and permeable; turns well; sharp tools required when planing; pinky-red heartwood; sometimes blue patches of darker colour are seen.

Gardening

This is a very attractive shade tree. It grows fast and easily from seed. It is drought-resistant but young trees are frost-sensitive.

GROWTH DETAILS

This is a single, straight trunk which branches high up into a few bare, main branches. These grow slightly upwards and outwards, with the leaves hanging towards the ends of thick twigs and branchlets on the outside of the canopy, to form a moderate to dense, semi-circular canopy.

Leaves   Compound, alternate leaves have 3 - 7 pairs of opposite, elliptic leaflets with a single leaflet at the tip. New leaves are coppery, turning shiny bright green, before they mature to blue-green above and paler below. They hang crowded towards the ends of the branchlets and twigs. Leaflets have a tapering tip and smooth margin.

Flowers   Inconspicuous, pink and white flowers grow in sprays at the ends of branches and twigs. They appear with, or before, the new leaves in spring. Male and female flowers grow on separate trees. (September to November). (Spray: 50 - 80 mm)

Fruit   The oval, plum-sized, fleshy fruit drops while it is still green. It ripens to pale yellow on the ground, giving off a strong fruity smell (January to March). Often woody stones, with two or three seed-holes, can be found nearby. (Fruit: 40 x 40 mm)

Seasonal changes
Deciduous. The leaves turn yellow-green before they drop, and the tree has long periods without leaves. The bark and stubby branchlets are very characteristic, making identification possible throughout the year.

Bark   The bark often peels in conspicuous, characteristic, rounded depressions, exposing a smooth pink-brown under-surface. In the forest the bark tends to form more regular blocks and has a pinkish-grey tinge.

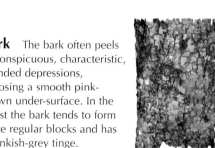

	Oct	Nov	Dec	Jan	Feb	Mar	Apr	May	Jun	Jul	Aug	Sep
Leaf												
Flower												
Fruit/Pod												

BUSHVELD-SAVANNAH – THORNVELD
Big Five – Marula

307

VELVET BUSHWILLOW

Combretum molle

BUSHWILLOW FAMILY
COMBRETACEAE

SA Tree Number 537

AFRIKAANS Fluweelboswilg, Basterrooibos **N. SOTHO** Mokgwethe **SISWATI** inKukutwane
TSONGA Xikhukhutsane **TSWANA** Modubatshipi **VENDA** Mugwiti **ZULU** umBondwe omhlope

The term **molle** originates from the word "mollis", meaning soft, referring to the soft leaves.

Where you'll find this tree easily

The Velvet Bushwillow grows singly among other species
of trees.

🌱 It is easiest to find in the Thornveld of the Bushveld-
Savannah (B), where it is one of the largest trees.

🌱 It can also be found in the Sand and Low-lying forests
of the Coast (C), Along Rivers (A), and the Woodland
of the Bushveld-Savannah (B).

A	B
C	**D**

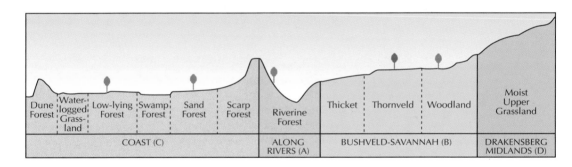

Dune Forest	Water-logged Grass-land	Low-lying Forest	Swamp Forest	Sand Forest	Scarp Forest	Riverine Forest	Thicket	Thornveld	Woodland	Moist Upper Grassland
COAST (C)						ALONG RIVERS (A)	BUSHVELD-SAVANNAH (B)			DRAKENSBERG MIDLANDS (D)

Striking features

- This is a single-trunked tree, with a dark, crooked trunk
  that branches fairly high into meandering branches,
  branchlets and twigs.

- **The irregular, dark green canopy stands out among
  the surrounding vegetation.**

- **The leaves are large and distinctly oval to rounded,
  and are easy to see individually even from 30 metres.**

- **The leaves are velvety with a distinct herringbone
  pattern of veins.**

- The bark is rough and dark grey and breaks up into
  regular blocks on older trees.

- It has characteristic, four-winged Bushwillow pod
  (January to June).

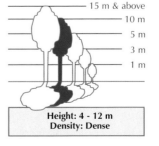

Height: 4 - 12 m
Density: Dense

Largest tree currently
registered

Diameter: 0,49 m
Girth: 1,54 m
Height: 11 m

EA Galpin
'Mosdene', Zyferkraal,
Dist. Potgietersrus

VELVET BUSHWILLOW

Combretum molle

Links with animals

The leaves are eaten by cattle and a wide variety of antelope. The caterpillars of 25 different species of butterfly feed on the leaves.

Human uses

The wood is used for fencing posts, implement handles, grain mortars and bowls for grinding peanuts. Leaves are used as a red fabric-dye, and roots as a yellow-brown dye. The fresh or moistened dry leaves are used to dress wounds and the root as an antidote to snakebite. Roots are used to induce abortion and to treat constipation. This tree is still used in traditional medicine today.

Gardening

This is an attractive garden tree, and mature trees are frost-resistant. It can be grown from seed and is suitable as a bonsai tree.

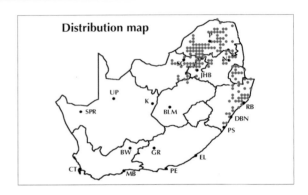

Distribution map

Coarse texture; yellow-brown heartwood; termite-proof; brittle when dry.

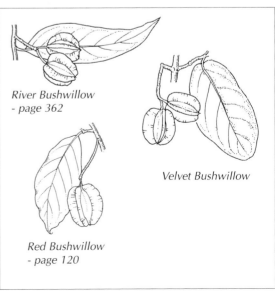

River Bushwillow - page 362

Velvet Bushwillow

Red Bushwillow - page 120

GROWTH DETAILS

This is a single-trunked tree with a crooked trunk that branches fairly high into meandering branches, branchlets and twigs. The moderate canopy is irregular and spreading.

Leaves Simple, opposite leaves are densely covered by velvety hairs when young, becoming smoother with age. The broadly elliptic leaf appears almost round and has a smooth margin and a rounded point with a fine, hair-like tip. The central and side veins and even intermediary veins stand out clearly on the under-surface. They are often hairy, and may be covered with reddish scales. (Leaf: 60 - 100 x 40 - 60 mm)

Pods The abundant four-winged pods turn from yellow-green to golden red-brown when ripe from January to June. Pods may remain on the tree for the whole season (January to June). (13 - 23 mm)

Flowers
Conspicuous, yellow-green spikes grow in the angles formed by the leaves. They are sweet-scented and appear before the leaves (September to November). (Spike: 40 - 90 mm; individual: 4 mm)

Bark The bark is grey-brown to black and breaks up into regular, small blocks, to reveal a reddish-tinted under-bark. The bark of new branches, branchlets and twigs has a reticulate pattern, like elephant skin. Twigs are covered by reddish hairs.

Seasonal changes
Deciduous. The leaves turn from copper to plum in autumn. It can be identified as long as the four-winged pods are present.

	Oct	Nov	Dec	Jan	Feb	Mar	Apr	May	Jun	Jul	Aug	Sep
Leaf	■	■	■	■	■	■	■					■
Flower												■
Fruit/Pod	■	■	■	■	■	■	■	■	■			

BUSHVELD-SAVANNAH – THORNVELD
Big Five – Velvet Bushwillow

311

BLACK MONKEY THORN ACACIA
Acacia burkei

THORN-TREE FAMILY **MIMOSACEAE**	**SA Tree Number 161**

AFRIKAANS Apiesdoring, Swartapiesdoring **TSONGA** Nkasinga **TSWANA** Mokgwa
ZULU Mbambampala, umKhaya wehlalahlathi

The term **burkei** refers to the naturalist/botanist Joseph Burke who catalogued the tree in the 1840s.

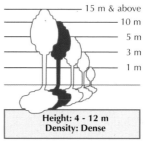

Where you'll find this tree easily

The Black Monkey Thorn Acacia grows singly, but where
one is found, others will be found in the vicinity.

🌶 It is easiest to find in the Thornveld and Woodland of
the Bushveld-Savannah (B).

🌶 It is also found in the Sand and Low-lying forests of the
Coast (C) and Along Rivers (A).

A	B
C	D

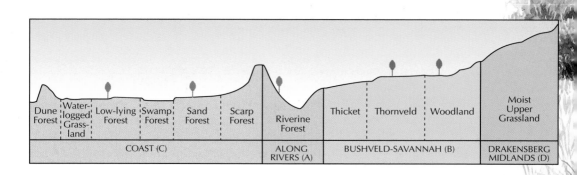

Dune Forest	Water-logged Grass-land	Low-lying Forest	Swamp Forest	Sand Forest	Scarp Forest	Riverine Forest	Thicket	Thornveld	Woodland	Moist Upper Grassland
COAST (C)						ALONG RIVERS (A)	BUSHVELD-SAVANNAH (B)			DRAKENSBERG MIDLANDS (D)

Striking features

- **This is the tallest of the umbrella trees in the
  Thornveld, being single-trunked, often high-branching,
  with a dense, dark green, semi-circular to deep-
  umbrella canopy.**

- The twice compound leaves are short and stiff, stand
  upright and hardly move in the wind.

- The bark is dark, rough, and forms deep, lengthways
  fissures exposing yellowish under-bark.

- The white flower-spikes bloom after the leaves have
  appeared from October to January.

- **The flat bean pods have a pointed tip and are dark
  brown when ripe.**

15 m & above
10 m
5 m
3 m
1 m

Height: 4 - 12 m
Density: Dense

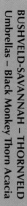

Largest tree currently registered

Diameter: 0,90 m

Girth: 2,83 m

Height: 14 m

EA Galpin
'Mosdene', Zyferkraal,
Dist. Potgietersrus

313

BLACK MONKEY THORN ACACIA

Acacia burkei

Links with animals

Insects often cause huge, dark swellings (galls) on the tips of branches that resemble rounded fruit. The dry pods have a high nutritional value and are eagerly eaten by cattle, game and Bushbabies. The green leaves are eaten by Black Rhino, Elephant, Giraffe, Kudu, Nyala and Impala, and fallen leaves are eaten by Steenbok and Grey Duiker. Monkeys eat the gum. These trees are favoured by nesting birds.

Human uses

The yellow-brown to dark-brown wood is fine-grained, strong, hard and heavy. The wood is used to make furniture and handles for tools. It makes good fence posts as it is termite-resistant, although it must be protected against wood-borers. This tree was believed to attract lightning.

Gardening

This tree can provide valuable shade in warm Sandveld areas, but the root systems are invasive. The seed germinates easily, but it is a slow-grower and prefers well-drained soil. The tree can withstand low temperatures but not cold wind. It is excellent as a bonsai tree.

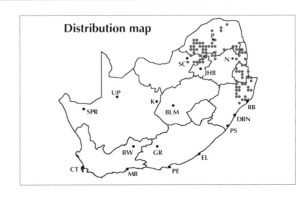

Distribution map

Look-alike trees The large leaflets of this tree can be confused with the Knob Thorn Acacia *(Acacia nigrescens)*, page 296, but the Knob Thorn has large, paired leaflets that may resemble butterfly leaves, and the knobs on the trunk are larger and prominent.

In the Thornveld, there are three other umbrella trees that can be confused with the Black Monkey Thorn. The Red Thorn Acacia *(Acacia gerrardii)*, page 260, is a smaller tree that has a paler green, moderate-umbrella canopy with long, droopy leaves and reddish bark.

The Scented Thorn Acacia *(Acacia nilotica)*, page 316, is also a much smaller tree, with a less dense, bottle-green, moderate-umbrella canopy, stiff leaves, dark brown, lengthways fissured bark, and distinct necklace-like pods.

The Umbrella Thorn Acacia *(Acacia tortilis)*, page 320, may grow very tall along rivers, but it has a flat, grey-green, thin-umbrella canopy of fine leaflets, hooked and straight thorns, and very tightly coiled pods.

GROWTH DETAILS

This is a single-trunked tree that branches to form a semi-circular to thick-umbrella canopy in the Thornveld areas. In Coastal Forests, it often branches high up and has a round canopy.

Leaves   Twice compound leaves are alternate and the leaf-stem is often covered in fine white hairs. The leaf may have 3 - 10 opposite or sub-opposite feather pairs, with fewer pairs in drier areas and more in wetter areas. There are 2 - 16 pairs of dark green leaflets that vary in shape and size, tending to be larger and rounder in the drier areas. The leaves are short and stiff, stand upright and hardly move in the wind.
(Leaf: 25 - 70 mm; leaflet: 4 - 20 x 2 - 12 mm)

Flowers   White flower-spikes in small groups appear long after the leaves in late spring or summer (October to January). (50 - 100 x 10 - 20 mm)

Pods   The flat bean pods have a pointed tip and turn red-brown to dark brown as they ripen. They are conspicuously veined, particularly when young. Ripe pods turn black and split open on the tree. They may remain on the tree until late autumn (December to May). (90 - 160 x 12 - 25 mm)

Thorns   Short, dark, sharply hooked thorns grow in pairs, far apart, below the leaf-buds. (3 - 9 mm)

Bark   The dark brown bark is rough and forms deep, lengthways fissures exposing yellowish under-bark. The branches often have dark, hooked thorns on knobs. Young branchlets are covered with fine, brown hairs that turn grey with age.

Seasonal changes

Deciduous. This tree may be difficult to identify in winter, but pods that remain on the tree help with identification.

	Oct	Nov	Dec	Jan	Feb	Mar	Apr	May	Jun	Jul	Aug	Sep
Leaf	▓	▓	▓	▓	▓	▓	▓	▓	▓			▓
Flower												
Fruit/Pod		▓	▓	▓	▓	▓	▓	▓				

315

SCENTED THORN ACACIA

Acacia nilotica

**THORN-TREE FAMILY
MIMOSACEAE**

SA Tree Number 179

AFRIKAANS Lekkerruikpeul, Swartsaadpeul **N. SOTHO** Mogohlo **SISWATI** isiThwethwe, umNcawe
TSONGA Nxangwa **TSWANA** Motšha **ZULU** umNqawe

The term **nilotica** refers to the distribution of the tree along the Nile River.

Where you'll find this tree easily

The Scented Thorn Acacia grows singly in small groups
or in large uniform groups, depending on the locality.

🌳 It is easiest to find in the Thornveld of the Bushveld-
Savannah (B), where it is one of the umbrella trees,
and is also common in the Moist Upper Grassland
of the Drakensberg Midlands (D), where it grows in
large stands.

🌳 It grows singly among other species of trees in other
areas of the Bushveld-Savannah (B), and can be found
Along Rivers (A), and in the Swamp, Low-Lying and
Scarp forests of the Coast (C).

A	B
C	D

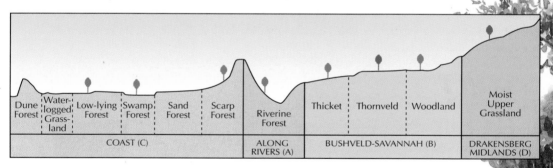

Dune Forest	Water-logged Grass-land	Low-lying Forest	Swamp Forest	Sand Forest	Scarp Forest	Riverine Forest	Thicket	Thornveld	Woodland	Moist Upper Grassland
COAST (C)						ALONG RIVERS (A)	BUSHVELD-SAVANNAH (B)			DRAKENSBERG MIDLANDS (D)

Striking features

• In the Thornveld, this single-stemmed tree branches
high up to form a dense, moderate-umbrella canopy.

• **The characteristic pods look similar to a beaded
necklace.**

• The bottle-green leaves are stiff and sturdy, and do not
move easily in the wind, despite small leaflets.

• **The flower-balls are yellow.**

• The thorns are paired, straight and white.

• The bark is dark brown and has deep lengthways
fissures.

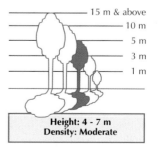

15 m & above
10 m
5 m
3 m
1 m

**Height: 4 - 7 m
Density: Moderate**

316

317

SCENTED THORN ACACIA
Acacia nilotica

Links with animals

The leaves are eaten by most browsers. The mature pods are eaten by Baboons, Black Rhino, Giraffe, Impala, Nyala and cattle, and seeds are dispensed in this way.

Human uses

The wood can be used as fence posts and to make furniture, especially riempie benches. Extracts of the unripe pods and bark were used for tanning. The gum is edible and can be used as glue. An extract of the bark was used to loosen phlegm, for treating eye diseases, as a tranquilliser and as an aphrodisiac. A root extract was used to cure tuberculosis, impotence, diarrhoea, haemorrhage, toothache, dysentery and gonorrhoea. Leaf extracts treated menstrual problems, eye infections, diarrhoea, sores caused by leprosy, stomach ulcers, indigestion and haemorrhage.

Gardening

This small tree will grow in most gardens. It is fairly frost- and drought-resistant and is easily grown from treated seeds, but grows slowly. The Scented Thorn Acacia attracts garden birds as it is always alive with insects and small reptiles. The tree starts to flower after five years.

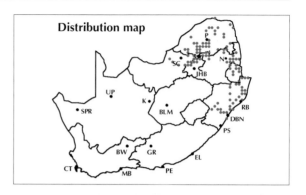

Distribution map

Durable; termite-resistant; fine texture; reddish-brown heartwood.

Look-alike trees   The Black Monkey Thorn Acacia *(Acacia burkei)*, page 312, is larger, with a striking dark green, dense, thick-umbrella canopy of larger rounded leaflets, hooked thorns, yellowish under-bark and pointed, flat bean pods.

The Red Thorn Acacia *(Acacia gerrardii)*, page 260, has a paler green, moderate-umbrella canopy, reddish bark and long, droopy leaves that form sleeves on thick branchlets.

The Umbrella Thorn Acacia *(Acacia tortilis)*, page 320, has a grey-green, thin-umbrella canopy, of fine feathery leaflets, hooked and straight thorns and tightly coiled pods.

The Paperbark Thorn Acacia *(Acacia sieberiana)*, page 348, has characteristically straw-coloured bark, which flakes off irregularly revealing deeper yellow under-bark. The thorns are straight and inconspicuous.

GROWTH DETAILS

In the Thornveld areas, this is a single-stemmed tree with branches that spread out to form a dense, fairly thick-umbrella canopy. In other areas, the canopy is rounder and the branches tend to droop downwards. The trunk is often crooked. The new leaves and twigs are green to reddish, and are covered by short, grey hairs.

Leaves The twice compound leaves are stiff, with 3 - 4 leaves clumped at the base of the thorns. They consist of 3 - 9 feather pairs and 8 - 20 pairs of leaflets. The leaflets are small, elliptic, and are bottle-green to bright green. The leaf-stems are hairy.
(Leaf: 40 - 50 mm;
leaflet: 4 x 1 mm)

Thorns The paired, white thorns are curved slightly backwards and are slightly hairy when young. The thorns grow from a single base and vary in size, with some being overdeveloped and others underdeveloped.
(50 - 90 x 4 mm)

Pods The long, narrow pods are characteristic. They are constricted between seeds, which gives the appearance of a beaded necklace. Young, green pods are covered with fine, reddish hairs, and turn black as they mature. The pods do not burst open but break up on the ground. Mature pods have a strong, sweet, "apple" scent irresistible to hoofed mammals (March to September). (120 - 200 x 31 - 15 mm)

Flowers The yellow, scented flower-balls with hairy stalks grow in groups of up to four on the new branchlets. The tree may flower most of the summer, although it is never covered in flowers (September to February).
(12 mm)

Bark The bark is reddish brown and smooth in young trees. In older trees, the bark is dark grey to black, and rough with lengthways fissures.

Seasonal changes

Semi-deciduous. Although these trees are difficult to identify without the pods, there are usually some pods on the tree all year round.

	Oct	Nov	Dec	Jan	Feb	Mar	Apr	May	Jun	Jul	Aug	Sep
Leaf												
Flower												
Fruit/Pod												

319

UMBRELLA THORN ACACIA

Acacia tortilis

THORN-TREE FAMILY
MIMOSACEAE

SA Tree Number 188

AFRIKAANS Haak-en-Steek, Withaakdoring **N. SOTHO** Mošu **SISWATI** isiThwethwe **TSONGA** Nsasani
TSWANA Mosu **ZULU** umSasane, isiThwethwe

The term **tortilis** refers to the twisted pods.

Where you'll find this tree easily

The Umbrella Thorn normally grows singly among other species of trees.

🌱 It is easiest to find as one of the umbrella trees in the Thornveld of the Bushveld-Savannah (B).

🌱 It can also be found in the Woodland of the Bushveld-Savannah (B), in the Sand and Low-lying forests of the Coast (C), and Along Rivers (A).

A	B
C	D

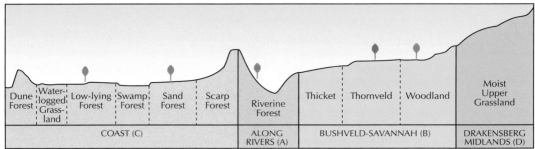

Dune Forest	Water-logged Grass-land	Low-lying Forest	Swamp Forest	Sand Forest	Scarp Forest	Riverine Forest	Thicket	Thornveld	Woodland	Moist Upper Grassland
COAST (C)						ALONG RIVERS (A)	BUSHVELD-SAVANNAH (B)			DRAKENSBERG MIDLANDS (D)

Striking features

- **This is one of the smaller umbrella trees in the Thornveld, with a particularly flat, thin-umbrella canopy of grey-green leaves.**

- The leaflets are very tiny, giving the umbrella canopy a fine feathery appearance.

- **There are some straight and some hooked thorns, singly or in pairs, in different arrangements on different branches.**

- Each pod is tightly coiled.

- In early summer the tree becomes covered in small, white flower-balls.

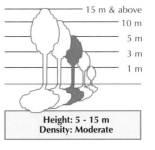

15 m & above
10 m
5 m
3 m
1 m

Height: 5 - 15 m
Density: Moderate

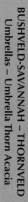

Largest tree currently registered

Diameter: 0,90 m

Girth: 2,83 m

Height: 17 m

Letaba Camp,
Kruger National Park

321

UMBRELLA THORN ACACIA
Acacia tortilis

Links with animals

The foliage is browsed by antelope and Giraffe. The pods are eaten by virtually every grazing or browsing mammal, often in preference to any other pod. The coiled pod shape makes it easy for grazers to pick up the pod without a mouthful of grit. The bark is also eaten by domestic and wild animals. Meyer's and Brownheaded Parrots relish the green seeds. Live plants are attacked by wood-borers and are often broken by Elephants.

Human uses

The wood makes good wagon beams, yokes and some furniture, if treated carefully. The gum is edible. The inner bark can be used to make rope. Bark is used in traditional medicine.

Gardening

It grows easily from seed and is extremely hardy, drought- and frost-resistant, but is rather slow growing. It is suitable as a bonsai tree.

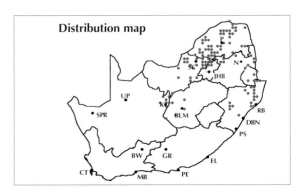

Distribution map

Rare; durable wood; reddish-brown heartwood; yellow sapwood; not suitable for turning.

Look-alike trees The Black Monkey Thorn Acacia *(Acacia burkei)*, page 312, is a much larger tree, with a striking dark green, dense, thick-umbrella canopy of larger, rounded leaflets, hooked thorns, yellowish under-bark and pointed, flat bean pods.

The umbrella form of the Red Thorn Acacia *(Acacia gerrardii)*, page 260, is the same size as the Umbrella Thorn Acacia, but has a paler green, moderate-umbrella canopy, with long, droopy leaves and reddish bark.

The Scented Thorn Acacia *(Acacia nilotica)*, page 316, has a less dense, bottle-green, moderate-umbrella canopy, with white thorns that curve slightly backwards, and necklace-like pods.

GROWTH DETAILS

This is a single-stemmed tree with a straight trunk. Branches come off horizontally to form a thick-umbrella canopy. Young trees tend to form a rounder canopy, with the thin branchlets and twigs intertwining.

Leaves   The twice compound leaves are grouped at the leaf-bud. The leaves are very small and delicate with 4 - 10 pairs of feathers and 5 - 15 pairs of leaflets. (Leaf: 20 - 30 mm; leaflet: 1 - 2 x 0,4 mm)

Flowers   Large numbers of sweet-scented, white flower-balls grow on older twigs, often shortly after rain (October to February). (5 - 10 mm)

Thorns   The sharp, white thorns are not always obvious. There are some straight and some hooked thorns, singly or in pairs, in different arrangements on different branches. (Straight thorn: 50 - 90 mm; hooked: 3 - 15 mm)

Pods   The pale brown, coiled pods hang in bunches. The pods do not split on the tree (December to June). (Pods up to 125 mm long when stretched out; 8 mm wide)

Bark   In mature trees the bark is dark grey and rough with deep, lengthways fissures. Younger trees have smoother, lighter bark.

Seasonal changes
This is a semi-deciduous tree.

	Oct	Nov	Dec	Jan	Feb	Mar	Apr	May	Jun	Jul	Aug	Sep
Leaf	▓	▓	▓	▓	▓	▓	▓	▓	▓	▓		
Flower	░	░	░									
Fruit/Pod		▓	▓	▓	▓	▓	▓	▓	▓			

323

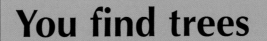

You find trees

BUSHVELD-SAVANNAH

– ROCKY OUTCROPS AND TERMITE MOUNDS

Once again two specialist Habitats tend to attract certain species of trees, and this makes them an easy place for newcomers to start. Develop a Search Image of these trees in this section, find them on Termite Mounds or Rocky Outcrops, and then you can look for them in the other places they grow in KwaZulu-Natal.

ROCKY OUTCROPS

TERMITE MOUNDS

Itala Game Reserve is one of South Africa's premier destinations, boasting a wide variety of magnificent Habitats.

CROW-BERRY KARREE
(COMMON CROW-BERRY)

Rhus pentheri

MANGO FAMILY
ANACARDIACEAE

SA Tree Number 391

AFRIKAANS Gewone Kraaibessie **N. SOTHO** Motšhakhutšhakhu **VENDA** Muṯasiri
ZULU inHlokoshiyane

The term **pentheri** is in honour of Dr A Penther, a Viennese botanist.

Where you'll find this tree easily

The Crow-berry Karree grows singly among other species
of trees.

- It is easiest to find on the Rocky Outcrops of the
  Bushveld-Savannah (B).
- It can also be found in the Low-lying Forest of the
  Coast (C), and Along Rivers (A).

A	B
C	D

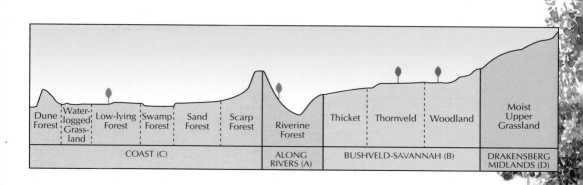

Dune Forest	Water-logged Grass-land	Low-lying Forest	Swamp Forest	Sand Forest	Scarp Forest	Riverine Forest	Thicket	Thornveld	Woodland	Moist Upper Grassland
COAST (C)						ALONG RIVERS (A)	BUSHVELD-SAVANNAH (B)			DRAKENSBERG MIDLANDS (D)

Striking features

- This is a small, sturdy, crooked-stemmed tree that
  branches low down to form a moderate semi-circular
  canopy.
- **The shiny, bright green, compound leaves have three
  leaflets, with margins that are often irregularly
  toothed along the upper third.**
- **The bark is dark brown and corky, breaking into
  deeply segmented blocks.**
- Thick, corky branches are visible between the leaves
  even in the outer canopy.

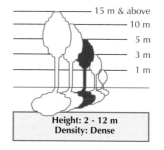

15 m & above
10 m
5 m
3 m
1 m

Height: 2 - 12 m
Density: Dense

CROW-BERRY KARREE
(COMMON CROW-BERRY)

Rhus pentheri

Links with animals

The roots of the tree are eaten by Vervet Monkeys, the bark by Black Rhino, and the leaves by Black Rhino, Impala, Nyala and Kudu. This tree provides fruit for birds throughout the year. Gurney's Sugarbirds nest in various Crow-berry and Karree *(Rhus)* species.

Human uses

The fruit of most types of Karree *(Rhus)* are edible by the handful, and taste like floury apples. Each fruit is a miniature, hollow version of a mango, and the taste comes from a thin layer of "jam" around the small, inner seed.

Gardening

This is an attractive garden tree. It is fairly frost- and drought-resistant.

Distribution map

Look-alike tree

The Fire-thorn Karree *(Rhus pyroides)* has very similar leaves but they are larger and paler, on long leaf-stems (45 mm), and it has smoother bark. See **Sappi Tree Spotting Highveld.**

Bark   The bark is dark brown and corky, breaking into deeply segmented blocks. The branchlets are covered by short, whitish hairs. The twigs may be spiny.

GROWTH DETAILS

This is a small, sturdy, single- or multi-stemmed tree with a crooked trunk. It branches low down to form a moderate, semi-circular canopy, with thick, corky branches and branchlets visible between the leaves in the outer canopy.

Leaves   The compound leaves have three elliptic leaflets and a hairy leaf-stem (20 - 30 mm). Young leaflets are also slightly hairy. Mature leaves are smooth and glossy, bright green above and slightly paler below. They have a yellow central vein and rounded tips. The margins are smooth or irregularly toothed along the upper third. (Central leaflet: 18 - 45 x 8 - 25 mm)

Flowers   Small, yellow, star-shaped flowers grow in sprays at the ends of the branches, in the angles formed by the leaves (August to March). (Spray: 35 - 45 mm)

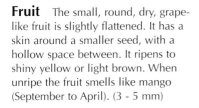

Fruit   The small, round, dry, grape-like fruit is slightly flattened. It has a skin around a smaller seed, with a hollow space between. It ripens to shiny yellow or light brown. When unripe the fruit smells like mango (September to April). (3 - 5 mm)

Spines   Scattered spines can often be seen on young branches.

Seasonal changes
Usually deciduous, but may be evergreen under favourable climatic conditions. The leaves turn yellow in Autumn.

	Oct	Nov	Dec	Jan	Feb	Mar	Apr	May	Jun	Jul	Aug	Sep
Leaf	■	■	■	■	■	■	■	■			■	■
Flower												
Fruit/Pod	■	■	■	■	■	■	■					■

329

HOOK THORN ACACIA
(COMMON HOOK-THORN)
Acacia caffra

THORN-TREE FAMILY MIMOSACEAE	SA Tree Number 162

AFRIKAANS Gewone Haakdoring, Katdoring **N. SOTHO** Motholo **TSONGA** Mbvhinya-xihloka
TSWANA Morutlhare **XHOSA** umThole, umNyamanzi **ZULU** umTholo

The term **caffra** refers to the Hebrew word 'Kafri', meaning 'person living on the land'.

Where you'll find this tree easily

The Hook Thorn Acacia often grows in groups.

🌳 It is easiest to find on rocky hill slopes of the Woodland of the Bushveld-Savannah (B), and the Moist Upper Grassland of the Drakensberg Midlands (D).

🌳 It can also be found in the Thornveld of the Bushveld-Savannah (B).

A	B
C	D

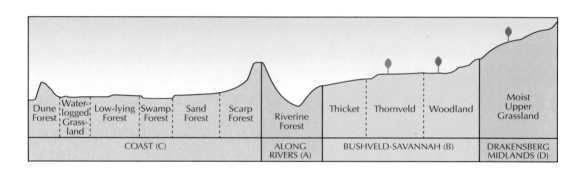

	COAST (C)					ALONG RIVERS (A)	BUSHVELD-SAVANNAH (B)			DRAKENSBERG MIDLANDS (D)
Dune Forest	Water-logged Grass-land	Low-lying Forest	Swamp Forest	Sand Forest	Scarp Forest	Riverine Forest	Thicket	Thornveld	Woodland	Moist Upper Grassland

Striking features

- It is a single-stemmed, V-shaped thorn tree which branches low down, so that the leaves sometimes obscure the trunk.

- The long, fine, twice compound leaves droop to form an irregular, soft, feathery canopy.

- **The hooked thorns are paired, and successive pairs are at right angles to each other.**

- **Early in spring the trees are covered by creamy-white flower-spikes.**

- The chocolate-brown, flat bean pods have pointed tips and grow in bunches.

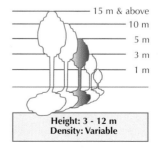

15 m & above
10 m
5 m
3 m
1 m

**Height: 3 - 12 m
Density: Variable**

331

HOOK THORN ACACIA
(COMMON HOOK-THORN)

Acacia caffra

Links with animals

This is a good fodder tree, the new leaves are particularly palatable.

Human uses

The wood is hard and makes good fence posts. It is also used to make tobacco pipes. The bark was used for tanning, and the bark, leaves and roots were believed to have magical properties. It was used to cleanse blood and to treat abdominal disorders in infants. This tree is still used in traditional medicine today.

Gardening

The Hook Thorn Acacia is easy to grow. It is an attractive tree that is frost- and drought-resistant, but grows slowly from seed. The seeds should be soaked in hot water before planting.

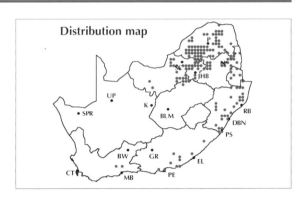

Distribution map

Look-alike trees

This tree may be confused with the Flame Thorn Acacia *(Acacia ataxacantha)*, page 108, which is a more scrambling tree, with scattered, hooked thorns (in no specific pattern) and purple-red pods.

The River Climbing Thorn Acacia *(Acacia schweinfurthii)*, page 19, is more creeper-like and has larger, dark green leaves (up to 190 mm); strong, hooked thorns that are arranged in rows on darker lines on the pale branchlets; creamy-white flower-balls (not spikes) and pale brown (not chocolate-brown) pods.

The Weeping Wattle *(Peltophorum africanum)* has larger, rounded leaflets, no thorns and pale, winged pods. See **Sappi Tree Spotting Lowveld**.

GROWTH DETAILS

This is a single-stemmed tree, often with a crooked trunk, that branches low down to form a V-shaped, irregular canopy. In areas of lower rainfall, the canopy is less dense than in areas where rainfall is high. The dark branches are usually obvious between the leaves. The long, drooping, twice compound leaves give the canopy a soft, feathery appearance.

Leaves   The large, twice compound, feathery leaves grow on thin, pale, reddish-brown twigs. There are 8 - 24 feather pairs, with 13 - 30 pairs of very small leaflets. The leaf-stem has small, hooked thorns. (Leaf: 60 - 230 mm; leaflet: 6 x 1,5 mm)

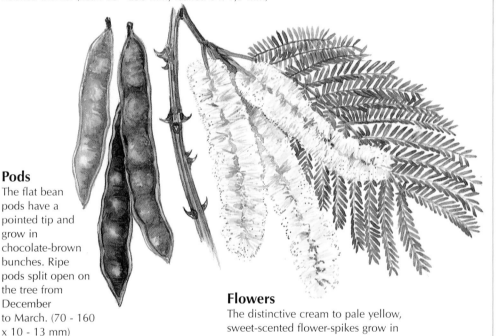

Pods
The flat bean pods have a pointed tip and grow in chocolate-brown bunches. Ripe pods split open on the tree from December to March. (70 - 160 x 10 - 13 mm)

Flowers
The distinctive cream to pale yellow, sweet-scented flower-spikes grow in bunches of 3 - 5, before the leaves appear (September to November). (60 - 140 mm)

Thorns   The short, hooked thorns grow in pairs at right angles to the next pair. Generally this is the least thorny of the thorn-trees in South Africa, although younger trees and branches tend to have more thorns. (5 mm)

Bark   The bark is dark grey-brown to black. It is rough and loosely peeling in places, showing light brown, streaky under-bark. New branches, branchlets and twigs are red-brown.

Seasonal changes
Deciduous. It is one of the first trees to come out in fresh green foliage in spring, and the leaves turn yellow and drop early in autumn.

	Oct	Nov	Dec	Jan	Feb	Mar	Apr	May	Jun	Jul	Aug	Sep
Leaf	■	■	■	■	■	■	■	■				■
Flower												
Fruit/Pod			■	■	■	■						

333

SPIKE-THORN (COMMON SPIKE-THORN)

Gymnosporia buxifolia (Maytenus heterophylla)

SPIKE-THORN FAMILY
CELASTRACEAE

SA Tree Number 399

AFRIKAANS Gewone Pendoring, Rooidoring **N. SOTHO** Mopadu **SISWATI** isiHlangu
TSONGA Xihlangwa **VENDA** Tshiphandwa **XHOSA** umQaqoba **ZULU** inGqwangane,
inGqwangane yehlanze

The term **buxifolia** refers to the shape of the leaves.

Where you'll find this tree easily

The Spike-thorn grows under widely different conditions.
It normally occurs singly among other species of trees.

🌱 It is easiest to find on Rocky Outcrops of the Bushveld-
Savannah (B) where it may be found in large uniform
groups.

🌱 It also occurs in most of the forests of the Coast (C),
Along Rivers (A), and in the Drakensberg Midlands (D).

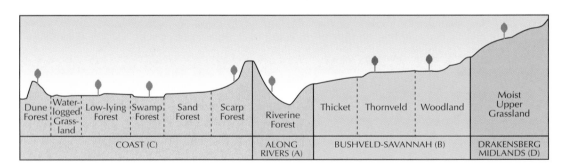

Dune Forest	Water-logged Grass-land	Low-lying Forest	Swamp Forest	Sand Forest	Scarp Forest	Riverine Forest	Thicket	Thornveld	Woodland	Moist Upper Grassland
COAST (C)						ALONG RIVERS (A)	BUSHVELD-SAVANNAH (B)			DRAKENSBERG MIDLANDS (D)

Striking features

* This is a single, crooked-stemmed, low-branching tree
with an angular, untidy outline formed by haphazardly
upward-growing branchlets.

* **The bark is characteristic in mature trees. It is dark
grey to brown and deeply furrowed, forming regular,
protruding blocks.**

* The pale grey-green leaves are clustered along the ends
of short, stubby twigs and branchlets forming "sleeves"
around them.

* **Abundant, white flowers smell like decaying meat in
spring.**

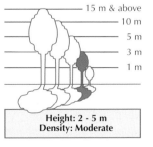

15 m & above
10 m
5 m
3 m
1 m

Height: 2 - 5 m
Density: Moderate

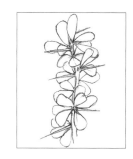

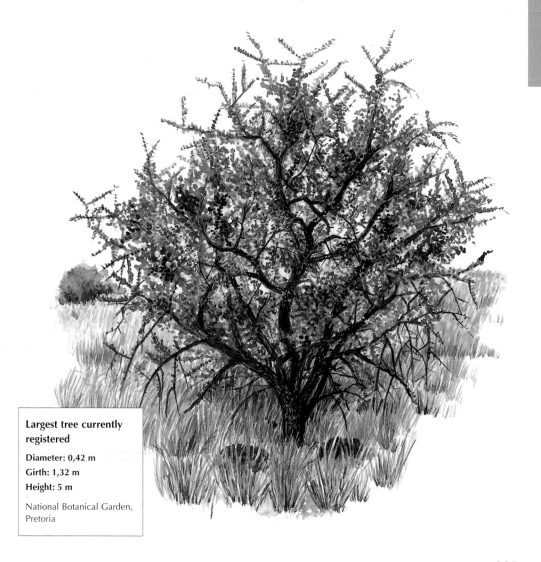

Largest tree currently registered

Diameter: 0,42 m
Girth: 1,32 m
Height: 5 m

National Botanical Garden, Pretoria

SPIKE-THORN (COMMON SPIKE-THORN)

Gymnosporia buxifolia (Maytenus heterophylla)

Links with animals

The contents of the fruit is eaten by birds such as the Cape White-eye. The flowers and young shoots are browsed by cattle in spring.

Human uses

The wood is used for carving and to make musical instruments, stools, spoons and knobkieries. It is widely used as a medicinal tree: the bark to treat dysentery and diarrhoea; the roots and thorns to treat colds, coughs and snakebites.

Gardening

This is not an attractive garden tree, and the smell of the flowers can be very offensive. However it is suitable as a bonsai tree.

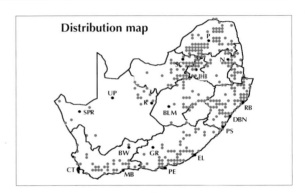

Distribution map

Colour varies from red to white; heavy, durable wood.

GROWTH DETAILS

The single, crooked trunk branches low down. It forms a moderate, irregular canopy, with large branches visible amongst the leaves. The branchlets grow at acute angles from the main branches. On the outside of the canopy they tend to grow haphazardly upwards like "hair standing on end", creating an angular, untidy outline. The leaves are tightly clustered along the ends of thick, stubby twigs and branchlets, forming "sleeves" around them.

Leaves The leaves are very variable in size and form. They are mostly elliptic with a very short leaf-stem, a broad tip and narrow base. The upper two thirds of the margin is often shallowly toothed. The upper-surface is pale grey-green and leathery. The net veining is visible on the under-surface. Young leaves have red edges. (Leaf: 10 - 90 x 4 - 50 mm)

Flowers From August to March, trees can be covered in clusters of white, star-shaped flowers growing on thick twigs. They are often strongly scented and smell like decayed meat to attract the flies that pollinate them. Similar male and female flowers grow on separate trees. (Individual: 2 - 7 mm)

Fruit A tough capsule encloses three seeds each covered in fatty pulp. Capsules grow in dense clusters close to the branchlets. Each capsule turns yellow to brown-red and bursts open when ripe from December to May. (3 - 10 mm)

Spines The straight spines are of variable length, but may be absent on some branches or trees. Young trees are generally more spiny than older trees. Leaf-buds grow just above the spines. Spines may often have leaves growing from them. (13 - 200 mm)

Bark The bark is dark grey to brown, rough and very deeply fissured to form regular protruding blocks in mature trees, and flat blocks in younger trees. The young branches and twigs are paler brown.

Seasonal changes

Evergreen. This tree is easy to identify throughout the year by its leaves and spines, and characteristic bark.

	Oct	Nov	Dec	Jan	Feb	Mar	Apr	May	Jun	Jul	Aug	Sep
Leaf												
Flower												
Fruit/Pod												

WEEPING BOER-BEAN

Schotia brachypetala

FLAMBOYANT FAMILY
CAESALPINIACEAE

SA Tree Number 202

AFRIKAANS Huilboerboon **ENGLISH** Fuchsia Tree **N. SOTHO** Molope **SISWATI** uVovovo
TSONGA Chochelamandleni, Nwavilombe **VENDA** Mulubi, Muṋunzwu **XHOSA** umGxam
ZULU iHluze, umGxamu

The term **brachypetala** means with short petals.

Where you'll find this tree easily

The Weeping Boer-bean grows singly.

🌱 It is easiest to find on the densely wooded Termite
Mounds of the Bushveld-Savannah (B).

🌱 It is also common along larger Rivers (A) and in the
Dune, Sand and Low-lying forests of the Coast (C).

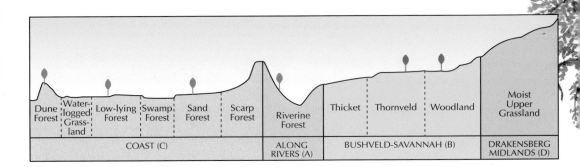

COAST (C)					ALONG RIVERS (A)	BUSHVELD-SAVANNAH (B)			DRAKENSBERG MIDLANDS (D)
Dune Forest	Water-logged Grass-land	Low-lying Forest	Swamp Forest	Sand Forest	Scarp Forest	Riverine Forest	Thicket	Thornveld	Woodland	Moist Upper Grassland

Striking features

- This is a single, crooked-trunked tree, branching low
  down into a few large branches to form a round, very
  dense, dark green canopy.

- On the canopy edge, branchlets and twigs tend to
  curve downwards.

- **The compound leaves often have four pairs of
  opposite, roundish leaflets with a pair of leaflets at
  the tip.**

- **Conspicuous, dense sprays of crimson flowers grow on
  older branches from August to November.**

- The brown, broad bean pods burst open on the tree
  from January to August.

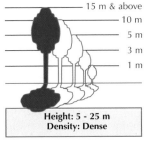

15 m & above
10 m
5 m
3 m
1 m

**Height: 5 - 25 m
Density: Dense**

Largest tree currently registered

Diameter: 1,05 m
Girth: 3,30 m
Height: 15 m

Nwanedi Resort,
Northern Province

WEEPING BOER-BEAN

Schotia brachypetala

Links with animals

Caterpillars of three charaxes butterflies feed on the leaves. The nectar is favoured by Baboons, Monkeys, Bees, other insects and especially by Sunbirds, such as the Greater and Doublecollared Sunbirds. Louries and Parrots eat the flower-buds and seeds. The leaves are eaten by Baboons, Giraffe, Kudu, Impala, Nyala and Black Rhino which also eat the bark. Vervet Monkeys eat the buds and seeds. The tree gets its name from the fact that the Spittle Bug sucks up sap and then ejects it as a froth, that drips from the tree.

Human uses

Roasted seeds are edible. The wood is used to make furniture and flooring blocks. Medicinal uses are recorded: bark extract for treatment of heartburn, pimples and diarrhoea, and to reduce swellings on the body; the smoke of burnt leaves inhaled to stop a bleeding nose; powdered leaves to speed up the healing process of tropical ulcers. The bark was used to make red dye for sangoma's cloaks and to ward off evil spirits.

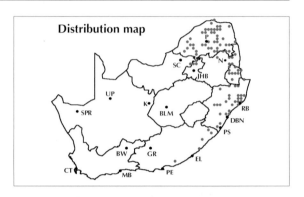

Distribution map

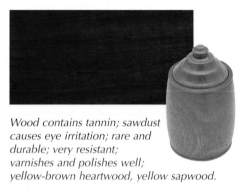

Wood contains tannin; sawdust causes eye irritation; rare and durable; very resistant; varnishes and polishes well; yellow-brown heartwood, yellow sapwood.

Gardening

This is a beautiful tree for the garden, germinating and transplanting well. The tree can withstand at least mild degrees of frost and long periods of drought.

Look-alike trees

The Dwarf Boer-bean (*Schotia capitata*) has very similar flowers, but it is a small shrub that is usually multi-stemmed, and the leaflets are smaller.

The White Milkwood (*Sideroxylon inerme*), page 342, also grows on termite mounds, but has simple, darker, shiny leaves and distinctive, blocky bark.

GROWTH DETAILS

It has a single, crooked trunk that is often gnarled and bent, and branches low down into a few large branches. The outer canopy, twigs and branchlets tend to hang downwards to form a rounded, very dense, dull, dark green canopy.

Leaves   The compound, alternate leaves have a pair of leaflets at the tip. There are four to six pairs of broadly elliptic to almost round leaflets which are opposite or sub-opposite, and have a slightly wavy margin. The central vein of each leaflet tends to be off-centre at the base, and the leaf-stem is winged. The leaves fall just before spring and are quickly replaced by new young leaves. (Leaf: 110 - 180; leaflet: 25 - 80 x 40 mm)

Flowers   Conspicuous, dense sprays of attractive, crimson flowers with prominent stamens grow at the end of the older branches. Flowers appear before or with the new leaves from August to November, but trees do not flower every year. (60 - 130 mm)

Pods   Brown, broad bean pods have a distinctly thickened edge. They burst open on the tree to reveal large, brown and yellow seeds (January to August). (60 - 160 mm x 40 mm)

Bark   The bark of younger trees is smooth and light brown. As the tree ages, the bark becomes darker and rougher.

Seasonal changes
Deciduous to semi-deciduous. The tree loses its leaves very late, and often over a very short period, just before the flowers appear. It is therefore easy to identify except for a short leafless period in early spring.

	Oct	Nov	Dec	Jan	Feb	Mar	Apr	May	Jun	Jul	Aug	Sep
Leaf												
Flower												
Fruit/Pod												

WHITE MILKWOOD
Sideroxylon inerme

MILKWOOD FAMILY
SAPOTACEAE

SA Tree Number 579

AFRIKAANS Witmelkhout, Melkhout **SISWATI** umNweba **TSONGA** Ximafana **VENDA** Muṭaladzi-vhufa
XHOSA umQwashu **ZULU** amaSethole, uMakhwelafingqane

The term **inerme** refers to the fact that the tree has no spines.

Where you'll find this tree easily

The White Milkwood is very widespread and normally
grows singly among other species of trees.

❦ It is easiest to find on the densely wooded Termite
Mounds of the Bushveld-Savannah (B), and in the
Low-lying Forest of the Coast (C).

❦ It is also common in most of the forests of the Coast
(C) and Along Rivers (A).

A	B
C	D

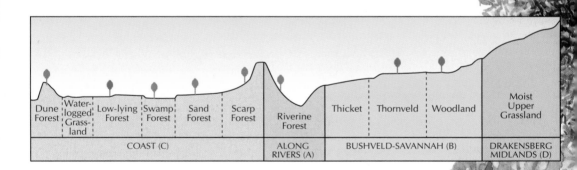

Dune Forest	Water-logged Grass-land	Low-lying Forest	Swamp Forest	Sand Forest	Scarp Forest	Riverine Forest	Thicket	Thornveld	Woodland	Moist Upper Grassland
COAST (C)						ALONG RIVERS (A)	BUSHVELD-SAVANNAH (B)			DRAKENSBERG MIDLANDS (D)

Striking features

• This large tree is single-stemmed with a thick trunk that
branches low down into several large branches to form
a dark green, dense, rounded canopy.

• **Leaves are leathery and shiny, with a conspicuous,
pale yellow central vein that can be seen from a
distance.**

• **The bark is light to dark brown and breaks into
distinct, rectangular blocks.**

• Leaves secrete small amounts of a milky latex when
broken off, or snapped in half.

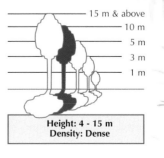

15 m & above
10 m
5 m
3 m
1 m

Height: 4 - 15 m
Density: Dense

342

Largest tree currently registered

Diameter: 1,02 m

Girth: 3,22 m

Height: 9 m

JU Blom
Renosterfontein,
Dist. Bredasdorp

343

WHITE MILKWOOD

Sideroxylon inerme

Links with animals

The fleshy fruit is not very palatable but is eaten by almost all fruit-eating birds and by Bats, Monkeys and Bushpigs. The leaves are also not very palatable. The flowers are eaten by Speckled Mousebirds.

Human uses

The wood is used for building boats, bridges, ploughs, hut poles, spoons and mills. A cupful of a root-bark infusion was drunk to banish bad dreams. The bark was used for gall-sickness in stock. Dried, powdered roots were taken for conjunctivitis, coughs and to treat fevers.

Gardening

This tree is suitable for coastal gardens. It can be grown from seed, and can withstand cold conditions.

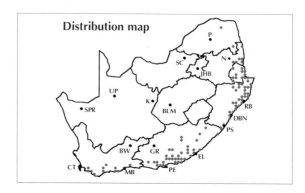

Distribution map

Very rare; yellow-brown heartwood; yellow sapwood; fine and even texture; very durable; turns well.

Look-alike tree The Coastal Red Milkwood (*Mimusops caffra*), page 154, has dark grey, coarse, fissured bark. The leaves are smaller, with rounded to square tips, and they form distinct rosettes at the tips of the branches.

GROWTH DETAILS

This can be a single- or multi-trunked tree with a thick crooked trunk that branches low down into several large branches to form a rounded, dense canopy.

Leaves   The simple, alternate leaves tend to be crowded towards the tips of the branches. The thick, leathery leaves are dark green above and distinctly paler below. They are elliptic and have a rounded to slightly pointed tip and a thickened margin. The central vein is conspicuous above and stands out below. The leaf-stem is distinct and about 20 mm long. (Leaf: 40 - 150 x 15 - 50 mm)

Fruit   The small, fleshy, berry-like fruit grows singly or in clusters between the leaves. It has a small, hairy tip and one to three yellow-brown seeds. The fruit turns black when ripe from February to September. (8 - 12 mm)

Flowers   Small, greenish-white, star-shaped flowers grow singly or in clusters on stalks in the angles formed by the lower leaves. They have an overpowering sweet smell. (October to April). (3 - 4 mm)

Bark   The bark is light to dark brown and smooth when young, but becomes darker and rougher with age and breaks into distinct rectangular blocks. The leaves are crowded towards the ends of thin twigs and branchlets.

Seasonal changes
Evergreen. This tree can be identified throughout the year.

	Oct	Nov	Dec	Jan	Feb	Mar	Apr	May	Jun	Jul	Aug	Sep
Leaf												
Flower												
Fruit/Pod												

You find trees

DRAKENSBERG-MIDLANDS – MOIST UPPER GRASSLAND

In the grassland very few species of tree flourish, because of the effects of fire and frost. As a result it is one of the simplest places to get to know a few trees. Check your position on the Maps, pages 406 - 409, and check Destination and Habitats Grids, pages 386 - 388 to be sure you know exactly which Ecozone you are in. Then you should easily be able to build up a Search Image of the two trees here.

Paperbark Acacia   p. 348
Sweet Thorn Acacia   p. 352

Paperbark Acacias are unusual and beautiful trees. They become a very special beacon to travellers through the Midlands as they do not grow above 900 metres.

PAPERBARK ACACIA

Acacia sieberiana

THORN-TREE FAMILY
MIMOSACEAE

SA Tree Number 187

AFRIKAANS Papierbasdoring, Verveldoring   **N. SOTHO** Mphoka, Mošibihla   **SISWATI** umNganduzi
TSONGA Nkowankowa   **TSWANA** Mokha   **VENDA** Musaunga, Muunga-luselo   **ZULU** umKhamba

The term **sieberiana** is in honour of Franz Wilhelm Sieber, a Bohemian botanist, plant collector and traveller of the early 18th century.

Where you'll find this tree easily

The Paperbark Acacia normally grows in loose, widespead groups.

❦ It is most easily found on the Moist Upper Grassland of the Drakensberg Midlands (D).

❦ It is also found in the Thornveld and Woodland of the Bushveld-Savannah (B), Along Rivers (A), and in the Low-lying Forest of the Coast (C).

A	B
C	D

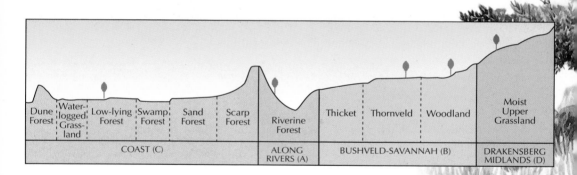

Dune Forest	Water-logged Grass-land	Low-lying Forest	Swamp Forest	Sand Forest	Scarp Forest	Riverine Forest	Thicket	Thornveld	Woodland	Moist Upper Grassland
COAST (C)						ALONG RIVERS (A)	BUSHVELD-SAVANNAH (B)			DRAKENSBERG MIDLANDS (D)

Striking features

- **This is a single-stemmed thorn tree with a moderately thick-umbrella canopy.**

- **The straw-coloured bark forms irregular flakes, revealing deeper yellow under-bark.**

- The twice compound leaves are yellowish-green and the ellipic leaflets are very narrow.

- Thick, flat pods hang in bunches and do not open on the tree.

- The thorns may not be conspicuous, but are straight and joined at the base when present.

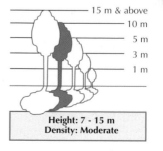

15 m & above
10 m
5 m
3 m
1 m

Height: 7 - 15 m
Density: Moderate

349

PAPERBARK ACACIA

Acacia sieberiana

Links with animals

The fallen pods and leaves are eaten by cattle and game, and in some parts of Natal it is planted as a fodder tree. Insects eat a large percentage of the seeds. The milk of cows that have eaten the pods has an unpleasant taste. The foliage, especially when wilted, contains a large amount of poisonous prussic acid and can be dangerous to stock. Many cases of poisoning are known. This tree attracts birds, especially the Barthroated Apalis, which gleans insects from flowers, leaves and tree-trunks. Sunbirds such as the Malachite, Greater Doublecollared, Scarletchested, Black and Collared, are also attracted to the tree.

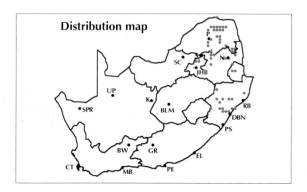

Distribution map

White heartwood and sapwood; coarse texture; varnishes well; saws cleanly if planks or logs are fed slowly and wood is not green; not suitable for turning.

Human uses

The wood is soft and easily destroyed by termites and borer beetles. The bark is very flammable. The gum is edible and has good adhesive properties. Bark and root extracts were used to treat arthritis and tapeworm infestations. Bark infusions were administered as enemas for pains in the back, and for chafing in the genital area. Root infusions were used as antiseptics and administered orally and as a wash to children with fevers or stomach ache.

Gardening

This is a fast-growing, attractive tree for the landscape garden. Although it is not very frost-resistant, it is probably more resistant than most other Acacias.

Bark

The bark is straw-coloured and corky, and forms flakes that may be large and obvious in some trees, and much smaller and almost inconspicuous in others.

GROWTH DETAILS

This is a single-stemmed tree with a straight trunk that branches low down into several large branches. These spread out horizontally to form a wide, moderately thick-umbrella canopy. Large branches are visible well into the canopy, and only form smaller branchlets and twigs high up. The branchlets are covered in golden hairs.

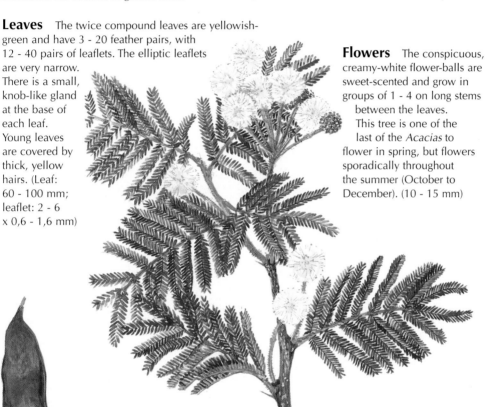

Leaves   The twice compound leaves are yellowish-green and have 3 - 20 feather pairs, with 12 - 40 pairs of leaflets. The elliptic leaflets are very narrow. There is a small, knob-like gland at the base of each leaf. Young leaves are covered by thick, yellow hairs. (Leaf: 60 - 100 mm; leaflet: 2 - 6 x 0,6 - 1,6 mm)

Flowers   The conspicuous, creamy-white flower-balls are sweet-scented and grow in groups of 1 - 4 on long stems between the leaves. This tree is one of the last of the *Acacias* to flower in spring, but flowers sporadically throughout the summer (October to December). (10 - 15 mm)

Pods   The stout, hard, woody, flat bean pods are hairy when young. The pods turn grey-brown when ripe and do not split open on the tree (March to June). (100 - 200 x 20 - 40 x 13 mm)

Thorns   The paired thorns are short, straight and white. However, they are not always well developed, and it may be difficult to see that this is a thorn-tree. (25 - 100 mm)

Seasonal changes
Deciduous. This tree can be identified by its bark throughout the year.

	Oct	Nov	Dec	Jan	Feb	Mar	Apr	May	Jun	Jul	Aug	Sep
Leaf												
Flower												
Fruit/Pod												

SWEET THORN ACACIA

Acacia karroo

**THORN-TREE FAMILY
MIMOSACEAE**

SA Tree Number 172

AFRIKAANS Soetdoring, Karoodoring **N. SOTHO** Mooka **SISWAT** isiNga **TSONGA** Munga
TSWANA Mooka, Mookana **VENDA** Muunga, Muunga-ludzi **XHOSA** umNga **ZULU** umuNga

The term **karroo** refers to the fact that this is the most conspicuous tree of the arid areas.

Where you'll find this tree easily

The Sweet Thorn Acacia is one of the most widespread
and common trees in South Africa.

- In KwaZulu-Natal it is found most easily in the Moist
  Upper Grassland of the Drakensberg Midlands (D),
  where it occurs in large, uniform groups of trees on the
  lower, grassy slopes of hills.

- It is also common in the Woodland and Thornveld
  of the Bushveld-Savannah (B), in the Waterlogged
  Grassland and Low-lying and Dune forests of the
  Coast (C), and Along Rivers (A).

A	B
C	D

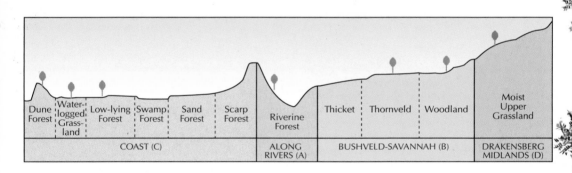

Dune Forest	Water-logged Grass-land	Low-lying Forest	Swamp Forest	Sand Forest	Scarp Forest	Riverine Forest	Thicket	Thornveld	Woodland	Moist Upper Grassland

COAST (C)	ALONG RIVERS (A)	BUSHVELD-SAVANNAH (B)	DRAKENSBERG MIDLANDS (D)

Striking features

- This is a single- or multi-trunked thorn tree that
  branches low down into several large branches to form
  a wide canopy.

- The bright green, twice compound leaves and straight,
  long, paired, white thorns contrast strongly with the
  dark, rough bark.

- **Many sturdy twigs in the outer canopy give this tree a
  spiky outline.**

- **The yellow, sweet-smelling flower-balls appear after
  rain, mostly from October to February.**

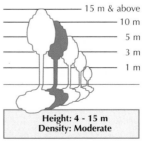

15 m & above
10 m
5 m
3 m
1 m

**Height: 4 - 15 m
Density: Moderate**

352

353

SWEET THORN ACACIA

Acacia karroo

Links with animals

This is a very good fodder tree, all parts of the tree being eaten by cattle and goats. Monkeys, Parrots and many other birds and insects are attracted to the flowers. Nitrogen-fixing bacteria are found on the roots of thorn trees. This increases the fertility of the soil in the vicinity and ultimately adds to the nutritional value of the grasses that grow there. Many grazers are attracted to these areas.

Human uses

The wood is used for building purposes. It was also used for spokes, wheels and yokes, as well as tool handles. The bark can be used to tan leather red. It is popular in certain areas for use as a Christmas tree.

Gardening

This is an attractive tree that is frost- and drought-resistant, and grows quickly. It is easy to grow from seed, but the seeds should be soaked in hot water before planting. It is suitable as a bonsai tree.

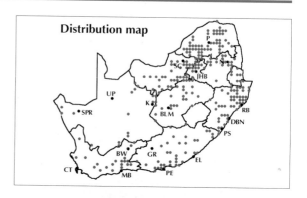

Distribution map

Durable, hard wood; yellow heartwood; tough.

GROWTH DETAILS

This single- or multi-stemmed tree often has a crooked trunk that branches low down. Multiple, small, sturdy, dark branchlets and twigs in the outer canopy give this tree a spiky outline. The moderate canopy is spreading but less dense in areas of lower rainfall. The young twigs grow in a zig-zag pattern, with the thorns on the angles. In the Coastal Forest this tree has a spindly form with a very straight trunk that branches high up to form delicate, thin branches and a moderate, irregular to umbrella-like canopy.

Leaves Twice compound leaves grow on small cushions in the angles of the thorns. There are 2 - 12 feather pairs, with 8 - 20 pairs of leaflets. (Leaf: 55 - 120 mm; leaflet: 3 - 10 x 1,5 - 5 mm). In the Dune Forest the leaflets are very fine (5 x 0,8 mm) and the leaves are shorter (about 30 mm).

Flowers The conspicuous, yellow flower-balls are sweet-scented and grow in sprays at the end of the twigs. This tree is one of the last of the thorn trees *(Acacias)* to flower in spring or early summer, often only after rain. It flowers intermittently throughout the summer. The trees may be covered in a mass of yellow flower-balls after good rains. (October to February) (10 - 13 mm)

Pods The bumpy bean pods curl into a sickle-shape. They split open on the tree when ripe, from January to May. Pods may stay on the tree for long periods. In the Coastal Forest the pods are constricted between the seeds giving them a beaded appearance. (50 - 130 x 6 - 13 mm)

Thorns The characteristic thorns are long, white and paired. The trees in the drier areas tend to be more thorny (30 - 150 mm). In the Coastal forests the thorns are long and swollen (up to 250 mm), and also grow on the main stem and large branches.

Bark The bark is dark red to black, rough and fissured lengthways, peeling loosely to reveal red under-bark. New branches, branchlets and twigs are smooth and red-brown. In the Coastal Forest the pale grey bark is smooth with white lines and narrow, widely-separated, lengthways fissures that are often reddish-brown.

Seasonal changes

Deciduous, but may be evergreen under favourable conditions. During drier periods and in drier areas, the leaves change into autumn colours before they drop.

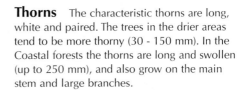

	Oct	Nov	Dec	Jan	Feb	Mar	Apr	May	Jun	Jul	Aug	Sep
Leaf												
Flower												
Fruit/Pod												

355

You find trees

ALONG RIVERS

The dense forests along the major rivers of KwaZulu-Natal are filled with a breathtaking variety of magnificent trees. But this Ecozone is for the well-established tree spotter only. However there are four trees which even a beginner will find easily, and these are listed below. There is a lot of competition on the river banks, so it is important to develop a clear Search Image from the Striking Features of each tree. Use the Seasonal Grid of each tree to help you know whether or not to look for fruit and flowers, and you should find the tree with very little trouble, along most rivers.

Brack Thorn Acacia	p. 358
River Bushwillow	p. 362
Sycamore Cluster Fig	p. 366
Tamboti	p. 370

The rivers of the Umfolozi Nature Reserve are fed by the Drakensberg to the east. They provide year-round water for forests that are far denser than the surrounding vegetation.

BRACK THORN ACACIA
Acacia robusta

THORN-TREE FAMILY MIMOSACEAE	SA Tree Number 183.1

AFRIKAANS Brakdoring **N. SOTHO** Mooka **TSONGA** Mvumbangwenya **TSWANA** Moga
XHOSA umNgampunzi **ZULU** umNgamanzi

The term **robusta** refers to the robust growth form of the tree.

Where you'll find this tree easily

The Brack Thorn Acacia normally grows singly among other species of trees.

🌲 It is most easily seen as one of the large trees growing Along Rivers (A).

🌲 It can also be found in the Sand and Low-lying forests of the Coast (C), as well in the Bushveld-Savannah (B), and the Moist Upper Grassland of the Drakensberg Midlands (D).

A	B
C	D

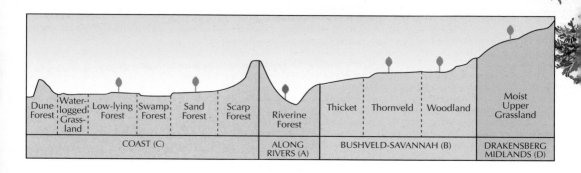

COAST (C)					ALONG RIVERS (A)	BUSHVELD-SAVANNAH (B)			DRAKENSBERG MIDLANDS (D)
Dune Forest	Water-logged Grass-land	Low-lying Forest	Swamp Forest	Sand Forest	Scarp Forest	Riverine Forest	Thicket	Thornveld	Woodland	Moist Upper Grassland

Striking features

- This is a large, upright thorn tree, with dense, dark green, feathery foliage, forming a spreading canopy.
- The branches stay thick, even towards their ends.
- **The leaves are relatively long and droopy for a thorn tree.**
- **There are prickly, dark "cushions" at the base of the new thorns and leaves.**
- The flower-balls are creamy-white and can be seen very early in the spring.
- The pods are thick and hang from the tree in prominent bunches.

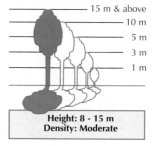

15 m & above
10 m
5 m
3 m
1 m

Height: 8 - 15 m
Density: Moderate

Largest tree currently registered

Diameter: 1,45 m

Girth: 4,55 m

Height: 16 m

Nwanedi Resort

BRACK THORN ACACIA

Acacia robusta

Links with animals

The leaves are browsed by Kudu. The flowers attract bees and butterflies.

Human uses

The wood is used for yokes and to make wedges to split other wood. The under-bark is used to make twine. The bark is used for tanning. This tree is still used in traditional medicine today. For example, steam from the boiled bark is inhaled to cure chest complaints and may also be used to treat skin ailments.

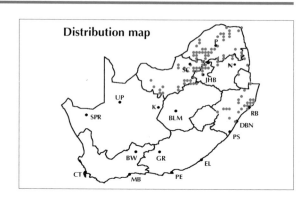

Distribution map

Dark heart-wood; paler sapwood; although tough, not suitable for timber; wood-borer beetles often found in wood.

Gardening

The Brack Thorn Acacia is very attractive in a well-watered, warm garden. It grows fast from seed, but is suitable as a bonsai tree.

Bark   The bark is dark grey, but paler on younger trees and branches. Older bark is closely grooved lengthways.

GROWTH DETAILS

This is a single-stemmed tree that divides into numerous large, upward-spreading branches, forming a dense, spreading canopy. Branches are thickened even towards their extremities, with the thick branches clearly visible in the canopy, giving the tree a robust appearance. In the Thornveld of the Bushveld-Savannah it often forms an umbrella-shaped canopy.

Leaves   The long, dark green leaves are twice compound and grow in clumps on prominent, dark, prickly "cushions". The leaflets grow at an acute angle to the leaf-stem, and tend to look half-closed. Leaves have 2 - 6 feather pairs, each consisting of 10 - 25 pairs of leaflets. (Leaf: 45 - 90 mm; leaflet: 7 - 12 x 3 - 4 mm)

Flowers
Conspicuous groups of up to 25 white flower-balls grow among the new green leaves in early spring (July to October). (15 - 20 mm)

Thorns   The straight, white, paired thorns grow from the prickly cushions that are joined at the base, which may be swollen. Some thorns may be underdeveloped. (70 - 110 mm)

Pods   The dark brown, slightly sickle-shaped pods are rounded at the tip. They grow in bunches and burst open on the tree when ripe. Pods may be seen on the tree during most of the summer (October to February). (70 - 160 x 13 - 30 mm)

Seasonal changes
Deciduous. The dark "cushions" remain on the branches even after the leaves have dropped, making identification possible even in winter.

	Oct	Nov	Dec	Jan	Feb.	Mar	Apr	May	Jun	Jul	Aug	Sep
Leaf	▓	▓	▓	▓	▓	▓	▓				▓	▓
Flower												
Fruit/Pod	▓	▓	▓	▓	▓							

RIVER BUSHWILLOW

Combretum erythrophyllum

BUSHWILLOW FAMILY
COMBRETACEAE

SA Tree Number 536

AFRIKAANS Riviervaderlandswilg, Vaderlandswilg **N. SOTHO** Moduba-noka **TSONGA** Mbvuva
TSWANA Moduba, Modubunoka **VENDA** Muvuvhu **XHOSA** umDubu, umDubi **ZULU** umDubu wehlanze

The term **erythrophyllum** refers to the red colour of the leaf in autumn.

Where you'll find this tree easily

The River Bushwillow grows singly, but where one is
found, others will often be found in the vicinity.

🌱 It is found almost exclusively Along Rivers (A)
throughout KwaZulu-Natal.

A	B
C	D

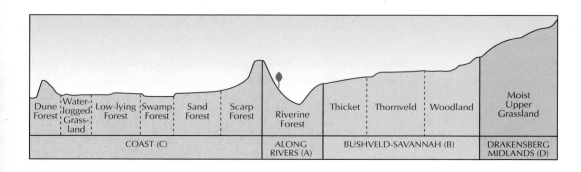

COAST (C)					ALONG RIVERS (A)	BUSHVELD-SAVANNAH (B)			DRAKENSBERG MIDLANDS (D)
Dune Forest	Water-logged Grass-land	Low-lying Forest	Swamp Forest	Sand Forest	Scarp Forest	Riverine Forest	Thicket	Thornveld	Woodland	Moist Upper Grassland

Striking features

- It is usually a single-trunked, wide-spreading, densely
  leafed tree.
- **The trunk and larger branches tend to meander, and
  old stems are often bumpy with irregular swellings,
  like cellulite.**
- The bark is smooth, pale yellowish and grey-brown,
  and flakes in irregular patches to expose rich, apricot-
  coloured under-bark.
- **It has typical, four-winged, bushwillow pods.**
- In the outer canopy new shoots are perpendicular.
  They carry pairs of simple, opposite leaves growing
  upright in a tight V-shape.

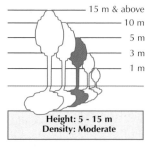

15 m & above
10 m
5 m
3 m
1 m

Height: 5 - 15 m
Density: Moderate

Largest tree currently registered

Diameter: 1,21 m

Girth: 3,80 m

Height: 16 m

W.G.F Neetling
Riverside Estate,
Dist. Pretoria

RIVER BUSHWILLOW

Combretum erythrophyllum

Links with animals

Leaves are eaten by Bushbuck. Fruit is eaten by Pied Barbets.

Human uses

The wood is used to make cattle troughs. The root is used as a purgative and as a cure for venereal disease, but may be very poisonous. This tree is still used in traditional medicine today.

Gardening

This is an attractive garden tree. Established trees are frost- and drought-resistant. The plant grows fast once established from seed. It is suitable as a bonsai tree.

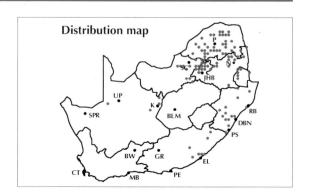

Distribution map

Yellow heartwood and sapwood; straight grain; turns well; suitable for carving.

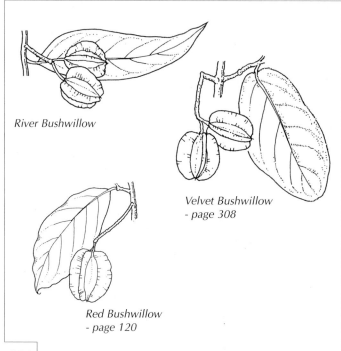

River Bushwillow

Velvet Bushwillow - page 308

Red Bushwillow - page 120

Bark The bark is yellowish, grey-brown and smooth, and peels irregularly to expose rich, apricot-coloured under-bark.

GROWTH DETAILS

This is a single-, sometimes multi-trunked tree with a crooked, trunk that branches low down to form a dense, spreading canopy. The trunk and larger branches of old trees are often bumpy with irregular swellings. Most older branchlets and twigs tend to hang down, but in the outer canopy new shoots are perpendicular.

Flowers   Inconspicuous, cream to yellow-green, roundish flower-balls appear just after the new leaves from August to November. (20 x 10 mm)

Leaves   In the outer canopy new shoots are perpendicular. They carry pairs of simple, opposite leaves growing upright in a tight V-shape. Simple, elliptic leaves are opposite on young twigs and tend to form whorls of three on older branches. They have a smooth margin, and the base and tip are tapering. The upper-surface of mature leaves is dark, shiny green, but young leaves are delicate green and often hairy. The under-surface of all leaves is slightly hairy. Leaves turn yellow and red in autumn. (Leaf: 50 - 130 x 20 - 65 mm)

Pods   The typical, four-winged bushwillow pods grow in abundance and turn pale brown to camel when they mature from January. Pods often stay on the tree until the next flowers appear in August. (10 - 15 mm)

Seasonal changes

Deciduous. The flaky bark and apricot under-bark, as well as the swellings on the trunk and the pods, are all characteristic and should aid identification throughout the year.

	Oct	Nov	Dec	Jan	Feb	Mar	Apr	May	Jun	Jul	Aug	Sep
Leaf												
Flower												
Fruit/Pod												

365

SYCAMORE CLUSTER FIG
(COMMON CLUSTER FIG)

Ficus sycomorus

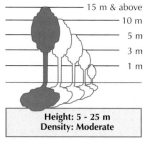

| **MULBERRY FAMILY** **MORACEAE** | **SA Tree Number 66** |

AFRIKAANS Geelstamvy, Gewone Trosvy **N. SOTHO** Mohlole, Mogo, Magobôya **TSONGA** Nkuwa
TSWANA Motšhaba **VENDA** Muṱole, Muhuyu-lukuse **ZULU** umNcongo

The term **sycomorus** is derived from the Greek word meaning fig-mulberry.

Where you'll find this tree easily

The Sycamore Cluster Fig grows singly.

🌿 It is common Along Rivers (A) and streams with permanent water.

🌿 It can also be found in the Dune, Swamp and Sand forests of the Coast (C).

A	B
C	D

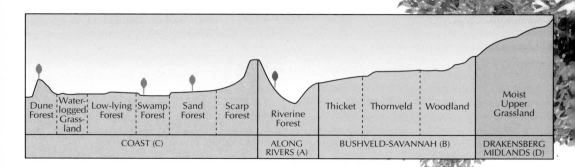

Dune Forest	Water-logged Grass-land	Low-lying Forest	Swamp Forest	Sand Forest	Scarp Forest	Riverine Forest	Thicket	Thornveld	Woodland	Moist Upper Grassland
COAST (C)						ALONG RIVERS (A)	BUSHVELD-SAVANNAH (B)			DRAKENSBERG MIDLANDS (D)

Striking features

- **This is a very large tree with yellowish-green to pink bark, growing on the banks of rivers with permanent water.**

- The bark is smooth and peels in thin papery sections to reveal pinkish under-bark.

- It has a fluted, relatively short, but massive trunk which is often buttressed and gnarled. Pale branches are clearly visible between the leaves, even towards the edge of the canopy.

- The canopy is wide, formed by simple, almost round leaves.

- **The fleshy figs grow in short, branched masses on the trunk and main branches.**

15 m & above
10 m
5 m
3 m
1 m

Height: 5 - 25 m
Density: Moderate

367

SYCAMORE CLUSTER FIG
(COMMON CLUSTER FIG)
Ficus sycomorus

Links with animals

Baboons, Monkeys and Bushbabies are very fond of the fruit on the tree. Many other animals eat the fallen fruit, e.g. Grey Duiker, Kudu, Nyala, Bushbuck, Impala, Bushpigs and Warthogs. Fish eat the fruit which fall in the water and it is also a favourite of fruit-eating birds. Black Rhino eat the leaves and fruit.

Human uses

The fruit is edible but very tasteless. Strong rope can be made from the inner bark. In Egypt mummy cases, made of this wood, were found intact after thousands of years. Dry wood was used as the base block when making fire by friction. Medicinally, the tree had many uses: the bark and latex to treat coughing, diarrhoea, inflamed throats; the milky latex for inflammation.

Gardening

This is a very attractive tree for a large garden, but it does have an invasive root system. It is best cultivated from cuttings and grows fairly fast. It is tender to frost, can withstand some cold, but needs substantial water. It does very well in a well-watered container, and is popular as a bonsai.

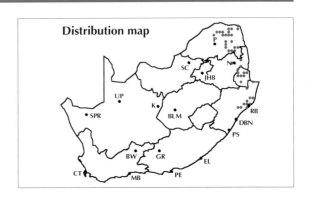

Distribution map

Rare wood; yellow-brown heartwood; grey sapwood; not suitable for turned articles; varnishes well.

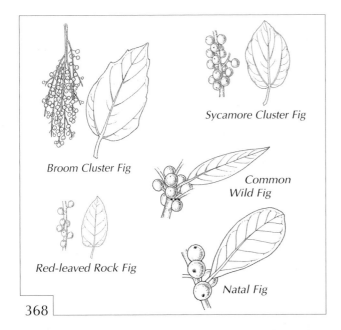

Sycamore Cluster Fig

Broom Cluster Fig

Common Wild Fig

Red-leaved Rock Fig

Natal Fig

Other common fig trees   The
Natal Fig (*Ficus natalensis*) is a strangler with aerial roots hanging from the branches. The similar leaves have a very short stem; the central vein stands out from the under-surface, but the side veins are not very obvious. The figs are hairless, have long stalks and turn yellow-red when ripe (September to March).

The Common Wild Fig (*Ficus thonningii*) is also a strangler with aerial roots. The leaves are small and dark green, and often have a long stem (up to 45 mm). The veins are prominent on both surfaces. The small, hairy figs (10 mm) have no stalks and turn red when ripe (August to December).

The Red-leaved Rock Fig (*Ficus ingens*) has very similar leaves but the margins are smooth and the figs grow on short stalks in the leaf-angles. (10 - 13 mm)

Also see the Broom Cluster Fig (*Ficus sur*), page 182.

GROWTH DETAILS

This is a very large, single-stemmed tree with a fluted or buttressed, relatively short trunk. The trunk branches low down, horizontally and then upwards to form a dense, wide-spreading canopy.

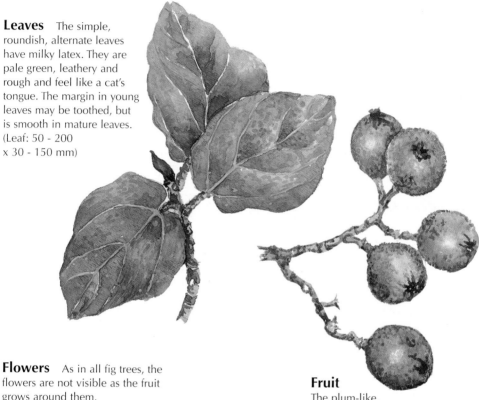

Leaves   The simple, roundish, alternate leaves have milky latex. They are pale green, leathery and rough and feel like a cat's tongue. The margin in young leaves may be toothed, but is smooth in mature leaves. (Leaf: 50 - 200 x 30 - 150 mm)

Flowers   As in all fig trees, the flowers are not visible as the fruit grows around them.

Bark   The yellowish-green to pinkish bark is smooth and peels in thin, straw-coloured, papery sections to reveal pinkish under-bark. In the forests the bark is often much greener, almost like that of a Fever Tree Acacia.

Fruit
The plum-like, fleshy figs grow in dense, short-branched clusters on the larger branches. They are covered in fine hairs and turn pinkish when ripe. The figs ripen throughout the year, and trees can produce up to four crops annually. (20 - 50 mm)

Seasonal changes
Evergreen to semi-deciduous. The leaves turn yellow and fall throughout the year. It is easy to recognise by its leaves and figs throughout the year.

	Oct	Nov	Dec	Jan	Feb	Mar	Apr	May	Jun	Jul	Aug	Sep
Leaf												
Flower												
Fruit/Pod												

TAMBOTI

Spirostachys africana

EUPHORBIA FAMILY
EUPHORBIACEAE

SA Tree Number 341

AFRIKAANS Tambotie, Sandelhout **N. SOTHO** Morekuri **SISWATI** umThombotsi, umThombothi
TSONGA Ndzopfori **TSWANA** Morukure **VENDA** Muonze **ZULU** umThombothi

The term **africana** means of Africa.

Where you'll find this tree easily

Tamboti grow as a single, tall tree, or in larger groups of
smaller trees, forming groves.

🌱 It is easiest to find Along Rivers (A).

🌱 It can also be found on stream banks and on clay areas
of the Woodland of the Bushveld-Savannah (B), and in
most of the forests of the Coast (C).

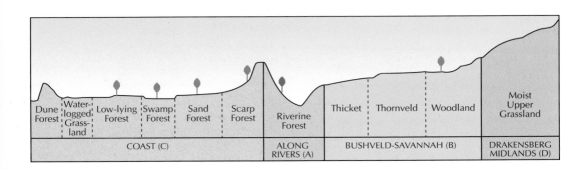

Striking features

- It has a single, straight, high-branching trunk.

- The narrow canopy is dense and usually has some red
leaves amongst the green.

- **The bark is characteristic dark brown to black, thick,
rough and deeply cracked into distinctive, very regular
rectangles.**

- **The simple, alternate leaves have finely toothed
margins and produce a white, milky, irritant latex
when broken off.**

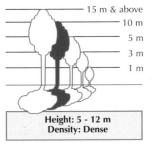

Height: 5 - 12 m
Density: Dense

Largest tree currently registered

Diameter: 1,85 m

Girth: 5,81 m

Height: 13 m

S van Schalkwyk
Diepkuil,
Dist. Thabazimbi

TAMBOTI

Spirostachys africana

Links with animals

The fallen seeds are eaten by Crested Guineafowl, Francolin and Doves. Black Rhino eat the young branches. Giraffe eat leaves on the tree and dry fallen leaves are eaten by Kudu, Nyala, Impala and Vervet Monkeys. The seeds are often infected with the caterpillars of the Knotthorn Moth (*Melanobasis*) which cause the seeds to jump when they straighten themselves inside.

Human uses

The milky latex is poisonous and extremely irritant. Toxic fumes from wood, used as firewood, can cause severe illness. The latex was used to treat boils and toothache, and to stupefy fish, making them easier to catch. Extracts of the roots and bark were used as an eye-wash, to cure stomach ulcers and for kidney ailments. The powdered bark was used as perfume, and pieces of the wood put among clothing act as insect repellent.

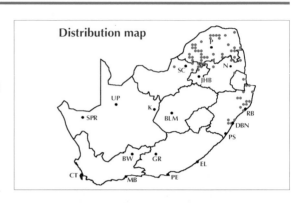

Distribution map

Hard wood; oily nature; turns easily; plane in direction of the grain; does not glue well; suitable for decorative veneer.

Gardening

This tree can be very attractive in a large garden. It is fairly drought- and frost-resistant. It grows well from seed but grows slowly.

The single, straight trunk is high-branching with main branches growing upwards. In Riverine Forests it forms a narrow, dense canopy. Young trees often have multiple stems. Young branchlets stand out above the canopy with leaves spirally arranged along the entire length of the branchlet. Being a member of the *Euphorbia* family, it produces a small amount of poisonous and irritant, milky latex when any part of the tree is broken.

Leaves   Simple, alternate, dull green leaves are arranged in a spiral along the branchlets. They have finely toothed margins and a short leaf-stem. New, red leaves are often visible among the older green leaves. Leaves show striking yellow and red autumn colours. (30 - 80 mm)

Flowers   In late winter, before the leaves appear, Tamboti trees have a distinct red sheen caused by the red flower-spikes (July to November). (15 - 30 mm)

Fruit
The dry, brown capsules are three-lobed, and open on hot summer days with an audible explosion. Seeds infected by Knotthorn caterpillars appear to jump, and are known as jumping beans. (Mature September to November). (10 mm)

Spines   Young trees often have conspicuous spines up to 150 mm, which make them look like a different species.

Bark   The bark is characteristic dark brown to black, thick, rough and neatly cracked into distinctive, very regular rectangles. In young trees the bark is smooth and grey and often has white patches.

Seasonal changes
Deciduous to evergreen, depending on Habitat. Flower-spikes have a red sheen; leaves redden before dropping; new leaves are red. The bark makes identification possible all year.

	Oct	Nov	Dec	Jan	Feb	Mar	Apr	May	Jun	Jul	Aug	Sep
Leaf												
Flower												
Fruit/Pod												

Family Features, Grids and Maps

All of these sections are designed to add to your knowledge base, rapidly and easily. They are also an inspirational centre, inviting you to travel to other places, check out other Habitats, and even try a few new hobbies!

Along the edges of swamps and lakes, the Wild Cotton Tree forms inpenetrable tangles of branches and stems. Above is a canopy of green, dotted with yellow hibiscus-shaped flowers.

Family Features

All living things have relatives that share certain distinctive features. In plants this can be similar growth form, seed dispersal mechanism, or leaf, flower, fruit or pod structure. Scientists classify plants by their flower features which can be minute details, hardly visible to the naked eye. As a pleasure-seeking tree spotter you will find that knowing some visible similarities between family members will help you build up methods of recognising new trees wherever you go in Africa or further afield. The scientific classifications tend to change quite regularly, so these statistics of world and South African distribution, are simply there to give you an idea of the family size and distribution.

The information includes the Ecozones where you are most likely to find each family member. This is shown by the letter A, B, C or D in brackets. With this information you can look for related trees in one area. Remember to check their Habitat distribution on the Ecozone Tree Lists, pages 32 - 35.

BUSHWILLOW *Combretaceae*
Worldwide – 60 genera, 400 species; South Africa – well represented with 5 genera, 41 tree species.
Family Features
• Leaves – simple
• Flowers – spiked
• Seeds – four-winged
Trees in this book
Red Bushwillow (B) p 120; River Bushwillow (A) p 362; Velvet Bushwillow (A, B, C) p 308

CABBAGE TREE *Araliaceae*
Worldwide – 54 genera, 650 species; South Africa – 15 tree species. Ivy family member; widely grown in gardens.
Family Features
• Leaves – conspicuous, large, palm-like
Trees in this book
Common Cabbage Tree (A, B, C, D) p 90

CAPE MYRTLE *Myrsinaceae*
Worldwide – 32 genera, 1 000 species, tropic and subtropic areas; South Africa – 5 shrub or tree species.
Family Features
• Leaves – simple, usually alternate, gland-dotted
Trees in this book
Cape Beech (A, B, C) p 206

CITRUS/BUCHU *Rutaceae*
Worldwide – 100 genera, 800 species, warm temperate areas; South Africa – 8 genera, 26 species. Some have medicinal properties.
Family Features
• Leaves – strong-scented, gland-dotted
Trees in this book
Small Knobwood (A, B, C) p 218; White Ironwood (A, B, C) p 242

COTTON *Malvaceae*
Worldwide – 43 genera, 1 700 species warmer areas; South Africa –3 genera, 8 shrub and herb species.
Family Features
• Leaves – lobed, star-shaped hairs, simple
• Flowers – five-petals, whorled, cup-like
Trees in this book
Wild Cotton Tree (C) p 88

CRANE-FLOWER *Strelitziaceae*
Worldwide – tropical Africa; South Africa – 5 species.
Family Features
• Leaves – stalked, simple, alternate, fan-like
• Flowers – resemble head of crane
Trees in this book
Natal Banana (A, C) p 82

DAISY *Asteraceae*
Worldwide – 200 genera, 2 000 species; South Africa – about 40 shrub and/or tree species.
Family Features
• Flowers – dense, clustered heads resemble single flower; attractive bloom in some species
Trees in this book
Camphor Bush (B, C) p 252; Coast Silver Oak (A, B, C) p 150

DOGWOOD *Rhamnaceae*
Worldwide – 51 genera, 600 species; South Africa – 7 genera, 20 tree species.
Family Features
• Leaves – shiny, simple, alternate
• Flowers – small, inconspicuous, nectar-rich
Trees in this book
Buffalo-thorn (A, B, C, D) p 292; Red Ivory (A, B, C, D) p 282

DRAGON TREE *Dracaenaceae*
Worldwide – 50 species; South Africa – 4 species.
Ancient tree history.
Family Features
- Leaves – long, tapering, parallel-veined,
  clustered at end of branch
- Flowers – lily-like
- Sap – red in certain species
Trees in this book
Large-leaved Dragon Tree (A, C) p 80

EBONY *Ebenaceae*
Worldwide – 2 genera, 485 species, mostly
tropical regions; South Africa – 2 genera, 35 tree
species. Wood traded by merchants in ancient
times.
Family Features
- Very variable
- Leaves – simple, smooth margin
Trees in this book
Bush Guarri (B, C) p 270;
Magic Guarri (B, C) p 256

ELM *Ulmaceae*
Worldwide – 16 genera, over 1 000 species,
tropical and temperate regions, mostly in
Northern Hemisphere; South Africa – 2 genera,
5 tree or shrub species.
Family Features
- Leaves – simple, alternate
- Flowers – small, greenish, stamen appears
  opposite each petal-like sepal
Trees in this book
Pigeonwood (A, B, C) p 194;
Thorny Elm (A, C) p 222

EUPHORBIA *Euphorbiaceae*
Worldwide – 2 000 species; South Africa –
100 species (2nd largest woody family).
Family Features
- Latex – milky or watery, often poisonous
- Leaves – simple, usually alternate, toothed
  margin
- Fruit – small, three-lobed capsule
Trees in this book
Mitzeeri (A, B, C) p 214; Rubber Euphorbia
(B, C, D) p 84; Tamboti (A, B, C) p 370;
Tassel Berry (A, B, C) p 124;
Tree Euphorbia (A, B, C) p 86

FLAMBOYANT *Caesalpiniaceae*
Worldwide – 162 genera, 2 000 species, mainly
tropics; South Africa – 50 species (one of the
largest woody families).
Family Features
- Leaves – compound, alternate, paired leaflets at
  tip, swelling at base of leaf-stem
- Flowers – large, showy, 5 symmetrically
  arranged petals.
- Seeds – encased in pods, usually cover more
  than one seed.
Trees in this book
Weeping Boer-bean (A, B, C) p 338

GARDENIA *Rubiaceae*
Worldwide – 400 genera, 5 000 - 6 000 species,
warmer parts of the world; South Africa –
47 genera.
Family Features
- Leaves – hairy pits in axils of veins (under-
  surface), untoothed margin, opposite or
  whorled
Trees in this book
White Gardenia (C, D) p 136;
Wild Medlar (A, B, C, D) p 176

LINDEN *Tiliaceae*
Worldwide – 44 genera, 500 species; South Africa
– 30 tree and shrub species.
Family Features
- Leaves – simple, alternate, 3-veined from base,
  toothed margin, star-shaped hairs
Trees in this book
Cross-berry Raisin (A, B, C) p 104

MAHOGANY *Meliaceae*
Worldwide – In Asia a well-known seringa; South
Africa – 6 genera, 20 tree and shrub species
Family Features
- Leaves – alternate, compound, crowded
  towards end of branchlets
- Flowers – stamens fused into a tube, 5 free
  petals
Trees in this book
Cape Ash (A, B, C) p 274;
Natal Mahogany (A, B, C)
p 278

Sweet Thorn
Acacia - p. 352

MANGO *Anacardiaceae*
Worldwide – 60 genera; South Africa – 10 genera, 80 species.
Family Features
- Leaves – three leaflets (Karree members only)
- Flowers – separate male and female flowers, on separate trees
- Fruit – edible in most species
- Bark – rich in resin
Trees in this book
Crow-berry Karree (A, B, C) p 326; Forest Karree (A, B, C) p 230; Marula (A, B, C) p 304; Red Beech (A, B, C) p 234; Wild Plum (A, C) p 246

MANGROVE *Rhizophoraceae*
Worldwide – 3 families, 5 species; South Africa – 3 species.
Family Features
- Leaves – simple, opposite, hairless
Trees in this book
Black Mangrove (C) p 160

MILKWOOD *Sapotaceae*
Worldwide – 40 genera, 600 species; South Africa – 7 genera, 22 species. Chewing gum made from rubber-like juice of one species.
Family Features
- Leaves – young leaves, rusty colour
- Latex – milky
- Fruit – fleshy
Trees in this book
Coastal Red Milkwood (C) p 154; White Milkwood (A, B, C) p 342

MULBERRY *Moraceae*
Worldwide – tropical and sub-tropical areas, 1 000 species; South Africa – *Ficus* genus, 35 species.
Family Features
- Leaves – alternate, rounded leaf-buds
- Latex – milky
Trees in this book
Broom Cluster Fig (A, B, C) p 182; Giant-leaved Fig (C) p 76; Sycamore Cluster Fig (A, C) p 366

MYRRH *Burseraceae*
Worldwide – 200 species, mainly Africa and Arabia; South Africa – 26 species. Linked to biblical times, produced frankincense and myrrh from resin.
Family Features
- Latex – milky
- Leaves – compound, aromatic
- Bark – thin, papery, flaky (some species)
Trees in this book
Red-stem Corkwood (A, B, C) p 94

MYRTLE *Myrtaceae*
Worldwide – large tropical and sub-tropical family, 2 000 species; South Africa – 25 species.
Family Features
- Leaves – simple, opposite, smooth margin
- Flowers – many stamens
- Fruit – tipped with remains of flower
Trees in this book
Water Berry (A, B, C) p 172

OLEANDER *Apocynaceae*
Worldwide – large family; South Africa – 14 genera, 40 tree species. Some species medicinal properties, others extremely poisonous.
Family Features
- Flowers – attractive
- Latex – milky or watery
Trees in this book
Common Poison Bush (A, B, C, D) p 186

OLIVE *Oleacee*
Worldwide – 40 genera, 300 species; South Africa – 5 genera, 15 species. Associated with humans since 3 000 BC.
Family Features
- Leaves – opposite, smooth margin
- Branchlets – raised, white dots
Trees in this book
Wild Olive (A, B, C) p 286

PALM *Arecaceae*
Worldwide – 140 genera, 1 000 species; South Africa – 7 shrub or tree species. Strongly associated with humans.
Family Features
- Flowers – small, spray enclosed in sheath
- Fruit – berry-like
Trees in this book
Date Palm (A, C) p 72; Lala Palm (A, C) p 78

PARA-NUT *Lecythidaceae*
Worldwide – 18 genera, 300 species; South Africa – 1 species.
Family Features
- Leaves – alternate, large and simple
- Flowers – beautiful, long sprays
Trees in this book
Powder-puff Tree (C) p 168

PEA *Fabaceae*
Worldwide – 437 genera, 11 300 species;
South Africa – 2 genera, 35 tree species.
Family Features
• Flowers – pea-like, broad, erect upper petal,
  two narrower wings on both sides, two lowest
  petals joined (boat-like keel)
• Seeds – encased in pods usually cover more
  than one seed.
Trees in this book
Climbing Flat-bean (A, C) p 100; Coral Tree
(A, B, C, D) p 210; Thorny Rope (A, B, D) p 226;
Umzimbeet (A, C) p 132

SNEEZEWOOD *Ptaeroxylaceae*
African family; South Africa – 1 species
Family Features
• Leaves – opposite, compound, single leaflet at tip
Trees in this book
Sneezewood (A, B, C) p 238

SPIKE-THORN *Celastraceae*
Worldwide – 60 - 70 genera; South Africa –
60 tree species, widely distributed.
Family Features
• Very variable
Trees in this book
Kooboo-berry (A, B, C) p 116;
Spike-thorn (A, B, C, D) p 334

STAR CHESTNUT *Sterculiaceae*
Worldwide – 50 genera, 1 000 species; South
Africa – 3 genera. Cocoa tree family member.
Family Features
• Leaves – star-shaped clumps of hairs (visible
  only with magnifying glass)
Trees in this book
Wild Pear (A, B, C, D) p 140

THORN-TREE *Mimosaceae*
Worldwide – 58 genera, 3 100 species, mainly
tropical regions; South Africa – 8 genera, 100 tree
species (3rd largest woody family).
Family Features
• Leaves – twice compound, the leaves of certain
  species fold up at night
• Flowers – balls or spikes, protruding stamens
• Seeds – protected by palatable bean-like pods
Trees in this book
Black Monkey Thorn Acacia (A, B, C) p 312;
Brack Thorn Acacia (A, B, C, D) p 358;
Fever Tree Acacia (A, C) p 74; Flame Thorn Acacia
(A, B, C) p 108; Flat Crown Albizia (C) p 190;
Hook Thorn Acacia (B, D) p 330;
Knob Thorn Acacia (A, B, C) p 296;
Large-leaved Albizia (A, B, C) p 300;

Paperbark Acacia (A, B, C, D) p 348;
Red Thorn Acacia (B, C) p 260;
Scented Thorn Acacia (A, B, C, D) p 316;
Sickle Bush (A, B, C) p 264;
Sweet Thorn Acacia (A, B, C, D) p 352;
Umbrella Thorn Acacia (A, B, C) p 320

VERBENA *Verbenaceae*
Worldwide – 73 genera, 2 000 species; South
Africa – 22 species. Chinese Hat plant is popular
garden exotic shrub; Tick Berry is noxious weed.
Family Features
• Leaves – aromatic when crushed
• Twigs – four-angled
Trees in this book
Tinderwood (A, B, C) p 128;
White Mangrove (C) p 164

WHITE PEAR *Icacinaceae*
Worldwide – 48 genera; South Africa – 2 genera.
Family Features
• Leaves – simple
• Flowers – bisexual, regular
• Fruit – berry-like
Trees in this book
White Pear (A, B, C) p 198

WILD ELDER *Loganiaceae*
Worldwide – 5 genera, 21 species; South Africa –
20 species.
Family Features
• Very varied
• Leaves – simple, opposite or in threes
• Flowers – bi-sexual
Trees in this book
Black Monkey Orange (B, C) p 146;
Forest Elder (A, C) p 112

WILD PEACH *Flacourtiaceae*
Worldwide – 80 genera, 500 species; South Africa
– 13 genera, 30 species (sub-tropical areas).
Family Features
• Fruit – edible
• Flowers – attractive (some species)
Trees in this book
Wild Mulberry (A, C) p 202

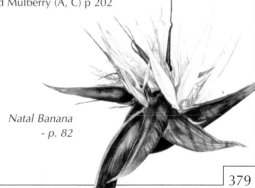

Natal Banana
- p. 82

Enjoy Tree Spotting

Tree spotting can be walking along the beach with the sand between your toes and a large hat to keep off the sun. Against the dunes is a thick carpet of the wind-swept, wind-shaped, Coastal Red Milkwoods. Perhaps you might catch sight of a monkey, or find the track of the bushpig, while birders might recognise the call of the Yellowstreaked Bulbul.

Bird-watching in nearby coastal swamps, you slosh along in sandled-feet, and find the cigar-shaped fruit of the Mangrove, plunged deep into the mud. Mudskippers loop back into the water, and crabs scuttle for holes in the sand.

At first light you might meet early-rising fishermen taking their boats out to sea. Among the trees the birds call – Cape Parrots, Hornbills, and perhaps a Green Coucal. With your rucksack full of oranges, you head into the cool of the forest, along a firm, smooth, sandy pathway.

Young, pale trunks, lichen-covered in pink and green, stand among gnarled old Toad and Cabbage Trees. The Thorny Elm and Thorny Rope present fearsome spikes that discourage your leaving the path to examine the huge fruit on the Monkey Thorns. Standing in quiet awe, you wonder why it has taken you so long to discover this primeval forest, it's smells, textures, colours, early humid coolness and peace.

The "Natal Parks" beckon. Under the stars, you lie beneath a huge, umbrella-shaped Black Monkey Thorn Acacia. Yesterday you watched a giraffe searching for the delicate, new shoots on a Knob Thorn Acacia, and getting its face covered in pollen for its troubles. It's amazing that so large an animal can effectively pollinate tiny, delicate flowers.

The dawn rises pink and gold, promising another day of looking for Black Rhino. Yesterday, you only glimpsed them as they sampled the air with raised upper lip, before thundering off into the Sickle Bush thickets. Later, you found where they had left deep tracks in the river mud after stripping leaves from the Cross-berry Raisin.

Perhaps you drive home through the KwaZulu-Natal Midlands. Here, over a century ago, sun-burned, peeling British soldiers must have stared in amazement at the Paperbark Acacias, that also appeared to be losing their skin in the African sun. At Howick, below the falls, the water gushes over rocks that have cooled thousands of human feet… a tree-shaded valley for collecting water, berries and firewood, and trunks for building and boats …Africa … people … history …trees.

This is the Green Province. A province of trees. Here, it seems, are the models Disney used for his scenes of Africa. Flat-crown Albizias stud the plains, and the coils of the Climbing Flat-bean are well suited to the pages of a storybook. But all flowers, textures, shapes and smells are real. Each tree is uniquely African. Each tells of the continent's mystery and cultural wealth, of Nature and the coming of humans. Each waits for your discovery. Each tree is ready to add enjoyment and enrichment to your journeys and holidays, to your life and your spirit.

Sycamore Cluster Fig
– page 366

DESTINATIONS – GENERAL INFORMATION

Along Rivers
Facilities

	TEL. NO.	LOCATION	AUTHORITY	Accommodation	Shop on site	Restaurant
Fundimvelo Nature Reserve	(0331) 95-2996	Empangeni	KZNNCS			
Goedetrouw Public Reserve	(0354) 42473	Eshowe	KZNNCS			
Hazelmere Nature Reserve	(0322) 33-2315	Tongaat	KZNNCS			
Kranzkloof Nature Reserve	(031) 764-3515	Kloof	KZNNCS			
Mfuli Game Ranch	(0354) 60-0620	Empangeni	P	•	•	•
Mhlopeni Nature Reserve	(033) 496-1722	Weenen	P	•		
Molweni Nature Reserve	(0331) 77-3659	Kloof	KZNNCS			
Oribi Gorge Nature Reserve	(039) 679-1644	Port Shepstone	KZNNCS	•		
*Palmiet Nature Reserve	(031) 86-1331	Westville	M			
Paradise Valley Nature Reserve	(031) 72-3443	Pinetown	M			
Shongweni Resources Reserve	(031) 769-1283	Pinetown	P			
Thukela Biosphere Reserve	(0363) 41938	Weenen	P/KZNNCS	•		
*Umbilo River Trail	(031) 21-1303	Durban	DPD			

Along Rivers
Outdoors

	Tree list	Caravan site	Camping site	Braai / Picnic area	Bird watching	Game	Hiking / Walking	Drives (own vehicle)	Drives (organised)
Fundimvelo Nature Reserve	•				•	•	•	•	
Goedetrouw Public Reserve				•	•			•	
Hazelmere Nature Reserve	•		•		•		•	•	
Kranzkloof Nature Reserve	•				•	•	•	•	
Mfuli Game Ranch					•	•	•	•	•
Mhlopeni Nature Reserve	•				•		•	•	
Molweni Nature Reserve	•				•		•	•	
Oribi Gorge Nature Reserve	•		•	•	•		•	•	
*Palmiet Nature Reserve	•				•	•	•	•	
Paradise Valley Nature Reserve	•			•	•		•	•	
Shongweni Resources Reserve	•			•	•		•	•	
Thukela Biosphere Reserve	•				•	•	•	•	
*Umbilo River Trail	•				•		•	•	

*Many of these destinations are actually in two or more Ecozones. They have been classified by the dominant zone that influences their tree distribution. The key for these grids is on page 388.

Bushveld-Savannah Facilities

	TEL. NO.	LOCATION	AUTHORITY	Accommodation	Shop on site	Restaurant
Assagay Nature Reserve	(031) 777-1000	Hillcrest	M			
Dlinza Forest Nature Reserve	(0358) 70-0552	Eshowe	KZNNCS			
Entumeni Nature Reserve	(0331) 47-1961	Eshowe	KZNNCS			
Hluhluwe Nature Reserve	(035) 562-0255	Hluhluwe	KZNNCS	•	•	•
Itala Game Reserve	(0388) 75239	Louwsburg	KZNNCS	•		•
Mkuze Nature Reserve	(0355) 573-0003	Hluhluwe	KZNNCS	•	•	
Ndumu Nature Reserve	(0331) 47-1961	Josini	KZNNCS	•	•	
Ntendeka Wilderness Area	(0386) 71883	Nongoma	SF			
Nyala Game Ranch	(0351) 92-8185	Empangeni	P	•	•	
Ocean View Game Park	(0354) 42473	Eshowe	KZNNCS			
Phinda Resource Reserve	(035) 562-0271	Sodwana Bay	P	•	•	•
Pongolapoort Nature Reserve	(0331) 47-1961	Josini	KZNNCS			
Queen Elizabeth Park	(0331) 47-1961	Pietermaritzburg	KZNNCS		•	
Tembe Elephant Park	(0355) 92-0001	Ndumo	KZNNCS	•		
Ubizane Game Ranch	(035) 562-0237	Hluhluwe	P	•		
Umfolozi Nature Reserve	(035) 562-0287	Mtubatuba	KZNNCS	•	•	
Windy Ridge Game Park	(0351) 92-8319	Empangeni	P	•		

Bushveld-Savannah Outdoors

	Tree list	Caravan site	Camping site	Braai / Picnic area	Bird watching	Game	Hiking / Walking	Drives (own vehicle)	Drives (organised)
Assagay Nature Reserve	•						•	•	
Dlinza Forest Nature Reserve	•			•	•		•	•	
Entumeni Nature Reserve				•	•	•		•	
*Hluhluwe Nature Reserve	•			•	•	•	•	•	•
Itala Game Reserve	•	•	•	•	•	•	•	•	•
Mkuze Nature Reserve	•	•	•	•	•	•	•	•	•
Ndumu Nature Reserve	•	•	•		•	•	•	•	•
Ntendeka Wilderness Area	•		•	•	•	•		•	
Nyala Game Ranch	•	•			•	•	•	•	•
Ocean View Game Park					•	•		•	
Phinda Resource Reserve	•				•	•	•	•	•
Pongolapoort Nature Reserve	•				•	•	•	•	
Queen Elizabeth Park				•	•			•	
Tembe Elephant Park	•				•	•		4x4	
Ubizane Game Ranch	•			•	•	•	•	•	
Umfolozi Nature Reserve				•	•	•	•	•	•
Windy Ridge Game Park	•		•	•	•	•	•	•	•

Pigeonwood
- page 194

*Many of these destinations are actually in two or more Ecozones. They have been classified by the dominant zone that influences their tree distribution. The key for these grids is on page 388.

Coast Facilities

	TEL. NO.	LOCATION	AUTHORITY	Accommodation	Shop on site	Restaurant
Amatikulu Nature Reserve	(0358) 70-0552	Tugela Mouth	KZNNCS			
Beachwood Mangrove Nature Reserve	(031) 25-1271	Durban	KZNNCS			
Bluff Nature Reserve	(031) 42-7030	Durban	KZNNCS			
Bonamanzi Game Park	(035) 562-0181	Hluhluwe	P	●		●
Burman Bush Nature Reserve	(031) 21-1303	Durban	DPD			
Cape Vidal	(035) 590-1404	St Lucia	KZNNCS	●		
Charter's Creek	(035) 550-1513	Lake St Lucia	KZNNCS	●		
*Clive Cheeseman Nature Reserve	(031) 21-3126	Kloof	WS	●		
Crestholme Nature Reserve	(031) 21-3126	Hillcrest	WS			
Dukuduku Forest	(0354) 42087	St Lucia	SAFCOL			
Durban Botanic Gardens	(031) 21-1303	Durban	M			
Empisini Nature Reserve	(0323) 937-0090	Umkomaas	M	●		
Enseleni Nature Reserve	(0351) 92-3732	Empangeni	KZNNCS			
False Bay Park	(035) 62-2911	Lake St Lucia	KZNNCS	●		
Fanie's Island	(035) 52-1431	Lake St Lucia	KZNNCS	●		
*Glenholme Nature Reserve	(031) 21-3126	Kloof	WS			
Harold Johnson Nature Reserve	(0324) 486-1574	Tugela Mouth	KZNNCS			
Hawaan Forest Reserve	(031) 561-1101	Umhlanga	KZNNCS			
Ilanda Wilds Nature Reserve	(031) 903-2121	Amanzimtoti	M			
*Ingwenya Nature Reserve	(0324) 52397	Tugela Mouth	WS			
Kenneth Stainbank Nature Reserve	(031) 469-2807	Durban	KZNNCS			
Kosi Bay Nature Reserve	(0331) 47-1961	Josini	KZNNCS	●		
La Lucia	(031) 561-1101	Umhlanga	KZNNCS	●	●	●
Lake Eteza Nature Reserve	(035) 590-1342	St Lucia	KZNNCS			
Lake Sibaya	(0331) 47-1981	Josini	KZNNCS	●		
Mapelane Nature Reserve	(035) 590-1407	St Lucia	KZNNCS	●		
*Mariannwood Nature Reserve	(031) 719-2215	Durban	M			
Mpenjati Nature Reserve	(039) 313-0531	Southbroom	KZNNCS			
*New Germany Nature Reserve	(031) 705-4360	Westville	M	●		
Ngoye Forest Reserve	(0331) 47-1981	Mtunzini	KZNNCS			
North Park Nature Reserve	(031) 764-3515	Queensburgh	KZNNCS			
*Pietermaritzburg Botanical Gardens	(0331) 44-3585	Pietermaritzburg	NBI			●
Pigeon Valley Park	(031) 21-1303	Durban	DPD			
Richards Bay Game Reserve	(0351) 753-2330	Richards Bay	KZNNCS	●		
Roosfontein Nature Reserve	(031) 86-1331	Queensburg	M			
Seaton Park	(031) 21-1303	Durban North	DPD			
Silverglen Nature Reserve	(031) 21-1303	Durban	DPD			
Skyline Nature Reserve	(03931) 50112	Uvongo	KZNNCS			
Sodwana Bay National Park	(035) 682-1502	Hluhluwe	KZNNCS	●	●	
*Springside Nature Reserve	(031) 765-1222	Hillcrest	M			
St Lucia Public Resort and Estuary	(03592) x 20	Mtubatuba	KZNNCS	●		●
Umbogovango Nature Reserve	(031) 949-2081	Amanzimtoti	AECI			
Umdoni Bird Sanctuary	(0323) 51227	Pennington	P			
Umhlanga Bush Nature Reserve	(031) 561-1101	Umhlanga	M			
Umlalazi Nature Reserve	(0353) 40-1836	Mtunzini	KZNNCS	●		
Uvongo Nature Reserve	(03931) 51222	Uvongo	M			
Vernon Crookes Nature Reserve	(0323) 974-2222	Umzinto	KZNNCS			
Virginia Bush Nature Reserve	(031) 21-1303	Durban North	DPD			

	Tree list	Caravan site	Camping site	Braai / Picnic area	Bird watching	Game	Hiking / Walking	Drives (own vehicle)	Drives (organised)
Amatikulu Nature Reserve	•		•			•	•	•	
Beachwood Mangrove Nature Reserve	•				•		•		
Bluff Nature Reserve				•	•	•		•	
Bonamanzi Game Park	•				•	•	•	•	
Burman Bush Nature Reserve	•				•		•	•	
Cape Vidal			•	•	•			•	
Charter's Creek	•				•	•			
Clive Cheeseman Nature Reserve					•		•	•	
Crestholme Nature Reserve						•	•		
Dukuduku Forest					•			•	
Durban Botanic Gardens	•				•		•		
Empisini Nature Reserve					•	•	•		
Enseleni Nature Reserve	•				•		•		
False Bay Park	•	•	•	•	•	•	•	•	
Fanie's Island	•	•	•	•	•	•	•	•	
Glenholme Nature Reserve					•		•	•	
Harold Johnson Nature Reserve	•		•	•		•	•	•	
Hawaan Forest Reserve					•	•	•	•	
Ilanda Wilds Nature Reserve					•	•		•	
Ingwenya Nature Reserve					•	•	•	•	
Kenneth Stainbank Nature Reserve	•				•	•	•	•	•
Kosi Bay Nature Reserve	•	•	•		•	•	•	4x4	
La Lucia	•	•	•	•	•				
Lake Eteza Nature Reserve						•		•	
Lake Sibaya	•				•	•	•	•	
Mapelane Nature Reserve	•	•	•		•	•	•	•	
Mariannwood Nature Reserve	•				•		•	•	•
Mpenjati Nature Reserve					•	•	•		
New Germany Nature Reserve					•	•	•	•	
Ngoye Forest Reserve	•				•			4x4	
North Park Nature Reserve	•			•	•			•	
Pietermaritzburg Botanical Gardens	•				•		•		
Pigeon Valley Park	•			•	•		•	•	
Richards Bay Game Reserve	•			•	•	•	•	•	
Roosfontein Nature Reserve	•			•	•		•	•	
Seaton Park	•				•		•	•	
Silverglen Nature Reserve	•			•	•		•	•	
Skyline Nature Reserve	•				•		•		
Sodwana Bay National Park	•		•	•	•	•		•	
Springside Nature Reserve							•	•	
St Lucia Public Resort and Estuary	•	•	•	•	•	•	•	•	
Umbogovango Nature Reserve	•			•	•		•	•	
Umdoni Bird Sanctuary				•	•		•	•	
Umhlanga Bush Nature Reserve					•		•	•	
Umlalazi Nature Reserve	•		•	•	•	•	•	•	
Uvongo Nature Reserve	•				•		•		
Vernon Crookes Nature Reserve	•				•	•		•	
Virginia Bush Nature Reserve	•				•		•	•	

Scented Thorn Acacia
- page 316

Drakensberg Midlands Facilities

	TEL. NO.	LOCATION	AUTHORITY	Accommodation	Shop on site	Restaurant
Albert Falls Nature Reserve	(03356) 91202	Pietermaritzburg	KZNNCS	•		
Chelmsford Nature Reserve	(0331) 43-3184	Newcastle	KZNNCS	•	•	
Coleford Nature Reserve	(031) 307-6345	Underberg	KZNNCS	•		
Craigie Burn Nature Reserve	(0331) 42-8 101	Mooiriver	KZNNCS			
*Doreen Clark Nature Reserve	(0331) 95-1111	Pietermaritzburg	KZNNCS			
Ferncliffe Forest	(0331) 42-1322	Pietermaritzburg	PPRD	•		
Fugitives' Drift	(034) 642-1843	Dundee	P	•		
Midmar Dam Public Resort	(0351) 47-1981	Howick	KZNNCS	•		•
Moor Park Nature Reserve	(0363) 23000	Escourt	KZNNCS			
Spioenkop Nature Reserve	(0331) 47-1961	Bergville	KZNNCS	•		•
Umgeni Valley Nature Reserve	(031) 21-1303	Howick	DPD	•		
Wagendrift Nature Reserve	(0363) 23000	Escourt	KZNNCS			
*Weenen Nature Reserve	(0363) 41809	Weenen	KZNNCS			

Drakensberg Midlands Outdoors

	Tree list	Caravan site	Camping site	Braai / Picnic area	Bird watching	Hiking / Walking	Game	Drives (own vehicle)	Drives (organised)
Albert Falls Nature Reserve	•	•	•	•	•			•	
Chelmsford Nature Reserve		•	•	•	•		•	•	
Coleford Nature Reserve					•	•	•	•	
Craigie Burn Nature Reserve	•		•	•				•	
Doreen Clark Nature Reserve	•			•	•		•	•	
Ferncliffe Forest	•			•	•	•		•	
Fugitives' Drift						•	•	•	•
Midmar Dam Public Resort		•	•	•	•	•	•	•	
Moor Park Nature Reserve				•	•	•	•	•	
Spioenkop Nature Reserve	•	•	•	•	•		•	•	
Umgeni Valley Nature Reserve	•			•	•	•		•	
Wagendrift Nature Reserve				•		•		•	
Weenen Nature Reserve	•	•	•	•	•	•	•	•	

*Many of these destinations are actually in two or more Ecozones. They have been classified by the dominant zone that influences their tree distribution. The key for these grids is on page 388.

DESTINATIONS AND HABITATS

On the previous pages destinations that have indigenous trees are grouped by the main Ecozone in which they occur geographically. However, many of these destinations have more than one Ecozone. The grids on this page summarise the Habitats that you will find at each destination.

A Along Rivers

Destination	Riverine	Thornveld	Woodland	Dune	Low-lying	Sand	Scarp	Swamp	Waterlogged	Moist Grassland
Fundimvelo Nature Reserve	•	•								
Goedetrouw Public Reserve	•	•								
Hazelmere Nature Reserve			•							
Kranzkloof Nature Reserve	•						•			
Mfuli Game Ranch	•	•	•							
Mhlopeni Nature Reserve	•									
Molweni Nature Reserve	•									
Oribi Gorge Nature Reserve	•						•			
Palmiet Nature Reserve	•	•								
Paradise Valley Nature Reserve	•					•			•	
Shongweni Resources Reserve	•							•		
Thukela Biosphere Reserve	•								•	
Umbilo River Trail	•					•				•

B Bushveld-Savannah

Destination	Riverine	Thornveld	Woodland	Dune	Low-lying	Sand	Scarp	Swamp	Waterlogged	Moist Grassland
Assagay Nature Reserve	•		•						•	
Dlinza Forest Nature Reserve			•				•			
Entumeni Nature Reserve			•				•			
Hluhluwe Nature Reserve	•	•	•				•			
Itala Game Reserve	•	•	•							
Mkuze Nature Reserve	•	•	•							•
Ndumu Nature Reserve	•	•	•			•				
Ntendeka Wilderness Area			•				•			
Nyala Game Ranch		•	•							
Ocean View Game Park			•		•					
Phinda Resource Reserve		•				•				
Pongolapoort Public Resource Nature Reserve		•	•							
Queen Elizabeth Park Nature Reserve		•	•							
Tembe Elephant Reserve		•								•
Ubizane Game Ranch		•				•				
Umfolozi Nature Reserve	•	•								
Windy Ridge Game Park	•	•	•							

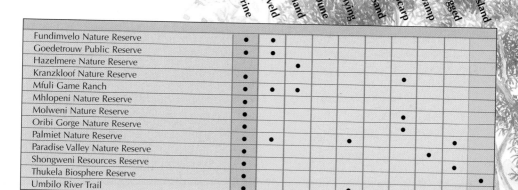

White Ironwood - page 242

Coast

	Riverine	Thornveld	Woodland	Dune	Low-lying	Mangrove	Sand	Scarp	Swamp	Waterlogged	Moist Grassland
Amatikulu Nature Reserve											•
Beachwood Mangrove Nature Reserve						•			•		
Bluff Nature Reserve				•						•	
Bonamanzi Game Park					•					•	
Burman Bush Nature Reserve					•						
Cape Vidal				•	•				•	•	
Charter's Creek					•	•				•	
Clive Cheeseman Nature Reserve								•			
Crestholme Nature Reserve								•			
Dukuduku Forest					•						
Durban Botanic Gardens					•						
Empisini Nature Reserve					•						
Enseleni Nature Reserve	•				•				•	•	
False Bay Park		•			•		•				
Fanie's Island					•	•			•	•	
Glenholme Nature Reserve					•					•	
Harold Johnson Nature Reserve	•				•						
Hawaan Forest Reserve					•						
Ilanda Wilds Nature Reserve			•		•						
Ingwenya Nature Reserve					•						
Kenneth Stainbank Nature Reserve					•						
Kosi Bay Nature Reserve									•		
La Lucia	•			•					•		
Lake Eteza Nature Reserve									•	•	
Lake Sibaya				•	•					•	
Mapelane Nature Reserve				•	•	•			•	•	
Mariannwood Nature Reserve					•						
Mpenjati Nature Reserve				•					•	•	
New Germany Nature Reserve					•						
Ngoye Forest Reserve								•			
North Park Nature Reserve					•						
Pietermaritzburg Botanical Gardens					•						
Pigeon Valley Park					•						
Richards Bay Game Reserve						•			•		
Roosfontein Nature Reserve	•				•						
Seaton Park					•						
Silverglen Nature Reserve					•						
Skyline Nature Reserve					•				•	•	
Sodwana Bay National Park				•	•	•	•		•	•	
Springside Nature Reserve	•				•				•		
St Lucia Public Resort and Estuary				•	•		•		•	•	
Umbogovango Nature Reserve					•						
Umdoni Bird Sanctuary					•					•	
Umhlanga Bush Nature Reserve					•				•		
Umlalazi Nature Reserve					•	•				•	
Uvongo Nature Reserve					•	•				•	
Vernon Crookes Nature Reserve								•			
Virginia Bush Nature Reserve					•						

Drakensberg Midlands

	Riverine	Thornveld	Woodland	Dune	Low-lying	Sand	Scarp	Swamp	Waterlogged	Moist Grassland
Albert Falls Nature Reserve		•								•
Chelmsford Nature Reserve										•
Coleford Nature Reserve										•
Craigie Burn Nature Reserve										•
Doreen Clark Nature Reserve							•			•
Ferncliffe Forest										•
Fugitive's Drift										•
Midmar Dam Public Resort										•
Moor Park Nature Reserve										•
Spioenkop Nature Reserve			•							•
Umgeni Valley Nature Reserve	•				•					•
Wagendrift Nature Reserve										•
Weenen Nature Reserve										•

KEY

Durban Parks Dept	DPD
KwaZulu-Natal Nature Conservation Services	KZNNCS
Private	P
Municipal	M
National Parks Board	NPB
Pietermaritzburg Parks & Recreation Dept	PPRD
State Forest	SF
Wildlife Society	WS

TREE LIST INVITATION

The grids on these pages are destinations to visit in KwaZulu-Natal which have the indigenous trees listed in this book. The Outdoors Grid has a column to indicate that Jacana has a tree list, for that particular destination. If you would like a copy of any list, contact Jacana at (011) 648-1157 or email - jacedu@iafrica.com.

Any organisation, which is open to the public, and has indigenous trees, and would like to add their name to this list for future editions, is welcome to contact Jacana at the same numbers.

Flat-crown Albizia - page 190

Tree names

A great deal of work has been done over the past 30 years on standardising and verifying the correctness of tree names in South Africa. Much of this important work was done by the Dendrological Society of South Africa. The majority of English names that are used in this book are taken from their booklet: *National List of Indigenous Trees*.

Currently, with the tremendous increase in local interest in our indigenous trees, there is a wave of new tree spotters who do not have the botanical background of the expert scientists who pioneered the field. In the research for this book, and the others in the **Sappi Tree Spotting** series, Jacana has encountered numerous people who would like the common usage names to be both functional and appealing. There are others who are making a strong appeal for names to stay the same.

Functional names

Many tree spotters have "evolved" through birding and will appreciate that the common usage names help them to recognise bird families. For example all kingfishers are kingfishers!

Many of the English names of trees do not have this advantage. There is nothing to link the Red Currant or Crow-berry to the other Karree family trees (*Rhus*) nor the Cross-berry to the Raisin (*Grewia*) family. There is no reliable link between the Thorn trees, which are *Acacias*, or the False-thorn trees, the *Albizias*.

Striking names

Many tree-spotters would like to see a simplification of some of the more cumbersome and less interesting names. Initially there were 17 occurrences of Common or Wild in the names of trees in this book. Out of 75 tree names, this represents 23%. When faced with a list of new-to-know trees, it is a help if the names themselves are striking!

History has a vote

Over the years many trees gained appeal through their names. Any change to this – even in translation – can take away that sense of identity.

To many aspirant, struggling tree spotters the one beacon of hope could well have been the Sycamore Cluster Fig. To find that it is now called the Common Cluster Fig feels like double trouble. The loss of charm seems very unfortunate.

New names

Jacana is aware of the implications of rashly introducing new terminology without scientific support, but we are also crucially aware of the difficulties that people, who spot trees for fun, are having.

The following trees are named in this book primarily under an easy-to-use title, and the Dendrological Society name is in brackets alongside. The list should be self explanatory but Jacana genuinely invite anyone interested in discussing this further to contact: (011) 648-1157.

Original name	*Changed name*		
Common Cluster Fig	Sycamore Cluster Fig	*Ficus sycamorus*	p. 366
Common Coral Tree	Coral Tree	*Erythrina lysistemon*	p. 210
Common Crow-berry	Crow-berry Karree	*Rhus pentheri*	p. 326
Common Hook-thorn	Hook Thorn Acacia	*Acacia caffra*	p. 330
Common Spike-thorn	Spike-thorn	*Maytenus heterophylla*	p. 334
Common Tree Euphorbia	Tree Euphorbia	*Euphorbia ingens*	p. 86
Common Wild Pear	Wild Pear	*Dombeya rotundifolia*	p. 140
Cross-berry	Cross-berry Raisin	*Grewia occidentalis*	p. 104
Flat-crown False-thorn	Flat-crown Albizia	*Albizia adianthifolia*	p. 190
Large-leaved False-thorn	Large-leaved Albizia	*Albizia versicolor*	p. 300
Natal Wild Banana	Natal Banana	*Strelitzia nicolai*	p. 82
Red Currant	Forest Karree	*Rhus chirindensis*	p. 230
Wild Date Palm	Date Palm	*Phoenix reclinata*	p. 72

Note: All *Acacias* have the word Acacia added to their common names.

Humans and Trees

Over millennia humans have used different parts of trees for thousands of culturally important functions. Food, medicine, music, tools, furniture, building transport and treasure carved out of wood are just a few of the ways that trees have shaped the progress of our evolution.

These lists are meant to inspire you to dream a while about the relationships we have had with trees, and how they have influenced your past life. Perhaps they will also inspire you to new activities that widen your interests, and include indigenous trees in your future too.

EDIBLE BERRIES AND LEAVES

The following berries are both edible and tasty:

Black Monkey Orange	p. 146
Broom Cluster Fig	p. 182
Coastal Red Milkwood	p. 154
Karrees (all)	p. 230, 326
Kooboo-berry	p. 116
Marula	p. 304
Mitzeeri	p. 214
Red Ivory	p. 282
Tassel Berry	p. 124
Water Berry	p. 172
Wild Medlar	p. 176
Wild Plum	p. 246

Young leaves of both the following trees can be soaked and cooked as a vegetable:

Pigeonwood	p. 194
Powder-puff Tree	p. 168

Leaves of the following tree can be boiled to eat with porridge:

White Pear	page 198

GUM AS NATURAL CHEWING GUM

Paperbark Acacia	p. 348
Sweet Thorn Acacia	p. 352
Umbrella Thorn Acacia	p. 320

COFFEE, TEA, JELLY, JAM, PORRIDGE, SAUCE ETC.

Buffalo-thorn	p. 292	seeds roasted for coffee substitute, or ground for porridge or meal
Common Cabbage Tree	p. 90	caterpillars on tree are edible; roots provide water
Flat-crown Albizia	p. 190	seeds make sauce
Marula	p. 304	oil from seeds is a preservative; fruit used for jelly and jam
Weeping Boer-bean	p. 338	roasted seeds are tasty
White Ironwood	p. 242	fruit makes chutney
Wild Olive	p. 286	leaves make tea
Wild Pear	p. 140	makes sour jelly

FERMENTING ALCOHOL

The following trees have fruit with sufficient sugar to allow fermentation:

Date Palm	p. 72	nutritious drink
Lala Palm	p. 78	nutritious drink
Magic Guarri	p. 256	brewed into beer
Marula	p. 304	brewed into beer and liqueur
Water Berry	p. 172	brewed into beer
Wild Medlar	p. 176	distilled into brandy

Jacana advise the utmost caution in eating fruit or any parts of plants from the wild, unless you are absolutely sure of the species. The "foods" listed here are not poisonous. However, Jacana can take no responsibility for tree spotters who test this information.

Another vital role played by trees has been their contribution as medicines. Tragically much of the indigenous knowledge is being lost forever as traditional methods are threatened by the advance of urbanisation. The trees listed below are still of particular importance to herbalists for their bark.

It is important to know that when all the bark is removed from any tree, that tree dies. This is because the main supply-line of food and water runs up and down the tree immediately under the bark. Highly skilled herbalists would never destroy a tree this way, nor would they remove a complete ring of bark which is as lethal to the tree. None the less, many trees die every year from inexperienced entrepreneurs collecting bark for sale in the cities.

Planting the following trees in parks, streets, schools and private gardens could be a real contribution to the availability of bark in urban areas:

The following treatments have been used for generations by African people and are still viable methods of dealing with a problem in the wild. As with the food lists, anyone testing this information does so entirely at their own risk. Always be sure you have no doubt about the plant you are using, as there are barks, roots, leaves and fruit that are poisonous to humans. These are listed below.

BUSH ILLNESSES AND INJURIES

Cross-berry Raisin	p. 104	hammered and soaked bark to dress wounds
Guarris (all)	p. 256 p. 270	natural antiseptic in the sap inhibits bacteria growth
Marula	p. 304	fruit high in Vitamin C
Sickle Bush	p. 264	chewed leaves to draw bites and stings
Velvet Bushwillow	p. 308	fresh, moist leaves to dress wounds
Wild Medlar	p. 176	fruit high in Vitamin C

BARK USED IN MEDICINES

Marula	p. 304
Natal Mahogany	p. 278
Red Beech	p. 234
Sneezewood	p. 238
Weeping Boer-bean	p. 338
White Ironwood	p. 242
White Pear	p. 198
Wild Pear	p. 140
Wild Plum	p. 246

POISONOUS TREES

The following trees are known to have parts that are either irritant or actually poisonous to humans.

Common Poison Bush	p. 186	the bark, latex & fruit are poisonous to mammals, but the fruit is eaten safely by birds
Powder-puff Tree	p. 168	poisonous fruit
Red Beech	p. 234	poisonous bark
River Bushwillow	p. 362	poisonous roots
Tamboti	p. 370	latex and wood-smoke are very poisonous
Tassel Berry	p. 124	roots are toxic

Water Berry
- page 172

Insect Repellent

Trees need to protect themselves from being eaten by insects. The soft, inner layer of the bark and leaves in particular are often defended by chemicals from large animal browsers. Some of these chemicals act as natural insect repellents and can be used to keep insects out of cupboards or clothing.

Sneezewood	p. 238	wood or sawdust
Tamboti	p. 370	a piece of wood in clothes; beware of irritant properties with very fresh wood or clothing close to the skin
Tinderwood	p. 128	leaves in cupboards

Perfume

Scents are traditionally associated with softer, non-woody plants. However, some trees use perfume to attract pollinators, or to protect themselves from being eaten.

Small Knobwood	p. 218	citrus-smelling seeds
Tamboti	p. 370	bark in small quantities is aromatic, but can become irritant

Glues

The gum from the following trees can be used as an adhesive, particularly when heated first.

Paperbark Acacia	p. 348
Red Beech	p. 234
Sweet Thorn Acacia	p. 352

Rope and Twine

For millennia humans have used the bark and tender new shoots of trees to make twine and rope, and to weave baskets.

Brack Thorn Acacia	p. 358
Broom Cluster Fig	p. 182
Climbing Flat-bean	p. 100
Large-leaved Albizia	p. 300
Red Thorn Acacia	p. 260
Sycamore Cluster Fig	p. 366
Umbrella Thorn Acacia	p. 320
Wild Pear	p. 140

Fire-making

In the past, people twirled sticks of certain kinds of wood on other types of wood to cause sufficient friction, and therefore heat, to make fire. The trees recorded as being used for this are listed below:

Fire blocks

Sycamore Cluster Fig	p. 366
Tinderwood	p. 128

Friction sticks

Broom Cluster Fig	p. 182

Fishing

Being a coastal area, there is a long tradition of usage of trees for supplementing human diet with fish.

Climbing Flat-bean	p. 100	fishing basket frames
Coastal Red Milkwood	p. 154	fish-traps
Coral Tree	p. 210	floats
Flame Thorn Acacia	p. 108	fish-traps
Mitzeeri	p. 214	fish-traps

Furniture

The wood of the following trees possess qualities which are ideal for futniture-making, such as durability, close grain, resistant to termites, and a smooth finish.

These trees are suitable for larger items of furniture eg. chairs, cabinets, tables:

Black Monkey Thorn Acacia	p. 312
Cape Ash	p. 274
Large-leaved Albizia	p. 300
Mitzeeri	p. 214
Red Bushwillow	p. 120
Red Ivory	p. 282
Umzimbeet	p. 132
Water Berry	p. 172
Weeping Boer-bean	p. 338

These trees are suitable for smaller items of furniture eg. stools and small tables:

Black Monkey Orange	p. 146
Kooboo-berry	p. 116
River Bushwillow	p. 362
Scented Thorn Acacia	p. 316
Spike-thorn	p. 334
Wild Olive	p. 286

Paperbark Acacia
- page 348

BOATS

Without trees it is possible that humans might never have found a way of leaving the shores on which they were born. All early boats were made of timber. However, only certain timber is suitable for boat-making as it has to be light but strong, not porous, and able to withstand the long-term effects of being submerged in water. The following trees are traditionally used for boat-making:

Coast Silver Oak	p. 150
Coastal Red Milkwood	p. 154
Coral Tree	p. 210
Water Berry	p. 172
White Mangrove	p. 164

WAGONS AND YOKES

Land travel too was dependent on products made from trees. The following are recorded as being useful for wagons parts and for yoking oxen:

Umzimbeet	p. 132
White Gardenia	p. 136

STICKS AND WEAPONS

Climbing Flat-bean	p. 100
Knob Thorn Acacia	p. 296
Kooboo-berry	p. 116
Red Ivory	p. 282
Small Knobwood	p. 218
Thorny Elm	p. 222
Umzimbeet	p. 132
White Gardenia	p. 136

MUSIC

Virtually every form of early music involved some part of a tree. From drums, to pipes, strings pulled across wooden frames, rattles, xylophones, pianos and violins, human music would sound very different had there never been trees. In early KwaZulu-Natal, the following trees were important for making instruments:

Black Monkey Orange	p. 146	fruit used to make the base of the marimba
Figs (large)	p. 182, 366	used for drums
Large-leaved Albizia	p. 300	used for drums
Spike-thorn	p. 334	thumping Instruments

DYES AND INKS

Colouring hides and skin, as well as baskets, ropes, cloth, walls and floors has been a central part of human culture that differentiates us from the other animals. The following trees can still offer pleasure for hand-dying paper or fabrics, woven baskets or unglazed clay work.

Kooboo-berry	p. 116	brown dye from the bark
Magic Guarri	p. 256	berries give a dark ink; roots dye baskets brown
Red Ivory	p. 282	bark gives a purple dye
Velvet Bushwillow	p. 308	roots give a yellow brown dye; leaves stain
Weeping Boer-bean	p. 338	bark gives a red dye
White Mangrove	p. 164	brown dye from the bark

GARDENING

Indigenous trees are ideally suited for gardens as they require minimum care, and attract birds and butterflies. The following information has been summarised to help you decide which trees will give you the most pleasure in your garden. The most important considerations before choosing a tree are how large the tree will be when grown, and whether it loses its leaves in winter or not. After that, it is a matter of choice as to the function of the tree in providing shade, acting as a hedge, or offering you the thrill of showy flowers or fruit in certain seasons.

Short trees - up to 6 metres

	height	Showy flower	Showy fruit/pod	Deciduous	Evergreen	Provide shade	Hedge or screen	Seed or cutting	Frost/Drought res.	Fast-growing	Ornamental	Invasive roots
Climbing Flat-bean	2 - 6 m	Oct - Nov	(P) Feb - Apr	•			•	s				
Cross-berry Raisin	2 - 6 m	Oct - Jan	(F) Jan - May	•				s	F/D		•	
Sickle Bush	2 - 6 m	Oct - Jan	(P) May - Sep	•			•	s/c	D			
White Gardenia	2 - 3 m	Oct - Feb	(F) All year		•			s/c	F/D			

Seed or cutting (S/C) indicates how you can propagate this tree.
Frost/Dought res. (F/D) indicates trees that are frost- and/or drought-resistant.

Medium trees - up to 10 metres

	Height	Showy flower	Showy fruit/pod	Deciduous	Evergreen	Provide shade	Hedge or screen	Seed or cutting	Frost/Drought res.	Fast-growing	Ornamental	Invasive roots
Black Monkey Orange	3 - 8 m		(F) Mar - Aug	•				s			•	•
Bush Guarri	4 - 10 m	Nov - Apr	(F) Mar - Dec			•		s	F/D			
Camphor Bush	2 - 9 m	Mar - Nov	(F) Mar - Nov		•				F/D			•
Common Cabbage Tree	3 - 10 m			•								•
Magic Guarri	3 - 7 m					•	•	s	F			
Powder-puff Tree	4 - 9 m	Nov - Jun	(F) Jul - Oct			•		c			•	•
Red Bushwillow	4 - 7 m		(P) Jan - May	•					F/D			
Red Thorn Acacia	3 - 10 m	Oct - Feb	(P) Dec - May	•				s	F/D			
Scented Thorn Acacia	4 - 7 m	Sep - Feb	(P) Mar - Sep	•				s	F/D			
Tassel Berry	3 - 7 m	Oct - Jan	(F) Jan - May			•		s	F			
Wild Medlar	2 - 8 m	Sep - Nov	(F) Nov - Apr	•				s/c	F/D			
Wild Olive	4 - 10 m	Oct - Feb	(F) Mar - Jul			•			F/D			
Wild Pear	3 - 9 m	Jul - Oct		•				s	F/D		•	

Red-stem Corkwood
– page 94

Tall trees - up to 18 metres

	Height	Showy flower	Showy fruit/pod	Deciduous	Evergreen	Provide shade	Hedge or screen	Seed or cutting	Frost/Drought res.	Fast-growing	Ornamental	Invasive roots
Black Monkey Thorn Acacia	4 - 12 m	Oct - Jan	(P) Dec - May	●				s				●
Brack Thorn Acacia	8 - 15 m	Jul - Oct	P) Oct - Feb	●				s			●	
Buffalo-thorn	3 - 12 m		(F) Feb - Jun	●				s	F/D		●	
Coastal Red Milkwood	4 - 16 m		(F) Jun - Jan			●		s				●
Coral Tree	4 - 12 m	Jun - Oct	(F) Sep - Feb					s/c	F		●	●
Crow-berry Karree	2 - 12 m	Aug - Mar	(F) Sep - Apr	●			●		F/D			
Forest Elder	3 - 18 m	May - Sep				●		s/c			●	
Hook Thorn Acacia	3 - 12 m	Sep - Nov	(P) Dec - Mar	●				s	F/D			
Kooboo-berry	3 - 15 m		(F) Jan - Jun			●			D			
Marula	5 - 17 m		(F) Jan - Mar	●		●		s	D		●	
Paperbark Acacia	7 - 15 m	Oct - Dec	(P) Mar - Jun	●						●	●	
Pigeonwood	5 - 15 m							s			●	●
Red ivory	3 - 15 m		(F) Jan - Apr	●					D			
Red-stem Corkwood	5 - 15 m	Oct - Dec	(F) Nov - Mar	●				s/c			●	
River Bushwillow	5 - 15 m	(P) Aug		●				s	F/D			
Small Knobwood	4 - 15 m		(F) Nov - Jun	●				s	F/D			
Sweet Thorn Acacia	4 - 15 m	Oct - Feb		●				s	F/D		●	
Tamboti	5 - 12 m	Jul - Nov	(F) Sep - Nov	●	●			s				
Tinderwood	2 - 15 m	Nov - Apr	(F) Feb - Jul	●				s/c			●	
Umbrella Thorn Acacia	5 - 15 m	Oct - Feb	(P) Dec - Jun	●				s	F/D			
Velvet Bushwillow	4 - 12 m		(P) Jan - Jun	●				s	F			
White Milkwood	4 - 15 m	Oct - Apr	(F) Feb - Sep			●		s				

Very tall trees - over 18 meters

	Height	Showy flower	Showy fruit/pod	Deciduous	Evergreen	Provide shade	Hedge or screen	Seed or cutting	Frost/Drought res.	Fast-growing	Ornamental	Invasive roots
Broom Cluster Fig	10 - 22 m		(F) Jun - Jan			●		c			●	●
Cape Ash	10 - 35 m		(F) Nov - Apr	●		●		s			●	
Cape Beech	3 - 20 m					●					●	●
Coast Silver Oak	4 - 25 m	Jul - Sep	(F) Nov - Jan	●			●	s	F/D			●
Flat-crown Albizia	10 - 25 m	Aug - Dec		●				s			●	
Forest Karree	3 - 25 m		(F) Dec - Mar	●				c	F/D			
Knob Thorn Acacia	5 - 20 m	Jul - Sep	(P) Dec - Jun	●				s	D			
Large-leaved Albizia	7 - 20 m	Aug - Jan	(P) Dec - Mar	●		●		s	D			
Mitzeeri	7 - 30 m			●								●
Natal Mahogany	5 - 20 m		(F) Dec - Mar			●	●	s/c			●	
Red Beech	10 - 25 m					●	●	s	D		●	
Sneezewood	7 - 35 m			●					D		●	
Sycamore Cluster Fig	5 - 25 m					●		c				
Umzimbeet	10 - 25 m	Dec - Mar	(P) Feb - Jul	●		●		s			●	
Water Berry	5 - 25 m	Oct - Jun	(F) Jun - Jan			●		s			●	●
Weeping Boer-bean	5 - 25 m	Aug - Nov	(P) Jan - Aug	●				s	D			
White Ironwood	10 - 30 m					●			D		●	
White Pear	5 - 20 m					●	●	● s			●	
Wild Plum	10 - 25 m	(F) Mar - Oct				●		s/c			●	●

MORE GARDENING AND BONSAI

TREES FOR COASTAL GARDENS

The following trees can withstand sandier soils and salt-laden winds.

Cape Beech	p. 206
Coast Silver Oak	p. 150
Coastal Red Milkwood	p. 154
Date Palm	p. 72
Fever Tree Acacia	p. 74
Lala Palm	p. 78
Lebombo Wattle	p. 1
White Milkwood	p. 342
Wild Cotton Tree	p. 88

TREES FOR SWAMPY AREAS

The following trees thrive with their feet near, or even in, water

Mangroves (all)	p. 160, 164
Powder-puff Tree	p. 168
Water Berry	p. 172

SHADE-LOVING TREES

These trees are unusual in that they can grow entirely in the shade.

Black Mangrove	p. 160
Large-leaved Dragon Tree	p. 80

GARDEN TREES FOR BIRDS

Birds can be attracted to trees for a number of reasons – insects or nutritious fruit as food, nectar in the flowers, or thorny branches for safer nesting. These trees are worth planting.

FRUIT AS FOOD

Kooboo-berry	p. 116
Mitzeeri	p. 214
Red Beech	p. 234
Sycamore Cluster Fig	p. 366
White Ironwood	p. 242

INSECTS AS FOOD

Cape Ash	p. 274
Figs (all)	p. 76, 182, 366
Mitzeeri	p. 214
Pigeonwood	p. 194
Red ivory	p. 282
Umzimbeet	p. 132

THORNY TREES FOR NESTING

Acacias (all)	p. 74, 108, 260, 296, 312, 316, 320, 330, 348, 352, 358
Sickle Bush	p. 264

Wild Olive
– page 286

INDIGENOUS LANDSCAPING CONTRACTORS AND CONSULTANTS

Bluff	
Eco Landscapes, Leanne O'Connor	(031) 466-2973
Michael Hickman	(031) 466-2043
Durban	
Landscape Studio, Frank Edwards	(031) 29-4146
Geoff Nichols Horticultural Services	(031) 23-3578
Gillitts	
Emerald Landscapes, Brendon Fox	(031) 764-0741
Hillcrest	
Enviropools, Phil Page	(031) 764-3156
Susan Petch	(031) 765-5227
Robyndale Landscapes, Rob Sandy	(031) 765-6113
Kearsney	
Designer Garden, Bruce Millican	(0324) 483-7863
Kloof	
Garden Line, Mary-Anne Paxton	(031) 764-3692
Link Hills	
Gavin Goldwyer Designs	082 659 5575
Mayville	
Plantnet, Wally Menne	082 444 2083

Mt Edgecombe	
Leitch Landscapes	(031) 502-2808
Northdene	
Garden Concepts, Judith Panton-Jones	(031) 78-3375
Pinetown	
Bruce Stead	(031) 700-2807
Rossburgh	
Indiflora, Johan Bodenstein	082 577 0898
Schagen	
Fishwick's Nursery, Neil Fishwick	(031) 733-4270
Westville	
Cowan & Van de Riet	(031) 86-6494
Harmony Landscapes, Mark Dennison	082 801 1955
Judy McKenzi	(031) 86-5678
Wandsbeck	
Karen Kelly	(031) 207-5148
Umhlali	
Gold Circle Gardens, Gill Theunissen	(0322) 91-8771

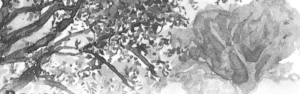

BONSAI

Some trees are ideal to grow as Bonsai from seeds or cuttings while others are not successful. Most people start with a full-grown tree bought from an expert and develop the hobby thereafter. Below are two lists of trees that are covered in this book. The first group are easy for beginners to grow. The second group you could grow if you have some expert help.

A useful contact in the Highveld is Bonsai Friend, Randfontein (011) 698-3002. They will tell you of a distributor near you in KwaZulu-Natal.

EASY TREES	
The following trees are the best species for beginners.	
Black Monkey Thorn Acacia	p. 312
Knob Thorn Acacia	p. 296
White Stinkwood	p. 13
Coral Tree	p. 210
Weeping Boer-bean	p. 338
Wild Olive	p. 286

TRY THESE TREES TOO	
It is possible to grow the following trees as Bonsai, however they need more specialised care.	
Buffalo-thorn	p. 292
Fever Tree Acacia	p. 74
Hook Thorn Acacia	p. 330
Marula	p. 304
Paperbark Acacia	p. 348
Umbrella Thorn Acacia	p. 320
Wild Mulberry	p. 202

FLOWER ARRANGING AND NURSERIES

Flower arranging

Flowers in a home are not just beautiful – they bring a sense of the pleasure of the outdoors into your living space. To use indigenous leaves, flowers, fruit and pods in your arrangements, whether in a vase or as a decoration on a table, can stimulate memories of the times you have seen them growing in the wild. Imagine a vase of Coast Silver Oak leaves that you saw Black Rhino browsing, or an Acacia branch in your lounge you saw Giraffe pollinating! However you might not be so keen to bring in the caterpillars with Mitzeeri leaves, even for the memory of a Giant Charaxes Butterfly!

FLOWERS	
Coral Tree	p. 210
Forest Elder	p. 112
Forest Karree	p. 230
Wild Pear	p. 140

LEAVES	
Bush Guarri	p. 270
Coast Silver Oak	p. 150
Forest Karree	p. 230
Magic Guarri	p. 256
Mitzeeri	p. 214
Red Beech	p. 234
Small Knobwood	p. 218
Waterberry	p. 172
White Ironwood	p. 242
White Milkwood	p. 342
Wild Olive	p. 286

PODS AND FRUIT	
Bushwillows	p. 308, 362
Forest Karree	p. 230
Kooboo Berry	p. 116
Mitzeeri	p. 214
Small Knobwood	p. 218
Umzimbeet	p. 132
Water Berry	p. 172
Wild Plum	p. 246
White Pear	p. 198

SPECIAL ARRANGEMENTS AND DISPLAYS	
Acacias (all) - thorns and pods	p. 74, 108, 260, 296, 312, 316, 320, 330, 348, 352, 358
Black Monkey Orange - fruit	p. 146
Common Cabbage Tree	p. 90
Date Palm - leaves & the husks of the fruit	p. 72
Lala Palm - fruit	p. 78
Marula - fruit	p. 304

Coral Tree
– page 210

398

Nurseries

The following nurseries in KwaZulu-Natal stock indigenous trees and will help you with detailed planting instructions.

Any nursery that would like to be included in this list, should contact Jacana (011) 648-1157.

KwaZulu-Natal nurseries	
Albert Falls	
Top Crop Nursery	(0335) 69-1333
Botha's Hill	
Dun Robin Nursery	(031) 777-1855
Chatsworth	
*Silverglen Medicinal Plant Nursery	(031) 404-5628
Durban	
*Afro Flora Nursery	(031) 47-4415
*P.L.A.N.T Depots	(031) 21-3126
*Wildlife Nursery	(031) 573-1054
*Wildlife Nursery	(031) 465-6179
Tropical Nursery	(031) 28-4925
Jungle Garden Nursery	(031) 207-7642
Durban North	
*Sharon & Robin Greaves	(031) 83-3406
Empangeni	
Aloe Ridge Garden Centre	(0351) 92-5894
Green Africa Nursery	(0351) 92-0065
Pick a Plant	082 935-9757
Eshowe	
*Eshowe Plant Depot	(0354) 42705
Zululand Nurseries	(0354) 42666
Gillitts	
Anders Nursery	(031) 767-3655
Greytown	
N.H. Farms Nursery	(0334) 71883
Hillcrest	
*Bella's Beauties	(031) 75-1158
Grabow Nursery	(031) 765-6003
Strangeways Inc	(031) 765-3255
Greenline Nursery	(031) 765-5250
Nursery Equipment Distributers	(031) 75-3255
Illovo Beach	
Illovo Nursery	(031) 96-2491
Ixopo	
Sutherland Seedlings	(0336) 34-1953
Kloof	
Kloof SPCA Nursery	(031) 73-1534
Margate	
Sebenza Wholesale Farm	(03931) 20378
Summerfield Nursery	(03931) 21895
Marina Beach	
Red Rhyno Farm	(039) 313-0620
Mid-Illovo	
*Gwahumbe Nursery	(0325) 81919
Mooi River	
*Shosholoza Nursery	(0333) 32830
Mtubatuba	
Maywood Nursery	(035) 550-1719
Mtunzinil	
*Twinstreams Nursery	(0353) 37-4836
Mtunzini Nursery	(0353) 40-1192
Munster	
*Indigiflora	(039) 309-1627
Mzumbe	
Follyfields Nursery	(039) 684-6277
Scottbrugh	
Woodpark Nursery	(0323) 20496
Pietermaritzburg	
*High Birnam Protea Nursery	(0332) 30-2354
*Natal National Botanic Gardens	(0331) 44-3585
*Val-lei Vista	(0331) 90-3527
McDonalds Garden Cntr	(0331) 42-2191
Jesmond Dene Nursery	(0331) 96-5000
Townbush Garden Pavilion	(0331) 47-1948
Pinetown	
*Geoff's Jungle	(031) 72-9097
Suregro Nursery	(031) 701-2668
Umhlali	
*Mwali Tree Sales	(0322) 525-8787
Driefontein Garden Pavilion	(0322) 525-8435
Umlaas Road	
*Cycad Centre	(0332) 51-0478
Uvongo	
South Coast Garden Pavilion	(03931) 21108
Joymac Nursery	(03931) 77289
Richards Bay	
*Richards Bay Indigenous Nursery	082 494 4481
Westville	
Gro-On Nursery	(031) 86-5678
Burgess Pavilion	(031) 86-4366
Plants-a-plenty	(031) 86-7455
Winterton	
*Thokozisa Nursery	(036) 468-1644
Tongaat	
Tongaat Plants	(0322) 92-3295

∗These nurseries are specialist indigenous nurseries.

DO YOU KNOW A RECORD-BREAKING TREE?

Dendrological Society of South Africa

The Dendrological Society (see page viii), compile a register of exceptionally large trees country wide. This means that they record large trees of different species. A large Broom Cluster Fig reaches 22 metres and is huge in anyone's eyes. A massive Sickle Bush, however, will tower at only 6 metres, but is still an exceptional tree for its kind. One of the great delights of learning about trees is the vast variety of shapes, forms and sizes in which they grow.

In some cases more than one large tree of a species is on the register. Jacana has chosen one tree per species from the register, and you will find their height, diameter and girth details, as well as the area where they grow, on the pages listed below. You can compare the more "normal" KwaZulu-Natal size of each tree in its height block.

Jacana

Jacana is keen to start a register which will record trees that have any historical or geographical significance within Southern Africa. You are invited to contact Jacana at (011) 648-1157 to discuss any trees of interest that might be included in a future publication.

LARGEST TREES CURRENTLY REGISTERED	
Black Monkey Thorn Acacia	p. 312
Broom Cluster Fig	p. 182
Brack Thorn Acacia	p. 358
Buffalo-thorn	p. 292
Cape Ash	p. 274
Coastal Red Milkwood	p. 154
Knob Thorn Acacia	p. 296
Large-leaved Albizia	P. 300
Natal Mahogany	p. 278
Marula	p. 304
River Bushwillow	p. 362
Sickle Bush	p. 264
Spike-thorn	p. 334
Tamboti	p. 370
Umbrella Thorn Acacia	p. 320
Velvet Bushwillow	p. 308
Weeping Boer-bean	p. 338
White Milkwood	p. 342
Wild Olive	p. 286

Readers should contact the Dendrological Society to obtain a form for registering very large trees. The Society publish their information in their journal the *Dendron*.

Coastal Red Milkwood – page 154

Insects, Birds, Trees and Birders

Trees, insects and birds are often mutually dependent on each other. Bees and butterflies mostly feed on sweet-scented flowers like those of the Thorn-trees, while flies tend to be attracted to more offensive smelling flowers such as those of the Spike-thorn. These flowers each have colours that attract specific insects that play an important role in their pollination.

Insects tend to avoid long, tube-like flowers, such as those of the Coral Trees, where they can get trapped. Birds with long bills, such as Sunbirds that can collect nectar from the tubes, distribute the pollen between the flowers. Insects attract insect-eating birds, and insect-eaters like Fly-catchers, Drongos and rarer birds such as the Yellowspotted Nicator, may often be found hunting near flowering or fruiting trees.

Many species of butterfly have evolved in such a way that their caterpillars only feed on certain kinds of trees. These caterpillars attract insect-eating birds like the Cuckoos, which in turn make these trees exciting for birders!

The following trees have definite associations with butterflies, and are well worth a binocular-search, to find the co-habiting wildlife – butterfly, caterpillar or bird species.

Trees and Butterflies

Brack Thorn Acacia	p. 358	Hutchinson's Highflier
Broom Cluster Fig	p. 182	Fig Tree
Buffalo-Thorn	p. 292	Hintza Pie, White Pie, Dotted Blue, Black Pie
Cape Ash	p. 274	White-barred Charaxes, Common Emperor Moth
Climbing Flat-bean	p. 100	Common Sailer
Coastal Red Milkwood	p. 154	Chief False Acraea
Common Cabbage Tree	p. 90	Charaxes spp.
Flame Thorn Acacia	p. 108	Satyr Charaxes
Flat-crown Albizia	p. 190	Blue-spotted Charaxes, Charaxes, Mirza Blue
Marula	p. 304	Green Lunar Moth
Mitzeeri	p. 214	Giant Charaxes, Morant's
Natal Mahogany	p. 278	White-barred Charaxes
Pigeonwood	p. 194	Blue-spotted Charaxes, Giant Charaxes
Powder-puff Tree	p. 168	Red-tab Policeman
Sickle Bush	p. 264	Satyr Charaxes
Tamboti	p. 370	Knotthorn Moth
Thorny Elm	p. 222	Charaxes, Forest King Charaxes

Trees and Butterflies

Thorny Rope	p. 226	Common Sailer
Tinderwood	p. 128	Natal Bar, Purple-brown Hairstreak
Umzimbeet	p. 132	Orange Playboy, Striped Policeman, Pondo Charaxes
Velvet Bushwillow	p. 308	Guinea-fowl, Morant's Orange
Water Berry	p. 172	Emperor Moth, Silver-barred Charaxes, Apricot Playboy, Morant's orange
Weeping Boer-bean	p. 338	Foxy Charaxes, Giant Charaxes, Large Blue Charaxes
White Ironwood	p. 242	Citrus Swallowtail, Constantine's Swallowtail, Green-banded Swallowtail
Wild Medlar	p. 176	Purple-brown Hairstreak
Wild Mulberry	p. 202	Common Orange Tip, African Leopard
Wild Pear	p. 140	Ragged Skipper
Wild Plum	p. 246	Common Hairtail, Eggar Moth

Because of the strong relationship between these trees and the insects, they are wonderful for spotting insectivorous birds. In particular watch out for all the Flycatchers, Drongos, Apalis and White-eyes.

BIRDS AND TREES

In the same way that butterflies and moths have developed associations with certain tree species, birds often show preferences for nesting, and for eating too! The following trees can help you find a long-sought-after species. Trees for spotting general insectiverous birds are on the previous page – only a few special species are covered here.

Black Monkey Thorn Acacia	p. 312	Nesting	Yellowbilled Hornbill
Broom Cluster Fig	p. 182	Fruit	Rameron Pigeon, Green Pigeon, Purplecrested Lourie, Blackcollared Barbet, White-eared Barbet, European Golden Oriole
Buffalo-thorn	p. 292	Fruit	Green Pigeon
		Nesting	Greater Doublecollared Sunbird
Cape Ash	p. 274	Fruit	Knysna Lourie, Purplecrested Lourie, Barbets, Hornbills, Rameron Pigeon
Cape Beech	p. 206	Fruit	Rameron Pigeon, Knysna Lourie, Bush Blackcap
Coastal Red Milkwood	p. 154	Fruit	Cape Parrots, Blackbellied Starling, Glossy Starling, Yellowstreaked Bulbuls, Knysna Lourie
Common Cabbage Tree	p. 90	Nectar	Sombre, Black-eyed Bulbuls, Knysna Lourie, Speckled Mousebird, Redwinged Starling
Cross-berry Raisin	p. 104	Fruit	Speckled Mousebird, Knysna Lourie
Crow-berry Karree	p. 326	Nesting	Gurney's Sugarbird
Flame Thorn Acacia	p. 108	Insects	Redbilled Woodhoopoe, Barthroated Apalis
Forest Elder	p. 112	Insects	Flycatchers
Knob Thorn Acacia	p. 296	Nesting	Red-billed Buffalo Weaver, Scarlet Chested Sunbird
Kooboo-berry	p. 116	Fruit	Purplecrested Louries, Green Pigeons, Cape Parrots
Lala Palm	p. 78	Nesting	Palm Swift
Large-leaved Albizia	p. 300	Seed	Brownheaded Parrot
Magic Guarri	p. 256	Fruit	Hornbill
Marula	p. 304	Nesting	Whalberg's Eagle
Mitzeeri	p. 214	Fruit	European Golden Oriole, Tinker Barbets
Natal Mahogany	p. 278	Seed	Crowned Hornbill, Grey Hornbill, Trumpeter Hornbill, Blackcollared Barbet, White-eared Barbet, Grey Lourie, Purple-crested Lourie, Blackbellied Glossy Starling,
Natal Banana	p. 82	Nesting	Golden-rumped Tinker Barbets
Pigeonwood	p. 194	Fruit	Rameron Pigeon, Delegorgue's Pigeon, Red-eyed Dove, Tambourine Dove
Powder-puff Tree	p. 168	Insects	Wattle-eyed Flycatcher
Red Bushwillow	p. 120	Seed	Brownheaded Parrots
River Bushwillow	p. 362	Fruit	Pied Barbets
Spike-thorn	p. 334	Fruit	Cape White-eye
Sweet Thorn Acacia	p. 352	Nesting	White-eared Barbet, European Golden Oriole
Sycamore Cluster Fig	p. 366	Fruit	Purplecrested Lourie, Rameron Pigeon, Green Pigeon, Purplecrested Lourie
Tamboti	p. 370	Seed	Crested Guineafowl, Francolins, Doves
Tassel Berry	p. 124	Fruit	Greenspotted Dove, Tambourine Dove, Green Pigeon, Louries, Hornbills, Barbets, Bulbuls, Mousebirds
Tinderwood	p. 128	Fruit	White-eyes, Bulbuls
Umbrella Thorn Acacia	p. 320	Seed	Meyer's Parrot, Brownheaded Parrot
Umzimbeet	p. 132	Nesting	Secretary Bird
Water Berry	p. 172	Fruit	Tambourine Dove, Green Pigeon
Weeping Boer-bean	p. 338	Nectar	Greater Sunbird, Doublecollared Sunbird, Marico
		Seed	Louries, Parrots
White Milkwood	p. 342	Nectar	Mousebirds, Rameron Pigeon
White Pear	p. 198	Fruit	Rameron Pigeon
Wild Olive	p. 286	Fruit	Rameron Pigeon
Wild Plum	p. 246	Fruit	Cape Parrot, Knysna Lourie, Cinnamon Dove

TREES VERSUS BROWSERS

All animals need protein as well as other nutrients, and varying amounts of these are contained in the leaves of different trees. Trees therefore, have to defend themselves against animals and insects that feed on their leaves. They have two main defences – mechanical and chemical.

The leaves of Thorn-trees are usually small, very palatable, and eagerly eaten. But, because of the mechanical thorn defenses, only a few leaves are eaten per meal. All the *Acacia* family – Umbrella Thorn, Knobthorn, Black Monkey Thorn, Fever Tree and Sweet Thorn, to name a few – fall into this category.

Trees with broad leaves and no thorns produce unpalatable tannin-like chemicals that taste like very strong, black tea. Among many others, these trees include the Marula, page 304, Red Bushwillow, page 120, Natal Mahogany, page 278, and Magic Guarri, page 256.

Trees like the *Euphorbia* family produce a poisonous latex. This includes the Tree Euphorbia page 86, Rubber Euphorbia, page 84, and Tamboti, page 370.

These chemicals act only as a deterrent to most of the African browsers, as the animals in turn have evolved mechanisms in their digestive systems to be able to cope with small quantities of the chemicals.

The tannins in the leaves are very similar to those found in a thin layer of wood just under the bark. The outer bark has little food value, but the under-bark is nutritious and often eaten by animals such as Elephant and Black Rhino, as well as some insects. To protect this layer, trees develop the chemicals which humans then use to tan leather. Tanned leather is indigestible even to bacteria and fungi.

This same under-bark and its chemicals are still in use today in traditional medicines. It is highly sought after by herbalists and healers. See page 391.

BLACK RHINOS AND TREES

Black Rhinos are a particularly favoured species in the game-watching culture of KwaZulu-Natal. Numerous groups, including the KwaZulu-Natal Nature Conservation Services, have invested skill, determination, money, science and energy to ensure the protection and productive future of these magnificent, prehistoric mammals. As long as they are given protection from human predation and the right Habitat for food, they breed very successfully.

Below is a list of trees covered in this book, that are particularly favoured by Black Rhinos.

Next time you are watching game, look out for these trees and you may find a Rhino. Or conversely, when you find the Rhino, look out for these trees!

Anyone interested in learning more about Black Rhinos can contact the African Rhino Specialist Group at Queen Elizabeth Park, Pietermaritzburg on (0331) 47-1961.

ALONG RIVERS (A)	
Coast Silver Oak	p. 150
Cross-berry Raisin	p. 104
Euphorbias (all)	p. 84, 86
Sneezewood	p. 238
Spike-thorn	p. 334
Wild Olive	p. 286
Wild Pear	p. 140

BUSHVELD-SAVANNAH (B)	
Dwarf Boer-bean	p. 340
False Horsewood	p. 220
Hook Thorn Acacia	p. 330
Red Ivory	p. 282
Red Thorn Acacia	p. 260
Sickle Bush	p. 264
Sweet Thorn Acacia	p. 352
Tamboti	p. 370
Weeping Boer-bean	p. 338

Tamboti
– page 370

Seed Dispersal

Many seeds need to move away from their parents. This can be to avoid competing for light and nutrition with the parent plant, or it can be to "find" a suitable place to grow.

Seeds and fruits are therefore designed to use various modes of transport. This often involves more than just the tree itself. There are many theories about the mechanisms, some scientifically proven, and others simply speculation. Below are a number of entertaining examples to add interest to your tree, bird and animal spotting.

- Some seeds or fruit have a wing, or wings, for flying on the wind
- Many types of trees invest in specialised, attractive food packages that then ensure they are dispersed and sown by animals – hoofed mammals, primates birds and insects.
- Others have built-in cork, or a raft to float in rivers.
- A few seeds that explode out of the fruit like mini-projectiles are launched out of the shade of the parent plant.

Wind-dispersed Seeds

ACACIAS – THORN-TREE FAMILY (P 379)

In most Acacias, neither the seeds nor pods are distinctly winged. However, in some species, the pods split open and are shaped like, and probably function as, small boomerangs with the seeds dangling on short threads. The pods are carried by whirlwinds, sometimes for kilometres. Watch for this, as scientific observations are not conclusive. In some Acacias the broad bean, papery pods split open, and are wing-like enough for strong gusts to blow them away from the parent tree.

ALBIZIA – THORN-TREE FAMILY (P 379)

The entire pod surrounding the seed acts as a wing.

Flat-crown Albizia	p. 190
Large-leaved Albizia	p. 300

BUSHWILLOW FAMILY (P 376)

The whole pod, containing the seed or seeds, is carried by the wind on large wing/s.

Red Bushwillow	p. 120
River Bushwillow -	p. 362
Velvet Bushwillow	p. 308

DAISY FAMILY (P 376)

Seed(s) have either a wing or fluffy parachute.

Camphor Bush	p. 252
Coast Silver Oak	p. 150

PEA FAMILY (P 376)

Each seed is individually winged.

Climbing Flat-bean	p. 100
Thorny Rope	p. 226

Bird-dispersed Seeds

OILY FRUIT

Oils are high in energy and are especially attractive to large or fast-flying birds that use lots of energy.

Spike-thorn	p 334
White Pear	p 198
Wild Olive	p 286

SUGARY / WATERY FRUIT

These fruits provide diluted food, but are usually available in large quantities, particularly in the summer, when many birds are breeding

Cabbage Trees (all)	p. 90
Cape Beech	p. 206
Common Poison Bush	p. 186
Giant-leaved Fig	p 76
Guarris (all)	p. 270, 256
Kooboo-berry	p. 116
Large-leaved Dragon Tree	p. 80
Mitzeeri	p. 214
Pigeonwood	p. 194
Red Ivory	p. 282
Tassel Berry	p. 124
Thorny Elm	p. 222
Tinderwood	p. 128
Weeping Boer-bean	p. 338
White Ironwood	p. 242
White Milkwood	p. 342

SUGARY / DRY FRUIT

Water in the fruit is re-absorbed as it ripens, leaving the entire sugar, and possibly oil content, wrapping the seed, like a coating of jam.

Karrees (all)	p 230, 326
Red Beech	p 120

Seeds Dispersed by Primates

The seeds of the following trees are dispersed and sown primarily by primates including humans, who have been part of the evolution of trees since time immemorial. In many types of trees, primates compete with fruit-eating birds. However, in the group listed below, the fruit has features particularly inviting to primates. Primates are attracted by the fruit's conspicuous size, a sour, sweet, or fruity taste and/or a fruity fragrance when ripe. A common feature shared by mammal-dispersed fruit is that they need to be processed using hands or teeth. This excludes many birds, other than Parrots, that cannot open hard shells. Also, no birds can suck big seeds or swallow large fruit whole.

DRY-PULP FRUIT

The pulp of several types has dry flesh firmly attached to the seed. Primates suck the seed for the taste and can be many metres away from the parent tree before spitting the seeds out.

Buffalo-thorn	p 292
Cross-berry Raisin	p 104
Date Palm	p 72
Wild Medlar	p 176

SUCCULENT FRUIT

When not fully ripe, these conspicuous fruit are not attractive to birds. The ripe fruits is astringent, sour or hard.

Black Monkey Orange	p. 146
Water Berry	p. 172
Wild Plum	p. 246

Seeds Dispersed by other Mammals

The whole process of interaction between plants and animals is well balanced in Africa. There are constant adaptations to changing local circumstances, that offer a win-win solution to both sides. The animals eat the pods and seeds because they not only contain more protein than grass and leaves, but also contain starches, sugars and minerals. Some time after eating, dung is dropped. This is usually away from the parent plant, and contains some whole undamaged seeds, that are already in an ideal medium for gemination.

Most seeds of the following trees grow inside dull coloured fruit or pods, with an apple-like or musky smell that is attractive to mammals. In order to germinate, many Acacia seeds need to pass through either the acids, or a soaking process, in the gut of animals.

Some pod segments may be designed to ride on muddy hooves. Watch for this as scientific observations are not conclusive, for example Fever Tree Acacia page 74.

DRY-PULP FRUIT

Most of these fruits have dry or floury pulp, digested by the animal, while the seed is passed intact.

Scented Thorn Acacia	p. 316
Sickle Bush	p. 264
Umbrella Thorn Acacia	p. 320

SUCCULENT FRUIT

In some trees the fruit is fragrant and succulent, and ferments, increasing the attractiveness.

Marula	p. 304

Forest Karree
– page 230

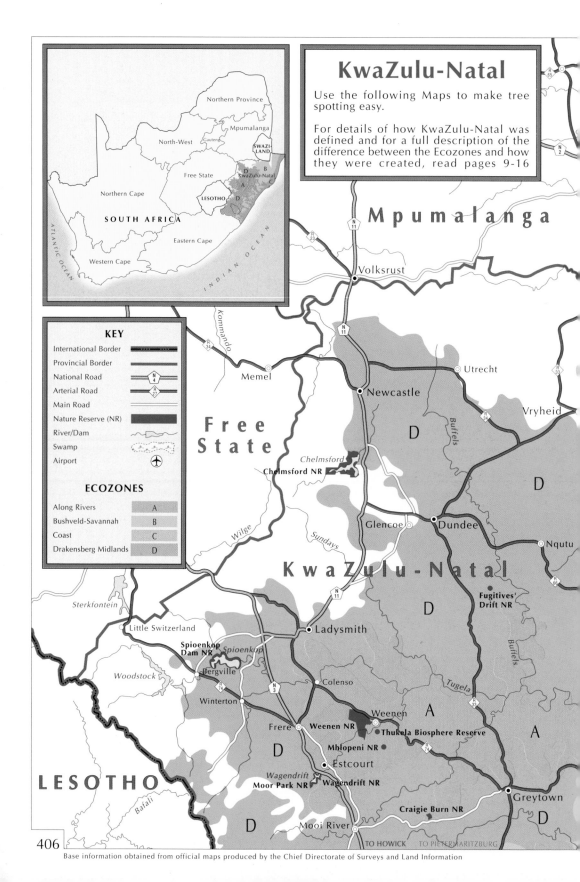

KwaZulu-Natal

Use the following Maps to make tree spotting easy.

For details of how KwaZulu-Natal was defined and for a full description of the difference between the Ecozones and how they were created, read pages 9-16

Mpumalanga

Volksrust

Utrecht

Memel

Newcastle

Vryheid

Free State

D

Buffels

D

Chelmsford
Chelmsford NR

Glencoe · Dundee

Nqutu

Wilge

Sundays

KwaZulu-Natal

N 11

D

Fugitives' Drift NR

Sterkfontein

Little Switzerland

Ladysmith

Buffels

Spioenkop
Dam NR   Spioenkop

Bergville

Woodstock

Colenso

Tugela

Winterton

Weenen

A

Frere   Weenen NR

Thukela Biosphere Reserve

A

Mhlopeni NR

LESOTHO

D

Estcourt

Wagendrift
Moor Park NR   Wagendrift NR

Bafali

Craigie Burn NR

Greytown

D

Mooi River

D

TO HOWICK   TO PIETERMARITZBURG

KEY

International Border	
Provincial Border	
National Road	N 4
Arterial Road	R 27
Main Road	
Nature Reserve (NR)	
River/Dam	
Swamp	
Airport	✈

ECOZONES

Along Rivers	A
Bushveld-Savannah	B
Coast	C
Drakensberg Midlands	D

Northern Province

Mpumalanga

North-West   Gauteng   SWAZI-LAND

Free State   B
KwaZulu-Natal   A
D

LESOTHO   C

Northern Cape   D

SOUTH AFRICA

Eastern Cape

Western Cape

ATLANTIC OCEAN

INDIAN OCEAN

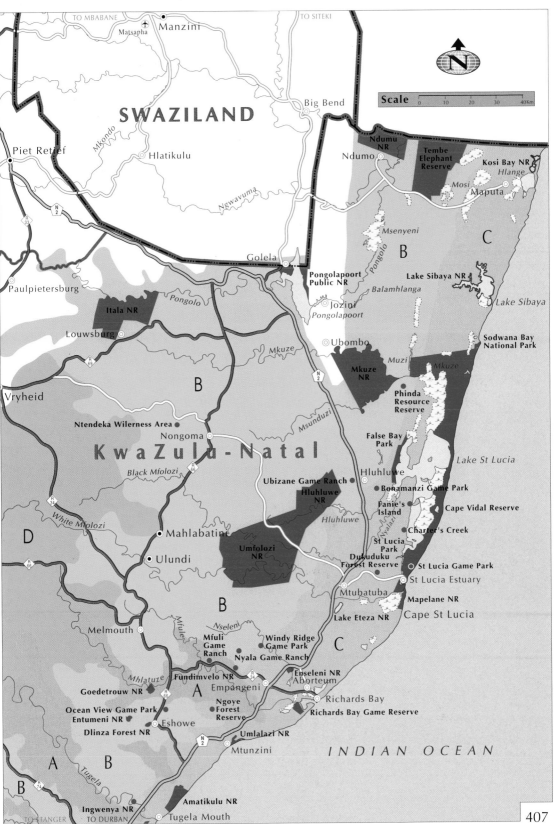

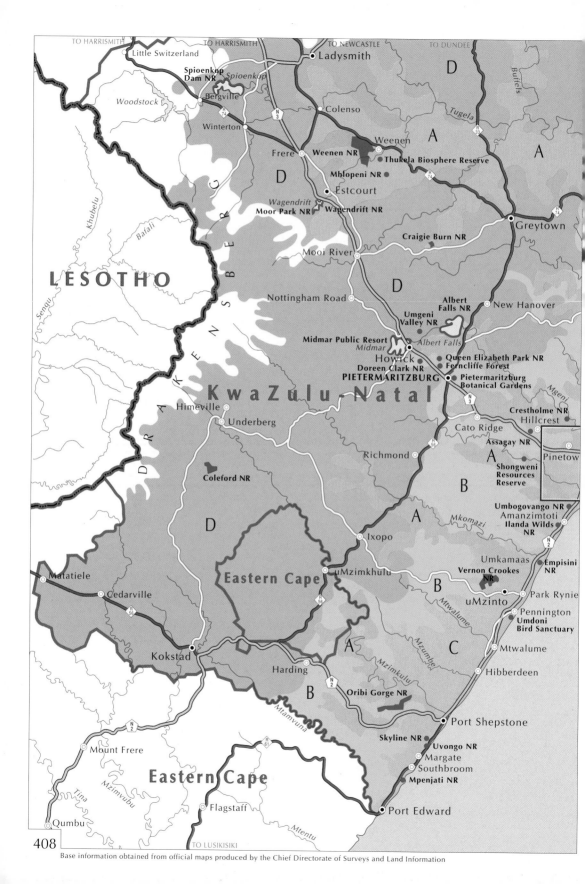

Base information obtained from official maps produced by the Chief Directorate of Surveys and Land Information

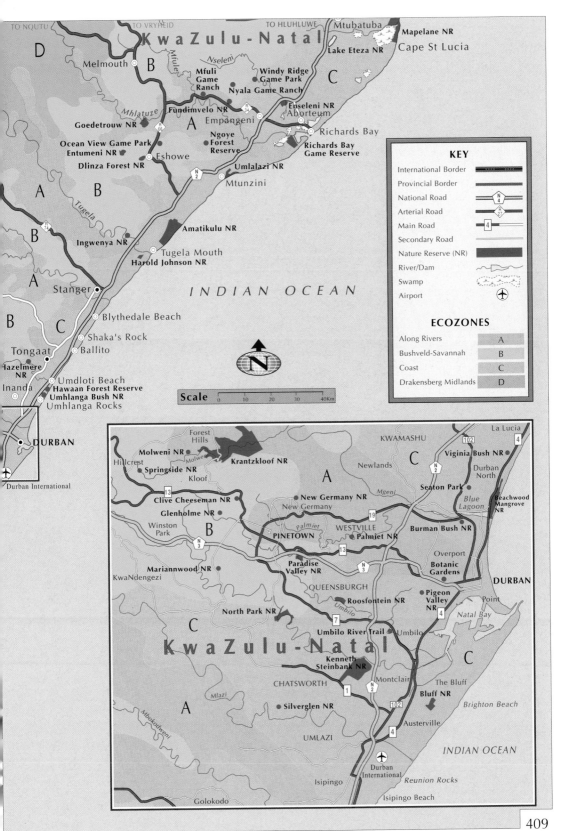

KwaZulu-Natal

TO NQUTU
TO VRYHEID
TO HLUHLUWE
Mtubatuba
Mapelane NR
Cape St Lucia

K w a Z u l u - N a t a l
Lake Eteza NR

D
Melmouth
B
Mfule
Nseleni
Windy Ridge
Game Park
Mfuli
Game
Ranch
Nyala Game Ranch
C

Goedetrouw NR
Mhlatuze
Fundimvelo NR
Empangeni
A
Enseleni NR
Aboretum

Ocean View Game Park
Entumeni NR
Eshowe
Ngoye
Forest
Reserve
Richards Bay
Richards Bay
Game Reserve

Dlinza Forest NR
Umlalazi NR
N2
Mtunzini

A
B
Tugela

B
Amatikulu NR

Ingwenya NR
Tugela Mouth
Harold Johnson NR

A
Stanger
INDIAN OCEAN

B
C
Blythedale Beach

Shaka's Rock

Tongaat
Ballito

Hazelmere
NR
Umdloti Beach
Hawaan Forest Reserve
Inanda
Umhlanga Bush NR
Umhlanga Rocks

DURBAN

Durban International

Scale
0   10   20   30   40Km

N

KEY

International Border
Provincial Border
National Road
Arterial Road
Main Road
Secondary Road
Nature Reserve (NR)
River/Dam
Swamp
Airport

ECOZONES

Along Rivers   A
Bushveld-Savannah   B
Coast   C
Drakensberg Midlands D

Forest
Hills
KWAMASHU
La Lucia
Molweni NR
Molweni
Krantzkloof NR
C
Viginia Bush NR
102
4
Hillcrest
Springside NR
Newlands
Durban
North
Kloof
A
Seaton Park
N2
Clive Cheeseman NR
Mgeni
Blue
Lagoon
Beachwood
Mangrove
NR
Glenholme NR
13
New Germany NR
New Germany
Palmiet
WESTVILLE
Burman Bush NR
Winston
Park
N3
B
PINETOWN
19
Palmiet NR
Overport
13
Botanic
Gardens
Marannwood NR
Paradise
Valley NR
N3
DURBAN
KwaNdengezi
QUEENSBURGH
Pigeon
Valley
NR
Point
North Park NR
Roosfontein NR
Umbilo
Natal Bay
C
7
Umbilo River Trail
Umbilo
K w a Z u l u - N a t a l
Kenneth
Steinbank NR
C
CHATSWORTH
1
N2
Montclair
The Bluff
Mlazi
Bluff NR
Brighton Beach
A
Silverglen NR
102
Austerville
UMLAZI
4
INDIAN OCEAN
Mbokodweni
Durban
International
Reunion Rocks
Isipingo
Isipingo Beach
Golokodo

409

Index

410

413

References

Acocks,J.P.H.,1988, *Veld Types of South Africa,* No 57, Botanical Research Institute, Pretoria.

Borchers, H., 1995, *Greening the KwaZulu-Natal Coast,* 2nd ed., 1996, Share-net, Pretoria.

Borchers, H., 1996, *Greening the KwaZulu-Natal Midlands,* Share-net, Pretoria.

Broomberg, B., 1985, *Trees in South Africa,* Apr-Sept, Page 23-24.

Broomberg, B., 1987, *Trees in South Africa,* Apr-Sept, Page 22-24.

Carr, J.D., 1976, *The South African Acacias,* Conservation Press (Pty) Ltd, Johannesburg.

Carr, J.D., 1988, *Combretaceae in South Africa,* Tree Society of Southern Africa, Johannesburg.

Coates Palgrave, K., 1977, *Trees of Southern Africa,* 1st ed., C. Struik, Cape Town.

Cooper, K.H., 1985, *Indigenous Forest Survey,* Wildlife Society of South Africa Conservation Division, Durban.

Cyrus, D. & Robson, N., 1980, *Bird Atlas of Natal,* University of Natal Press, Pietermaritzburg.

Everard, D. A., Midgley, J.J. & van Wyk, G.F., 1995, *Dynamics of some Forests in KwaZulu-Natal ,* South Africa, Based on ordinations and size-class distributions.

Geldenhuys, C.J., 1992, *Richness, Composition and Relationships of the Floras of Selected Forests in Southern Africa,* CSIR Division of Forest Science and Technology, Pretoria.

Henderson, L. & Musil, K.J., 1987, *Plant Invaders of the Transvaal,* Promedia Publications, Pretoria.

Huntley, B.J., 1965, *A Preliminary Account of the Ngoye Forest Reserve,* Zululand, J.S. Afr. Bot. 31: 177-205.

Hutchings, A., Scott, A.H., Lewis, G. & Cunningham, A.B., 1996, *Zulu Medicinal Plants – An Inventory,* University of Natal Press, Pietermaritzburg.

Journal of Dendrology, 1991, *National Register of Big Trees.*

Low, A.B. & Rebelo, A.G., (Eds), 1996, *Vegetation of South Africa, Lesotho and Swaziland* (with accompanied vegetation map), Department of Environment Affairs and Tourism, Pretoria.

Lowveld Plant Specialist Group, 1994, *Checklist of the Trees and Shrubs recorded at Mapelane, Natal.*

Moll, E.J., 1968, *A Plant Ecological Reconnaissance of the Upper Umgeni Catchment,* J.S. Afr.Bot. 34: 401-420.

Moll, E.J., 1968, *A Quantitative Ecological Investigation of the Krantzkloof Forest, Natal,* J.S. Afr.Bot. 34: 15-25.

Moll, E.J., 1968, *An Account of the Plant Ecology of the Hawaan Forest, Natal,* J.S. Afr.Bot. 34: 61-76.

Moll, E.J., 1978, *A Quantitiative Floristic Comparison of Four Natal Forests,* S. Afr. for J. 104: 25-34.

Moll, E.J., 1992, *Trees of Natal,* University of Cape Town, Eco-lab Trust Fund, Cape Town.

Moll, E.J., & Cooper, K.H., 1968, *Notes on an Area of the Karkloof Forest,* Natal, African Wildlife 22, 49-57.

Moll, E.J., & White, F., 1978, *The Indian Ocean Coastal Belt,* in Werger, M.J.A., (Ed), Biogeography and ecology of Southern Africa, W. Junk, the Hague, P. 561-598.

Mountain, A., 1990, *Paradise Under Pressure,* Southern Book Publishers (Pty) Ltd, Johannesburg.

Palmer, E. & Pitman, N., 1972 & 1973, *Trees of Southern Africa,* 3 Vols, A.A. Balkema, Cape Town.

Pooley, E., 1993, *The Complete Field Guide to Trees of Natal, Zululand & Transkei,* 1st ed., Natal Flora Publications Trust, Durban.

Roberts, D.C., 1993, *The Vegetation Ecology of Municipal Durban, Natal,* Floristic Classification, Department of Geographical and Environmental Sciences, University of Natal, Durban.

Rutherford, M.C. & Westfall, R.H., 1994, *Biomes of Southern Africa: An Objective Categorization,* National Botanical Institute, Claremont.

Steyn, Marthinus, 1994, *S.A. Acacias Identification Guide,* Promedia Marks Street, Waltloo.

Steyn, Marthinus, 1996, *S.A. Ficus Identification Guide for Wild Figs in South Africa,* Promedia Marks Street, Waltloo.

Taylor, R., 1991, *The Greater St Lucia Wetland and Park,* Parke-Davis.

Trendler, R. & Hes, L., 1994, *Attracting Birds to your Garden in Southern Africa,* Hirt &Carter (Pty) Ltd, Cape Town.

Van Wyk, B. & van Wyk, P., 1997, *Field Guide to Trees of Southern Africa,* Struik Publishers (Pty) Ltd, Cape Town.

Van Wyk, B.E., van Oudtshoorn, B. & Gericke, N., 1997, *Medicinal Plants of South Africa,* 1st ed., Briza Publications, Pretoria.

Venter, F. & J.A., 1996, *Making the Most of Indigenous Trees,* 1st ed., Briza Publications, Pretoria.

Von Breitenbach, F., 1995, *National List of Indigenous Trees,* 3rd ed., Dendrological Foundation, Pretoria.

Ward, M.C. & Weisser, P.J., 1991, *Checklist of Vascular Plants in Sodwana – Kosi-Bay area,* National Botanical Institute, Pretoria.

Watt, J.M. & Breyer-Brandwijk, M.G., 1962, *Medicinal and Poisonous Plants of Southern and Eastern Africa,* 2nd ed., E & S Livingstone Ltd, Edinburgh and London.

Wirminghaus, J.O., 1990, *A Checklist of the Plants of the Karkloof Forest, Natal Midlands,* Dept. of Zoology and Entomology, University of Natal, Pietermaritzburg.